MW01057013

STEPHEN STILLS

CHANGE PARTNERS

David Roberts

First published: October 2016

ISBN: 978-1911346005

Proofreading: Matthew White
Design: Poppublishing
Cover photo: Gijsbert Hanekroot/Getty Images
A full list of acknowledgements appears at the back of this book

Red Planet Publishing Ltd,
Manor Lodge, Grass Yard, Kimbolton, PE28 0HQ
For more information visit www.redplanetzone.com

Printed in the United States of America

For Janet, Andy, who first introduced me to the music of Stephen Stills, my 'brother' in music Neil, who convinced me I *must* write this book, and Kendall's 'alcoholic nut farm' dream that reinforced the notion that I was destined to do it.

INTRODUCTION

If the yardstick of a successful career is leaving an enduring musical legacy, then Stephen Stills is right up there. That's certainly true if the 2012 sci-fi movie *Prometheus* is anything to go by. The year is 2093, when a scene in director Ridley Scott's prequel to *Alien* has off-duty spaceship captain Janek (played by Idris Elba) startling Meredith Vickers (Charlize Theron) by playing a tiny accordion. When Vickers compares the sound of "the thing" to "a dying cat," an affronted Janek responds by revealing that "this thing" once belonged to Stephen Stills.

"Am I supposed to know who that is?" responds Vickers. As she walks seductively away, Janek lifts up the prized squeezebox and accompanies himself singing Stills' biggest solo hit single, 'Love The One You're With.'

And it was that earworm of a song that rekindled my own personal obsession with music, an obsession that had diluted to a mere passing interest after the demise of The Beatles a year earlier. To this British teenager, 'Love The One You're With' sounded cool, sexually confident, and very American. It was a breath of fresh air in 1971. Not since the gorgeous harmonies of the then fading Beach Boys had I got so excited about what was coming out of the USA.

And Stills was clearly not just a one-hit wonder. I immediately bought as much of his music as I could afford and read every word that British music papers *Sounds, New Musical Express*, and *Melody Maker* would print about him. Here in the dark, austere bleak British winter was a personality to aspire to. He appeared to have confidence in bucket loads, had a blonde, rugged, hippie sensibility, spoke with measured arrogance, and could play the guitar like a veteran blues man.

Having immersed myself in the music of my first two Stills records (CSN&Y's *Déjà Vu* and his debut solo album), I was also fascinated by every detail of the LP packaging. No one looked more cocksure or confident than Stephen Stills. There he was, nonchalantly gazing out from the cover of *Déjà Vu* in a confederate (naturally) American Civil War soldier's uniform, then seated picking at a guitar in the Colorado snow, cigarette wedged in his little finger while seemingly playing to a pink toy giraffe on the front of his first solo LP. Cool!

Like first love, first albums always left an indelible impression on my baby boomer generation. When *Déjà Vu* and *Stephen Stills* made their debut on my parents' single-speaker Russian-made record player, they soon vied for attention with offerings around that time by Bowie and solo Beatles and, of course, retrospective purchases of the CSN debut and Buffalo Springfield releases. If The Beatles had once, imperiously, meant everything to me, now, aged 17, I was captivated by what was happening across the Atlantic. The musical differences seemed clear. If the British offered up invention and an in-your-face grittiness, the new wave of singer-songwriter artists and bands across the Atlantic had absorbed all that and were exuding a worldly-wise, exciting assurance. The West Coast music scene, in particular, was reflecting the political temperature of the early 70s and delving back into the American folk movement for inspiration. Stills, though, wasn't your archetypal singer-songwriter. His songs had great emotional stories and he could clearly write biting protest lyrics, but his ability to play a whole range of instruments and master a whole range of different genres was just as impressive and exciting. That said, my devotion to Stills wasn't slavish and I wasn't overly enamored with his second solo album, my head increasingly turned by the Eagles, Little Feat and his old compadre

Neil Young. What he did next however, was to create what is still today my favourite album of all time. Handpicking a bunch of extraordinarily gifted musicians, he assembled Stephen Stills' Manassas and released a double album featuring music genres from all over the Americas. Country, bluegrass, rock, blues, and Latin genres showcased some of his best songs in what everyone calls Americana today. And all of a sudden Stills was in England promoting the album. The family reel-to-reel tape recorder was pressed into action to capture his appearances on the BBC and a ticket was duly acquired for what turned out to be a stunning Manassas concert at north London's Rainbow Theatre. My devotion as a fan increased further when I discovered that the formation and rehearsals for *Manassas* had taken place in England and some of Stills' best studio recordings had been made in London. All the British music papers and, when trips to London enabled me to buy it, *Rolling Stone*, were championing Stills and feeding my fix and filling my scrapbooks.

I would certainly lap up a ton of great music from him after 1972, but Manassas that year was the peak of my devotion. It was a devotion that ebbed and flowed but never really vanished completely in later life.

But in my career in the book business I regularly pondered, where was the Stills biography or autobiography I craved? Crosby – tick, Nash – tick, and Young – tick, tick, tick! Dare I attempt to fill that void, I often wondered. Stephen Stills is clearly not a man who spends too much time daydreaming about the past. The prospect of interviews doesn't excite him – there was a polite but firm 'no' when he was approached about this book via his manager Elliot Roberts – and he wasn't even much involved in the creation of his own recent box set, curated by Joel Bernstein and Graham Nash.

The release of the four-disc anthology, *Carry On*, in 2013 prompted Stills to admit to *Rolling Stone* magazine that it was probably his equivalent of an autobiography, explaining that although he had enjoyed reading Keith Richards' *Life* (2011), other rock-star memoirs "bore the shit out of me." Music writer Jeff Tamarkin provoked an equally damning response that same year when Stills revealed, "I find interviews and talking about myself the most loathsome activity in the world. So no, I'll never write one of those stupid autobiographies."

But he's far from being the curmudgeon all this might indicate. The enormous ego and intensity of his 1970s self has long since evaporated, replaced by the self-deprecating and relaxed (and often downright funny) self in his seventies.

Despite his protestations, he has tried to write his own story. But you sense the staying power and slog of hunching over a typewriter on the tour bus appeals less than picking up a guitar and doing what comes effortlessly with his 21st-century blues project, The Rides.

This, then, is an unauthorized biography of several different people, all of them Stephen Stills. At various times he has been band leader, guitarist, workaholic, egomaniac, blues man, poetic songwriter, and laid-back, carefree family man and father of seven. The steely, blue-eyed blonde kid with the big white guitar has evolved into a gravel-voiced LA blues man who, you feel, would make the perfect voice-over candidate for the next Disney blockbuster.

So, the most complicated and hard to pin down member of the CSN&Y conglomerate finally gets his story told. The satisfaction and responsibility of writing it have been huge. Stills' career has not been without its problems, but the unconditional love, protection, and support of his fans tells me that I better have got the facts right! As for the man himself: If you read this Stephen, I hope you will look kindly on my efforts and perhaps find my order of events helpful in finally writing your memoirs one day. Over to you…

CHAPTER 1
The Blue-Eyed Injun'

Though born in Texas, the southern states of Louisiana and Florida was where Stephen Stills felt most at home as a young boy. "I mean, my origins—according to my aunt, I'm basically a blue-eyed Injun' from Louisiana," he once revealed to *Guitar World*. "And after the Civil War, my great-great-grandmother gravitated to southern Illinois, where my father was from. But I've got relatives that look so much like 'gator swamp guys. Duane Allman and I had the same kind of bond. All of us crackers—we're all just a tribe."

A song-writing career peppered with references to the Civil War must surely have been influenced by tales of how his ancestors had been forced north from their property and lands in Louisiana by the Union Army led by General Tecumseh Sherman. Coincidentally, Sherman had earlier begun his Civil War career at the Battle of First Manassas in Virginia (aka the First Battle of Bull Run). It was a fact noted by Stephen more than a century later when naming his new band and album after the city which experienced the first major battle during that bloody period in American history. But Sherman's implementation of the infamous aggressive 'scorched earth' policy of routing the Confederate southern states meant only a temporary personal retreat for the Stills clan.

In the 1930s, still adrift from their spiritual home in the south, southern Illinois was home to the Stills family. Son of a school teacher, the young William Stills met and married Talitha and set about building a career in engineering. Despite the economic depression that gripped the nation, he studied hard at University and worked as an engineer before World War II and in the construction industry after it. Seemingly most of the couple's free time was spent taking in big band concerts and supplementing their income by booking some of the acts around the Champaign area of Illinois. And as his son Stephen would later reveal in a *Sounding Out* BBC TV interview, it wasn't just the local talent that William Stills took care of.

"My Dad was into the big bands. He used to book them when he was in college. He booked Paul Whiteman and Benny Goodman and Fletcher Henderson, and all those people through the mid-west."

When William and Talitha started their own family, Hannah was born in Illinois, but when Talitha fell pregnant again their new son would be born where work dictated William move to.

And so, on January 3, 1945, Stephen Arthur Stills was born in Dallas, Texas. Although Stephen's first months coincided thankfully with the end of World War II, 1945 was still a year of horrific headlines. At the time of little Stephen's birth, Adolf Hitler was still very much alive and decorating German soldiers with their medals while around 4,000 prisoners were being liberated in the Polish death camp, Auschwitz. In February, American troops were gaining a significant victory on the Pacific island of Iwo Jima, but by August the war still wasn't done until the Japanese city of Hiroshima had been obliterated by a single atom bomb.

On a much lighter note, and more relevant to Stephen's future, the first solid-body electric guitar hadn't even been built. Can you imagine a world without them now? Well, Les Paul only finally perfected that minor miracle in 1947.

Stephen Stills may have been born in Texas but his family didn't stay there long. After a spell in Illinois once more, at least this branch of the Stills family tree was back home to their southern roots in Louisiana. Here was where the childhood music education and influences began. Covington, with a population of around 5,000 back when Stephen was a boy, is located at a fork of the Bogue Falaya and the Tchefuncte River. Tantalisingly, Covington was across the other side of Lake Pontchartrain from New Orleans. The Bogue Falaya River was where Stephen learnt to fish and, as his song 'Old Times Good Times' noted, boated up the river in a pirogue and once got lost aged seven.

Unsurprisingly in a household filled with the music of Bix Beiderbecke, The Dorsey Brothers, Paul Whiteman, Cole Porter, and Lead Belly, he quickly (and literally) found his musical feet. When interviewed for *American Songwriters.com* by Paul Rollo, Stephen recalled his very young self tap dancing immediately after learning to walk. One of his clearest memories was of being three years old, sitting on a chair with tap shoes on and tapping rhythms onto a metal board. The first instrument he mastered was not guitar, but the drums. "Rhythm is my thing," he said.

At the age of eight or nine his parents came to the same conclusion. "My father bought me drums because somebody gave me some drumsticks, and then the furniture was being destroyed. He went to the pawnshop and found a really cool Slingerland [drum] kit," he revealed to Lydia Hutchinson for *Performing Songwriter Be Heard*.

"I think Don Henley tells the same kind of story about beating pencils on a book in class," he later told Tavis Smiley.

Now armed with a set of pearl gray Slingerland Radio Kings, most other forms of music practice paled into insignificance. Although there was a piano at home, Stephen didn't enjoy the lessons he had to endure. "My teacher, this very proper lady, had a thing about Brahms, which I could never get into that much," he remembered when downloading his childhood to Dave Zimmer for *Crosby, Stills & Nash - The Authorized Biography*.

Certainly, as far as the piano was concerned, his musical influences were closer to home. "My maternal grandmother was a movie-house piano player and just fabulous. She had the greatest touch and phrasing. She played the nickelodeons during the Depression. And what *she* was doin' was more my style."

The first guitar of any kind he ever held in his hands was a baritone ukulele that belonged to a kid across the street, but his love affair with the real thing would take a while to develop.

With plenty of encouragement from his parents and grandparents Stephen's feel for music was evident, but a problem that would hamper him for the rest of his life was already having an impact.

Stephen remembers the first time he was aware anything was wrong was aged nine. "This was in 1954 and a little truck came to the school to give the children physicals. The doctor noticed a hearing loss in my right ear and told my parents to 'keep an eye on it'." The deafness would get progressively worse until, late on in life, he discovered the ideal type of hearing aids.

Up to this point, any burgeoning musical talent Stephen possessed was minimal. But he was about to get exposure to a variety of new types of music, all courtesy of his father's itchy feet. Triggered by the birth of new baby daughter Talitha Junior and the inspiration of a new construction project in Tampa, Florida, William Stills uprooted the family and moved them 600 miles west to the Sunshine State. Stephen remembered his father back then as "a sarcastic son of a bitch" at times who definitely influenced his own character and reputation as a cranky so and so. Maybe that crankiness was already showing itself in Stephen at an early age. His mother evidently thought so. Believing that an extra dose of manners and discipline wouldn't go amiss, William and Talitha picked out a military establishment as the next stepping stone in their son's frequently changing education.

"I went to so many schools I was the perpetual stranger," he responded when quizzed by *Mojo*'s Sylvie Simmons in 2013. His future schooling would be both varied and exotic, in keeping with his father's own perpetual motion when it came to employment opportunities. Real estate, engineering, lumber, molasses, and the booking of those big bands in earlier times made for a colorful CV. And so Stephen began a toughening-up phase in his life when he was enrolled in the Admiral Farragut Academy in St. Petersburg. He is on record as admitting that it was something he needed at the time: "I was behaving like a goon and my mother wanted to turn me into a gentleman."

If the strict code of conduct at the Academy was a shock to his system, that feeling didn't last long and he soon began to adapt and absorb all the good things the place had to offer. Marching in the drill team, the ordered environment, even the dress code, would all contribute something to his demeanor and band management skills in his twenties. Confidence, control, and the drive to get things done were all characteristics honed at the Admiral Farragut Academy and, somewhat bizarrely, used to good effect in the laid-back West Coast rock vibe a decade later.

During his time at the Academy the guitar–as opposed to all the other instruments he'd been tinkering with–became the center of his attention. His roommate had a guitar that Stephen practiced on until his fingers bled and he was often at his neighborhood friend Michael O'Hara Garcia's home listening to records by Woody Guthrie, Robert Johnson, Muddy Waters, and the 'new' rock 'n' roll sound of Chuck Berry. While Stephen picked out a tune on an old Stella steel-stringed guitar, Michael would try to emulate the lazy blues vocal of bluesman Jimmy Reed on one of the two teenagers' favorite records, 'Baby What You Want Me To Do.' Stephen's heroes at the time also included Elmore James, Howlin' Wolf, Bo Diddley, and some non-blues artists.

"I liked pre-Nashville Appalachian country music, the real stuff. I also liked Motown, The Shirelles, and the girl groups," he said later.

Interestingly, also among Michael Garcia's family record collection was the music of local bluesman Tampa Red. As a teenager, Stephen believes he met the once famous bluesman. Then in his early sixties, Stephen saw him busking during a shopping trip to Tampa. "His skin was mottled, his hair was kinda red, and he was blind," Stephen later recalled in an interview with CSN biographer Dave Zimmer. "He had an old black Silvertone guitar and played the most dangerous, the *baddest* music I had ever been exposed to. I'd sit down next to him, and I was this scruffy little white kid, but he talked to me, showed me how he played slide guitar with a knife." Clearly this encounter with the man famed for his single-string slide playing must have been a defining moment in shaping Stephen's own career-long love of the blues guitar. Tampa Red would die a destitute 77-year-old in 1981.

In the summer, Stephen left Admiral Farragut Academy and spent many happy days driving a tractor through the peach trees around his Uncle Sidney's farm. He did not know it at the time, but as he strained hard to sing loudly above the racket of the Massey Ferguson's engine he was developing the vocal chords of a rock singer. That summer he also began to read for fun. His Aunt Veda was a retired Southern Illinois University history professor.

"In the farm-house attic she had every copy of *Time* magazine since its inception," Stills remembered fondly. "I read all about World War II through that. The writing was really good back then."

Tampa's Woodrow Wilson Junior High was where 'the perpetual stranger' was schooled next when summer ended. And he must have felt that 'stranger' tag greatly as the Benedictine monastery and school of St. Leo Academy, near Dade City, swiftly became his next port of call. Aside from that institution's more trivial claim to fame educating actors Desi Arnaz and Lee Marvin, St. Leo's had a reputation for progressive policies and in 1889 had ended racial segregation on campus long before it was legal to do so in the state of Florida. However, that didn't stop it from being another strict regime, but, as most tough establishments have, it had one saving grace. St. Leo's boasted, as Stephen recalled, "a very good vocal coach" and he and friend Michael Garcia found themselves singing (in Latin) the High Mass in the choir under the expert and helpful tutelage of choir director Donald Kteusch. Now the teenage Stills was able to add proper vocal coaching in how to sing lead first baritone, lead second baritone, and even tenor to his raucous vocal stretching exercises aboard the Massey Ferguson.

By this time a bright, brand-new decade had dawned–the (not yet swinging) Sixties–and radio was becoming an increasingly important musical fix for American teenagers. Michael Garcia and Stephen Stills were no exception.

"Stephen and I became dedicated fans of the late-night blues shows of Big Hugh Baby and John R. on WLAC Nashville," Michael noted in the essay he wrote to accompany Stephen's *Carry On* box set. "On weekend nights, the old tube radio in our black 1940 Packard sedan would blast out the sounds of Slim Harpo, Little Willie John, Muddy Waters, and a new rhythm and blues group called James [Brown] and The Famous Flames."

When he wasn't listening to music Stephen was playing it, trying his best to emulate the latest records in a variety of genres. Although Peter, Paul and Mary and all the blues numbers were top of his list to mimic, by now, to his ears, Elvis Presley had lost his authenticity and he detested what he referred to as "fake black music."

His ambitions at this point were probably limited to maybe joining a band and enjoying life. A Budweiser or two and a few swigs of Bourbon at the local drive-in would have constituted a typical night out, as his buddy Michael revealed. Practicing and getting all the licks off pat from the endless output of blues numbers Stephen was hearing took up most of the rest of his available time. Writing songs probably wasn't something that crossed his mind. But even at this early stage there were fragments of information being squirreled away that would form the songwriter in him. He remembered his English teacher especially well as she inspired his lyrical alliteration on his 1969 recording 'Helplessly Hoping.' "She was a real knock-out. So much so that she got all the football players to stand up and read poetry, trying to impress her with how sensitive we were and how much we loved this awful stuff."

His formal education wasn't done yet as he swapped St. Leo's for yet another hall of learning at Gainesville High and began to seek out other like-minded teenagers to play music with. He helped out on drums with a local outfit called The Radars, who had a lead guitarist who made a big impression on him at the time, as he later explained to *Guitar Player* magazine: "His name was Chuck Schwin, in Tampa, Florida. He was a very fine guitar player, he played a Fender. There was a whole little bunch of us who were into kind of a combination of all the blues guys and others including Chet Atkins, Dick Dale, and Hank Marvin: a very weird cross section of far- out guitar players."

But Stephen was no slouch with the guitar himself, and his general enthusiasm got him an invitation to join a local band called The Continentals. His switch to guitar, Stephen later noted jokingly, was, as all drummers know, to avoid scratching and banging a prized automobile. "You can have a nicer car if you don't have to worry about drums. They're a pain in the neck! That was part of it. The other part was that I rather fell in love with Chuck Berry!"

He wouldn't ever leave playing drums behind entirely, but his constant level of practicing and improvement on guitar now had an outlet–his first proper audiences.

"My very first guitar was a Kay, mahogany, sunburst acoustic thing–it was very tinny. In the rock and roll band, when I switched from drums to guitar, I borrowed it–it was their version of a jazz guitar, acoustic electric, and I played rhythm on that," Stephen told *Guitar World*.

The Continentals were no big deal in Florida and had been created in order to satisfy teenager Jeff Williams' brother's assignment of getting a band together for the local fraternity party. Drummer and leader of The Continentals, it was Jeff who first spotted Stephen's potential, and after a swift audition invited him to join. Significantly, The Continentals already had one guitar player–another southern boy on his way to a famous career as a rock star, Don Felder. The talented Felder, who would go on to be a key member of the Eagles and co-write 'Hotel California,' remembers the newcomer's audition well. "Stephen came by this fraternity house, plugged in his guitar, and we thrashed away on E for a while. Then he played 'La Bamba' and a couple of other things. It was real good. And all of a sudden Stephen was in the band." Felder, who has remained friends and is a close neighbor and golf partner to Stephen these days, thought their dual lead guitar partnership "pretty funky." Gigging regularly around Gainesville, Florida, caused a few practical problems as Stills later remembered. "We played fraternity parties at the University of Florida and bars where I would lie about my age, which was virtually impossible because at 15 I looked maybe 11."

These must have been wild and exciting times for Stephen and Don, but it was Felder's mother who drove the two young guitarists to their Continentals bookings. On one occasion, when it is assumed Mrs Felder *wasn't* on driving duties, The Continentals played the Palatka prom, sleeping over at a hotel and getting drunk and partying the night away playing cards. "Stephen was a little more wild and crazy than the rest of us," admitted Felder, but it was his independence and drive that most impressed his friend. After four short months Stephen left The Continentals, replaced by another future Eagles guitarist, Bernie Leadon.

Stephen obviously shared Don Felder's view of his 'wild and crazy' side, as he admitted to Dave Zimmer. "We knew how to get nuts in the south, and boy could we drink! ... Some of the stuff we did was right out of *American Graffiti* and I was the [Richard] Dreyfuss character."

Yet another school of learning beckoned in 1961–this time Plant High in Tampa–where Stephen studied selectively by day and bagged groceries and worked at a racetrack to earn a few dollars in his spare time. Despite his out-of-school activities resembling a mash-up of *West Side Story* and *American Graffiti*, he continued to show a focused streak where music was concerned. But at Plant High his ambition and determined plan to become director of the 125-piece school orchestra was derailed when he was disciplined, wrongly as it turned out, for stealing another student's books. He was so deeply hurt and frustrated by the injustice of the punishment that he refused a subsequent invitation to take charge of the school's 30-piece band instead and quit Plant High.

His next move needed to be a dramatic one to escape the bad feelings associated with his Plant High experience. His family moving to South America gave him the perfect opportunity.

His father, mother, and both his sisters had already moved out of Florida for another move connected to William Stills' business dealings. Their destination, Costa Rica, would provide their son with a wonderful extra chunk of his music education, but once Stephen arrived he realized that Latin America rather lacked the excitement and scene he was used to as a 16-year-old teenager in the US. Although he subsequently described Costa Rica's capital city San Jose, where he wound up, as "beautiful, filled with art, culture and music" and compared it favorably with Paris, he soon discovered the place had some deficiencies. "In Latin America, there were no cheeseburgers or rock 'n' roll then," he pointed out.

So, once enrolled in a private school with all the other American State Department kids at Colegio Lincoln (aka La Escuela Lincoln in Costa Rica), he got his head down and worked enthusiastically at his studies by day and swapped his spare time Florida rebel-rousing for simple guitar practice.

"There was nothing in Costa Rica at night except ballroom dancing and drive-in cafes," he later told *Mojo*'s Sylvie Simmons. "So after homework, I'd go into the bathroom and develop that [Merle] Travis picking, or whatever kind of picking mine was, until my sister would come and yell at me."

He had by this time already seen how guitarist Chet Atkins 'picked' at close quarters, having taken in a demonstration at a local music store before also discovering the astonishing ability of Merle Travis on record. Now he put the two styles together.

Merle Travis had a syncopated style of finger-picking the guitar strings that attracted Stephen immediately, but the Kentucky country music star was not an obvious guitar hero. His career peaked in the 1940s, but the late 50s, early 60s folk revival in which his music gained a new audience was how Stephen would have picked up on the man famous for penning and first recording Tennessee Ernie Ford's monster hit 'Sixteen Tons.'

Not content with his old acoustic guitar, by now Stephen remembered hankering for something louder, as he later told Tavis Smiley in a TV interview. "Just finger- picking at first, I couldn't wait to get an electrified guitar so that I could get that thing where you incorporate the amplifier into the music that you're making."

The culture shock of inactivity in Costa Rica soon drove Stephen to make his own entertainment. Along with some school friends he put his energy into a project to create their own US-style drive-in movie. A patch of land was cleared, a movie projector borrowed, and a screen of white bed sheets erected. And when that wasn't filling his teenage free time he was checking out two musicians that would broaden his musical education. At the local hotel he was able to sample some of the local Latin and jazz that he would quickly try to adapt into his bathroom guitar sessions. Seeing bass guitarist Pala White and Pibe Hines on keyboards perform as part of the hotel's ensemble proved to be a valuable experience. As he later revealed in Anthony Fawcett's *California Rock, California Sound*, "Pala was a gentle soul and he taught me the underpinnings of Latin music. He taught me positions on the bass and that little anticipated beat, before the downbeat, which influences the way I play bass today." The practical side of Stills' piano-playing would also be enhanced by watching Hines in action. "He had the Erroll Garner influence, you know, and he taught me how to get a good spread–from what I first learned when I was eight or nine to playing fifths, and with my left hand and being able to manipulate octaves."

By late 1962, Stills had accumulated and absorbed an unusually varied mixture of sounds. The fact that he was by this time more than just a proficient guitarist can be proven by his first ever recording session for his song 'Travelin',' captured for posterity by the Voice of America United States Information Agency, in San Jose. There's an astonishing clarity to his vocal and the 16-year-old teenager sounds, well, amazingly, like the Stephen Stills we are all familiar with today. The guitar-playing is perhaps the most impressive aspect and pretty much bears his distinctive hallmark already. His lyrics don't amount to much but they are delivered with an almost cute sincerity, and he is at least writing about a subject he knows only too well … travelling and moving. The recording is featured as track one on his box set *Carry On*. Stills was taken aback when he listened again to the 2 minutes and 19 seconds of 'Travelin',' where, it has to be said, the word 'Lord' appears rather too many times. Nevertheless, he was rightly impressed with his young self.

"Oh my god, I was in shock! The song is kind of silly, but it's all I knew, about moving from one place to the next. 'Lord' is used more as an adjective than in a religious way. But the thing that shocked me was that my finger-picking style emerged almost completely whole while I was in Costa Rica."

The song–very much in the contemporary folk style of Peter, Paul and Mary–was fortunately recorded very cleanly and professionally, as Stills explained to Jeff Tamarkin for music.mag.com.

"One day a fellow said to me, 'I've got a whole apartment full of electronic gear, all the good stuff. I'll record you because nobody has yet.' I was 16, and he wasn't kidding: it was wall-to-wall, two rooms of electronic equipment. He had good microphones and maybe an Uher or a Grundig reel-to-reel recorder. It came out beautifully, and I don't know how it survived, but my sister saved it. The guitar style emerged whole—exactly the way I play now. Don't know if I have the jackhammer thumb I used to—I've developed a little carpal tunnel—but that's amazing."

Meanwhile, away from the music he was receiving home education in the form of lessons in Spanish from his mother over the kitchen table and enjoying and hating, in equal measure, his time studying subjects at Colegio Lincoln. Although he found math and the sciences to be "a crushing bore" he excelled in English and history. Teacher David Steinberg, now a journalist at the *Albuquerque Journal*, remembered his young student well.

"Stephen Stills was a high school senior in 63. I was told his parents were living in El Salvador, where his father was in the molasses-exporting business. It was unclear to me why Stephen was attending school in Costa Rica. I believe he was staying with family friends, and as I recall he drove a sports car to and from school. He really became animated on Fridays in my American history class when I invited students to bring American pop songs and musical instruments to class; I saw it as cultural history in a relaxed Friday afternoon, end-of-the-school-week setting. I do remember Stephen, playing an acoustic guitar, contributing folk songs, among them 'Puff The Magic Dragon.'

Steinberg also remembered the only time he recalled Stills singing at school and his love of horses: "For the senior prom, Stephen took the stage to sing a few songs with fellow seniors Ramon Coll and Rodrigo Barahona. I think it was fairly impromptu. And also for the senior trip, I was one of the chaperones on the class visit to Playa del Coco on Costa Rica's west coast. I do remember him playfully riding a horse, bareback, in the shallow waters along the beach."

The teacher-pupil relationship was such that the young 22-year-old Steinberg did meet Stills' parents and stayed with them in El Salvador for a few days and met Stephen's older sister in Mexico City. "Stephen gave me their phone numbers and addresses for my bus trip back to the US after the school year."

Stephen's schooling, family life, and guitar-playing were all pretty normal for a teenager at this point, but as he would point out in a BBC interview a decade later, South America was a volatile place to live at times with governments falling, rising, and falling again. "I had to dodge machine-gun bullets myself because me and my Dad were in town and everybody started shooting and I was off hanging out and I was trying to get home and it was one of those 'get back to the hotel alive' kind of things. It was nitty gritty."

In spite of the ever-present but infrequent dangers, he looks back on his time in Costa Rica mostly favorably, but with one big exception. "Going to Central America at that age, it opened my brain up. But it also cost me my rock band. I would have been a much better electric rock player, much earlier! I didn't get any good [on electric guitar] until I was 50! But it was a great mind-opening experience."

After passing his high school finals in December 1963, he left Colegio Lincoln and Costa Rica. During his absence from the US almost half a million people had attended a civil rights rally in Washington, DC to hear Martin Luther King speak, the world, never mind the US, had recoiled in horror at the death of President John F. Kennedy, and the simmering tensions down in south Vietnam were about to unleash more doom and gloom on a nation wondering what dramatic headlines they were about to wake up to next.

When Stephen returned to the US the music scene was changing rapidly. Aside from having hits, musicians were now having those chart hits by singing protest anthems. A new dawn in music was breaking, which had recently seen Bob Dylan walk out of *The Ed Sullivan Show* when told he could not sing his 'Talkin' John Birch Society Blues,' but bigger still was the news of The Beatles' arriving in the US for the very first time on February 7, 1964.

Although Stephen's idea had been to return to the US and enrol at the University of Florida in Gainesville, things didn't work out as planned. Soon after his arrival back in Florida he quickly realized that he was simply duplicating studies he had already completed in educational establishments he'd attended a couple of years previously. So he quit classes for good.

One can only imagine the eschewing row when he returned to touch base with his family again.

"So I went back to Latin America and had a tremendous fight with my father about being semi-sensible and using my brains," says Stephen of an important crossroads in his young life.

Make a living as a musician? There were hundreds of thousands of teenagers across America, about to fall under the spell of The Beatles and The Rolling Stones, feeling just like he did.

CHAPTER 2

'A Young Sprite In Greenwich Village'

His next move would see the now 18-year-old Stephen Stills head for New Orleans. When he applied for and got the job as a bartender in the first establishment he called on, along Bourbon Street, he had more than just bartending in mind. The Bayou Room had a small stage where he hoped his employer, a man with an eye patch, would give him a gig. But with a strip joint near the bar entrance he had his work cut out to keep the peace.

"I had to keep all the farmers from Arkansas from clawing the B-girls. A couple of times, I had to pull out a gun and I would hear, 'Who is this nine-year-old with a .45?!'"

Although the bar owner resisted Stephen's first requests for a slot performing on the stage, he soon conceded when a second voice started bending his ear.

Chris Sarns was another young, hopeful musician trying to capitalize on the then boom in folk music. His arrival at the

Bayou Room coincided perfectly with the owner's insistence to Stephen that he didn't book single performers–only groups. So Stephen (who favored Bob Dylan) and Chris (who was into The Kingston Trio) became a duo playing what Stephen referred to as "just lame folk."

It was hard work as Sarns recalled to Dave Zimmer: "We'd do five sets a night until all hours of the morning and made somewhat of a living. We ate a lot of these cheap little hamburgers."

For the rest of that spring and summer of 1964 the duo plodded on performing, but not necessarily the material they wanted to play. Stills, in particular, was becoming frustrated that he couldn't mix up the folk songs with just the occasional blues number. While he did moonlight at a black roadhouse playing drums in another band, he again felt self-conscious about just how young and out of place he looked: "I really did look like I was about nine."

After six months at the Bayou Room and occasional coffee-house gigs, Stephen found a convenient way out. Having already said goodbye to Chris Sarns, he followed his friend to New York, a vibrant hub of the folk scene, on the back of an invitation to hitch a ride with an East Coast folk group visiting the Bayou Room. Stephen didn't need asking twice. The day after his conversation with the Augmented 7th saw him tag along on the long journey north to New York, and more specifically Greenwich Village.

Arriving in the village he sought out Chris Sarns again and began to familiarize himself with the local folk circuit and clubs playing any kind of music. But it was the sound emanating from across the Atlantic in Liverpool that was making the biggest noise when he first arrived in NYC. "There was a movie house down the street and *A Hard Day's Night* came on. And everyone just went 'Yeh!'" remembered Stills of the August release of The

Beatles' film debut. Nevertheless, folk was still a hugely popular scene in the Village.

"We had missed that first wave of people, you know, Dylan and all those, but you could always go play," he recollected in an interview with Simon Harper for *Clash* in 2011. "Every night was open mic night, and you passed the hat, and I did fine. On the way home from work, I walked past the immortal Blue Note [club] and got to stop in and see Miles [Davis] and Dizzy Gillespie and Thelonious Monk and, god, every week there was somebody incredible. The Village Gate [club] was around the corner—I saw Nina Simone there. And then Simon and Garfunkel...Lenny Bruce was at the Cafe Au Go Go."

There's little doubt, of all the new sounds and personalities he experienced in Greenwich Village, who impressed him the most. Three names stand out in the many interviews Stephen gave on the subject: "Freddy [Fred Neil] and Timmy [Tim Hardin] and Richie Havens are probably more responsible for my style on guitar, along with Chet Atkins, than anybody else..."

When Havens passed away in 2013, Stills recalled their time together in NYC to *The Daily Telegraph*: "Richie Havens was one of the nicest, most generous, and pure individuals I have ever met. When I was a young sprite in Greenwich Village, we used to have breakfast together at the diner on 6th Avenue next to the Waverly Theatre. He was very wise in the ways of our calling. He always caught fire every time he played."

On the subject of breakfast, Stephen recalls how his meals were dependent on how many dollars there were in the hat from the five or six little clubs he would play regularly. "I would hope that I would make 15 cents in the first couple of sets so I could go across the street and have a slice of pizza for breakfast. And I'd work from about 7.30 until about 4.30 or 5 in the morning. It rained a lot and it was cold, and I got sick a lot. I was 20 maybe 19 years old and had no idea what in the hell I was doing! I just knew there was something there."

And there were a lot of other musicians trying to get a break just like him on the circuit. John Sebastian, Cass Elliot, and Phil Ochs were all competing for the folk dollar and there was a whole extra scene involving performers like Woody Allen and Lenny Bruce. "I even met Richard Pryor when he was just starting out. I took in all of the influences by osmosis, I guess," Stephen reflected.

He would also add Henry Diltz to the list of 'teachers' that helped his musical development. Diltz, whose incredible talent as a professional photographer is evident in this book, was a member of another popular Greenwich Village outfit, The Modern Folk Quartet. "Henry Diltz and the MFQ had an influence on how I looked at harmony singing ... and Henry taught me a lot about playing the banjo."

The plethora of clubs enabled Stills to perform outside the folk circuit at basket houses, where the blues got an airing. He'd turn up at the Bitter End, Four Winds, Gaslight, and Night Owl for a few dollars more, which enabled him to at least get a permanent roof over his head. On one such blues date he met kindred spirit John Hopkins, and when the two hit it off quickly they rented an apartment together.

It was probably during his apartment share with Hopkins that Stephen first experienced the siren call of the female folk singer who would play a significant part in his life a few years later. At any rate, he was certainly staying with "a friend" at this time, who just happened to own a copy of the recently released LP *Judy Collins 3*. Stills remembered being instantly entranced by the album sleeve portrait photo of the girl with "cornflower eyes," as he described her. "I spent a whole year, shivering in winter, listening to that voice," he recalled fondly.

Befriending John Hopkins would be practical in more ways than one. Through Hopkins, Stephen discovered that he had a look-a-like also playing the circuit locally. That look-a-like would turn out to be a Washington, DC-born blonde-haired banjo player called Peter Thorkelson, who had been told the same story. When the two 'look-a-likes' met at the Four Winds cafe they began a friendship that would quickly turn into an unnamed trio, performing with John Hopkins. But when Thorkelson (later to be anointed a Monkee as Peter Tork) left for California and Hopkins drifted off to Long Island, Stephen reunited the Bayou Room duo of Stills and Sarns.

It wasn't long before Stephen and Chris were head-hunted for a new project. New York impresario Eddie Miller was putting together a vocal folk revue outfit. His most recent claim to fame had been the composition of that year's big pop-folk hit 'Don't Let The Rain Come Down' for The Serendipity Singers. Miller began collecting together a bunch of talent that included Stephen, although ultimately not the unfortunate Sarns, who was drafted soon after. A mighty struggle then eschewed between Miller, who had formed the choral group, and the owner of the Café Au Go-Go, Howard Solomon. When Solomon won the battle to take over the group they became the Au Go-Go Singers and were booked to begin a residency at his club.

The Café Au Go-Go, situated at 152 Bleecker Street, was a 375-seater basement club that would help launch the careers of a number of rock acts besides Stephen. Grateful Dead, Cream, Blood, Sweat & Tears, The Mothers of Invention, The Yardbirds, and Jimi Hendrix would all find a New York City showcase for their talents here in the Sixties. Additionally, it became a haven for the Sixties' blues revival and encouraged jazz and comedy talent too. Demolished in 1977, the Café Au Go-Go once competed heavily for business with The Bitter End (still standing) across the street. So when their rivals had a resident group, The Bitter End Singers, Howard Solomon daubed his new protégés the Au Go-Go Singers and booked them for an initial 20-date run in August and September 1964. At last Stills was getting some steady work. "That was called a straight job, a day job. And I also got a lot of good training out of the cat, who was the arranger for that, a fellow by the name of Jimmy Friedman."

But the Au Go-Go Singers didn't make much money. The $500 weekly wage shared between ten members, from manager Solomon, hardly covered their expenses when on tour outside of New York City. If money was short the experience for Stephen was still a good one, as it meant regular work and the chance to record an album, *They Call Us Au Go-Go Singers*. At odds with his unbelievably youthful looks, Stephen delivered a rasping, soulful vocal on the folk-blues track he wrote titled 'High Flyin' Bird.' The rest of the album was mainly a throwback to the folk scene at a time when beat music, through the British Invasion, was grabbing the attention of teenagers across America. But, Like Stephen, another young member of the soon-to- be-outdated Au Go-Go Singers was making the most of his opportunity. Almost a year older than Stephen, Ohio-born Richie Furay would also contribute positively to the group's album with a confident, emotional reading of Tom Paxton's folk standard 'Where I'm Bound.'

Although the LP, on the Roulette label, was a commercial flop, it helped Stills and Furay to focus their minds on bigger and better projects ahead and how they might shed their folk shackles. A meeting with country music obsessive Gram Parsons would encourage them (Furay more so than Stills) to begin exploring another seemingly outdated genre.

Significantly, an album that would probably have disappeared from sale completely in the 21st century still has a life today thanks to Stills and Furay. *They Call Us Au Go-Go Singers* carries stickers on the CD case advertising the "First Recordings of Stephen Stills and Richie Furay."

By April 1965, the members of the Au Go-Go Singers had had enough and played their last gig at the Café Au Go-Go. As the group fragmented, a new outfit was formed featuring Rick Geiger, Roy Michaels, Michael Scott, and Jean Gurney, who had been The Bay Singers before their adventures in the Au Go-Go Singers. Calling themselves The Company, the group were spotted in their new form by the Rollins & Joffe talent agency and invited to tour Canada. Seeing another opportunity to broaden his horizons, and get a weekly wage doing it, Stephen asked to join and was added to the line-up. Little did he realize, as he set off with The Company for the short tour north, that the trip would provide an encounter with his most enduring partner in music.

CHAPTER 3
Monkee Business

"I was in a little folk group that got sent across Canada in a station wagon with the big bass fiddle sitting down the middle. And we were doing a set in Fort William, Ontario, and the club owner comes up on a Saturday night and says there's this visiting guy that we've had before with his band and we want him to do a set between your two sets. So great ... We listened to him for a minute and he's doing exactly what I planned to do when I got back to New York City, which is pick up an electric guitar and start writing my own songs."

That was how Stephen described his first encounter with Neil Young when talking to Tavis Smiley on his TV show in 2013. Toronto-born Young had scraped together a series of gigs, including one in particular that would see the two meet at the Fourth Dimension coffee house in Fort William, when Neil's trio, The Squires, were booked to support Stephen's 'little folk group' The Company. Stills and Young immediately hit it off and enjoyed each other's company over a beer or three before taking stock of their respective careers to date. The Squires were performing a variation of the kind of music Stephen was familiar with that he found excitingly different.

"Neil was playing folk rock before anybody else," Stephen maintained later when interviewed by John Einarson. "He had his big Gretsch guitar, a rock 'n' roll band that had just switched from playing 'Louie Louie' to playing the popular folk songs of the day with electric guitar, drums, and bass. It was an interesting band because they could go right from 'Cotton Fields' to 'Farmer John'."

Neil Young was similarly impressed with Stephen: "We got on quite well right away. Stills' voice was phenomenal. His guitar-playing was marginal. He was the rhythm guitarist and didn't really get into playing lead guitar until the Springfield. He had been with several singers in the Au Go-Go Singers and the whole hootenanny thing in New York, so he was voice-oriented, had voice training, and knew harmony."

There was definitely a feeling of camaraderie between the two and the instinct both had that they should stay in touch after the encounter in Fort William. Addresses were exchanged and The Company and The Squires both went their separate ways. Bizarrely, in the gap before the two would meet again, Stills would become more and more certain that he wanted to "go electric" and follow Neil's lead, while Neil became convinced that he wanted to become a coffee-house folkie like Stephen.

By this time, like most everybody else, Stephen had come under the spell of the records being released by The Byrds. Their fusion of folk and Dylan and rock and Beatles was now the kind of music he wanted to pursue. Several factors were combining to draw him in the direction that kind of music was coming from.

A move to the West Coast was calling.

One trigger was disappointment. He almost hitched up with New York friend and fellow musician John Sebastian. In an interview with TravelingBoy.com's Timothy Mattox, Stephen lamented, "I wanted to play bass for The Lovin' Spoonful, when I was in New York. But they got somebody else and that's what sent me to California as a matter of fact." Joining John Sebastian in The Lovin' Spoonful would have been a fast track into the big time. They were smashing the *Billboard* Hot 100 Top 10 with their debut hit 'Do You Believe In Magic' that August, when Stephen was contemplating his next move. His migration west was confirmed when a family crisis intervened. On hearing that his mother had left his father and moved back to New Orleans from El Salvador with his sister Ticita, Stills' plans must have accelerated.

So instead of heading out west on his own, he invited his mother and Ticita to go with him, traveled via New Orleans, and set out to settle everyone down in their preferred destination of San Francisco.

While based in San Francisco, Stephen took in the developing music scene that fall and another opportunity to be part of a band came to nothing. Mesmerized by the performance of a young Grace Slick at a Great Society gig he attended, Stills considered approaching her with an invitation to create a new band. "She was married to the drummer [Jerry Slick] of the band. [The Great Society] was terrible and I was just too shy to ask her if she wanted to get some good musicians and form a *real* band," he later admitted to Dave Zimmer. Grace Slick would very quickly find herself in a *real* band when Jefferson Airplane recruited her.

Sensing all along that L.A. might be a better place to build his faltering career, Stephen moved south. Despite the continued difficulty in finding a new home for his talents, he did, by this time, have some saleable songs. A new song would showcase his ability to write some observational, topical lyrics. 'Four Days Gone' was penned by Stills after meeting a draft dodger on the run. Less interesting, but at least financially lucrative, was 'Sit Down I Think I Love You.' Selling the publishing rights on it and a couple of other songs was something he clearly had to do to make ends meet at the time. With the one-off payment he received from the celebrated music executive Chuck Kaye he could at least eat and put a roof over his head. "I was starvin'!" he later confessed.

Yet another attempt to form a band fell by the wayside when an association with Van Dyke Parks, who was already involved with local bands Frank Zappa and The Mothers of Invention and The Beach Boys, failed to take off. The Van Dyke Parks Band, featuring guitarists Stills and Alabama singer-songwriter Steve Young, was a fleeting project, although Parks, with his shared love of Latin music, would remain a friend and useful contact.

Stephen's own fascinating recollections of Frank Zappa at this time were recorded in an interview with *Classic Rock*: "We were planning bands and we all lived in this little neighborhood off Sunset Boulevard, Orange Grove Avenue. He heard me play at some coffee house or something and he came up to me in the middle of the street and starts reading me the lyrics to 'Who Are The Brain Police?,' but he was so intense and overwhelming about it. I was like, 'Woah, that's cool.' He was really pretty out there at the time. Now, of course, he'd be considered middle of the road. I thought it was great. I went to a few sessions just because we used to just pop in on each other's sessions back then. You didn't have some three-hundred pounder at the door saying, 'Who the fuck are you?' He was directing a full orchestra and I heard these tracks before he got on to yelling over the top of them and they were just marvelous. I thought he was a genius. He suffered a lot after he broke his leg. He was the first person I know who didn't allow smoking in his studio. Which I thought was great."

Still no nearer to forming the rock 'n' roll band he wanted, Stephen did, however, get a few bookings as a duo alongside another guy heading west to escape the Greenwich Village folk scene, Ron Long. One night Stills and Long traveled out to Huntington Beach to play a gig at The Golden Bear and ran into yet another former Village folkie, Peter Thorkelson.

"The way I ran into him again was that Ron Long and I had a duo called the Buffalo Fish, which was the song of Ron's old group—Shaggy Gorillas Minus One Buffalo Fish. We would sing half rhythm and blues and just horse around a lot. They billed us as "funky folk-rock and comedy." So we were booked into the Bear and we were really terrible for the whole gig except for two nights. Those two nights Peter got up and played piano with us."

The reunion would prove life-changing for Peter. At The Golden Bear he was singing and playing his banjo when the management would give him a slot, backing up visiting musicians and washing dishes. When Peter expressed a wish to keep in touch with Stephen and Stephen told him over breakfast one morning that he'd call him if anything turned up, work wise, it set off a sequence of events that would lead Peter Tork to lucrative TV stardom as a member of a group that would rival even The Beatles for popularity.

The Monkees were a group assembled by Hollywood producers Bob Rafelson and Bert Schneider to capitalize on the success of The Beatles' movies *A Hard Day's Night* and *Help!* In a ground-breaking move, Rafelson and Schneider created their own group when they were unable to secure the services of current hot properties The Lovin' Spoonful and Britain's Dave

Clark Five. When auditions for the wacky actor/musicians they were seeking were advertised in showbusiness magazine *Daily Variety*, Stephen Stills went along in January 1966, having heard about the auditions from the Modern Folk Quartet's Jerry Yester.

Whether out of frustration that he was no nearer to forming a band or joining one, or simply thinking he sensed an opportunity, Stephen presented himself at the auditions that began in the fall of 1965 and ended in early 1966. More than 400 hopefuls competed for the parts from a small ad headed 'Madness!!' Any individuals interested were requested to call a number to attend an interview for 'Folk & Roll Musicians, Singers, for acting roles in new TV series. Running parts for 4 insane boys, age 17-21. Want spirited Ben Frank's-types. Have courage to work,' the ad stressed.

Stories circulated for years that Stills had been turned down for a role in the show because he had a gap in his teeth or his hair wasn't right, but as he later insisted, his motives behind auditioning wasn't to push to be a Monkee at all.

"I never tried out for them! I have said this a million times! I went in there to sell my songs. Do you think in my wildest dreams I wanted to be a damn fake Beatle on television? I was already writing songs, and I figured—I was young and dumb—that the only way I could get to them was a cattle call. I got in there and said, 'I've got all these songs.' And they said, 'That's already been fixed.' I said, 'What, you've got some Tin Pan Alley [person] writing all the songs?' and they said, 'Yeah.' I said, 'I don't want this job, but I know a guy you might like,' and that turned out to be Peter Tork."

So, Peter got the call Stephen had promised him if anything turned up.

"After he went down for the first interview, I asked him how he felt he did and he said, 'Well, it looks good. I'll see how things go.' And they kept calling him back. He liked Michael Nesmith. That was the first thing that happened."

Peter Tork duly convinced the interviewers that he had the perfect blend of comedy and music they wanted to join Davy Jones, Mike Nesmith, and Micky Dolenz in The Monkees. Stephen was left to continue his search for anyone who might want to make music with him.

For a time, Stephen's base in L.A. was the opulent Fountain Avenue home of Barry Friedman, a music businessman a few years older than Stephen. Friedman, who would later change his name to Frazier Mohawk, was already well connected. As a publicist, he'd handled the press conferences for The Beatles for their Hollywood Bowl performance in 1964 and had been hired by Brian Epstein to promote his top female Liverpudlian solo artist, Cilla Black, on the West Coast.

When Stills and Friedman were introduced by Dick Davis, a mover and shaker working at local music venue the Troubadour, Stephen was still a guest at Davis's apartment. Friedman immediately got what Stephen was all about, later describing him as "the kind of guy you know is going to make it, no matter what," and offered Stephen a roof over his head while he assembled a band. At least he now had support and easy access to a telephone, and he and Friedman rang round everyone they could think of to recruit band members to their project.

But even a call to Neil Young came to nothing when Stephen rang Neil's mother Rassy, only to be told that he'd broken up his band, was living with a folk singer, and she didn't know where he was herself. "She was really vexed with him," Stephen recalled.

The first signs that Stephen and Barry might finally be getting the band together they wanted didn't initially start out any more successfully than any of the other recent failed attempts. The first crucial name on the team sheet was that of Stephen's Au Go-Go Singers buddy Richie Furay. Richie, as it turned out, had been trying to contact Stephen, having met Neil Young in Greenwich Village and started covering the Young song 'Nowadays Clancy Can't Even Sing' in his dates at The Bitter End. Furay's letter to Stephen took a long time to reach him in L.A. "I sent it to his Dad in El Salvador," Richie explained to Dave Zimmer. "That's the only address I had on him. But the letter came back to me with postage due. It was one cent short! So I sent it out again with the right postage and waited to hear."

This time the letter, although going via Stephen's temporary San Francisco address, wasn't returned to sender and finally found its addressee.

By the time the letter arrived, Stephen was getting desperate to find another singer/guitarist to share the load in his imagined band line-up. Furay, he decided, would be the perfect fit. So, taking no chances, he phoned him and stretched the truth a little to get him out to California, telling the keen but cautious Furay that he had already assembled a band he wanted him to join. "I didn't really have a group yet," admitted Stephen, "but I figured Richie might not come if he knew it was just me."

The lie worked and Furay headed west, only to discover the disappointing truth that there was no group and precious little else to sustain him apart from Stills' continued focus on making something happen.

If Stephen's anxiety about a lack of progress had been high before, it was doubled following the arrival of the unemployed Furay. They were at the heart of the burgeoning West Coast scene, surrounded by dozens of great music clubs and venues, and had the support of a man in the know, but the delay and frustration in getting anything off the ground was obviously beginning to effect Stephen. Here's how Denny Doherty of The Mamas & The Papas remembers Stephen's state of mind in an extract from Barney Hoskyns' *Hotel California*: "I'm sitting in Barney's Beanery and in walks Stephen Stills. He looks kinda down, so I ask him what he's doing. He says 'Fuck all, man, I ain't doin' nothin'. 'Two or three weeks later I walked into the Whisky and Bam! There he is with a band. I said to him, 'What the fuck? Did you add water and get an instant band?'"

CHAPTER 4
Follow That Hearse

In their quest to assemble a perfect band, indeed any kind of band, Stills, Furay, and Friedman needed a break, and on April 6, 1966 they got one. As fate would have it, two other musicians who were out of work and leaving L.A. that day would share in one of those great, fortuitous moments in rock history.

The group that Neil Young and bass guitarist Bruce Palmer had until recently been members of, The Mynah Birds, had just split up and the duo had invested in an old 1953 Pontiac hearse to enable them to drive from Toronto to the land of musical opportunity, L.A. On arrival they then spent five days without accommodation, sleeping in the hearse and using gas-station bathrooms at night, and on Neil Young's insistence, trying to reconnect with the guy he'd remembered from Fort William, Stephen Stills. All Young knew was that Richie Furay had told him Stephen was hanging out in L.A. So they asked around at clubs like The Trip and Huffs on Sunset Strip, but on the sixth day they gave up and decided to head north to San Francisco to experience the newly-born Haight-Ashbury hippie scene.

As Young and Palmer hit a traffic jam on Sunset Boulevard, a white van containing Stills, Furay, and Friedman was crawling slowly in the opposite direction. When he gazed out of the van's window and saw a hearse with a Canadian license plate, Stephen had no doubt about the identity of the occupant. "I knew exactly who it was before I even saw who was driving. Neil had another hearse that had died in Thunder Bay, but this one was a Pontiac he'd driven all the way to California, and when I pulled behind him, he was actually looking for 77 Sunset Strip!" he later joked, to *Vintage Guitar*.

A highly illegal U-turn enabled the van to inch up behind the hearse, and after much yelling, horn honking, and frantic waving, Stills, Friedman and Furay attracted the attention of the startled Young and Palmer. When both vehicles found their way out of the busy traffic and into a Ben Franklin store parking lot, they got out in an excited huddle (and some introductions for Palmer and Friedman) before heading off to Friedman's home for a party and the inevitable jam session. It's hard to quantify how much this reunion meant to the various personnel, but for Neil Young it was the perfect culmination to his Hollywood experience. It's hard to imagine now just how exciting and unattainable that experience must have seemed to the Canadian. To have found the guy that he'd clearly not forgotten and tried to track down was a joyful bonus. For Stephen it was relief that in that moment in the parking lot he had found the kindred, driven spirit who would help him realize his dreams.

The song that became the catalyst for them forming a band was 'Nowadays Clancy Can't Even Sing.' Neil had played his song to Richie back in New York; then Richie had begun performing it in his solo gigs and Stephen and Richie had worked out an exciting harmony blend. Now Neil could really see the potential of what they could do together—with Palmer on bass—and exciting plans were made to join forces.

The new group was still one member short. They needed a drummer, and a friend of Stephen's, Billy Mundi, looked like he might be the answer until the real deal turned up in the form of Dewey Martin. He came well recommended by The Byrds' manager Jim Dickson, who had heard on the Hollywood grapevine that Stills and co. needed a drummer to complete their line-up. His career had already seen him as the go-to drummer for Nashville stars Patsy Cline, Buck Owens, Carl Perkins, and George Jones. His CV also included drumming for Roy Orbison, Faron Young, and a recent stint in The Dillards. The oldest and most experienced of the five-man line-up, Dewey Martin (another Canadian) meant that the two original US members were now outnumbered. A trivial observation, perhaps, but factions and feuds would become a repetitive theme in the soap opera surrounding this band. Stephen Stills was unquestionably the leader as they faced their first big decision: What shall we call ourselves?

CHAPTER 5

"Fluid and Bluesy... Fuzzy and Angry"

The naming of Stephen, Richie, Neil, Bruce, and Dewey's new band would be one of those finger-snapping, back-slapping moments when everyone agrees on a great idea at once. Grabbing their attention was a nameplate on a steamroller that was re-surfacing the Hollywood streets: It read 'Buffalo Springfield.' Exactly how they spotted it varies, depending on who you ask. Dewey Martin suggested the band-naming occurred around the time he auditioned at Fountain Avenue, with Stephen telling Dave Zimmer that the sign was somehow gleefully removed from the steamroller as a souvenir. "Neil and Barry [Friedman] had stolen a 'Buffalo Springfield' sign off the steamroller for Barry's house. They put it up. We all looked at it on the wall and a light went off. That's how we came up with the name.

"We thought it was pretty apt," Stephen added when interviewed years later on the Tavis Smiley TV show, "because Neil Young is from Manitoba which is buffalo country, and Richie

Furay was from Springfield, Ohio… and I'm the field!" he joked.

They had a name–well two actually, as locally they were also known as The Herd for a time–but no money to speak of, and Canadians Neil and Bruce didn't even have the working permits or paperwork required to earn a living in California. All they did have was a shared feeling that their respective careers had stalled. But with at least some experience of performing and recording and an enthusiastic will to succeed, it didn't take them long to rehearse a set of songs they could play on stage.

They didn't have to travel far for their first gig. On April 11, 1966 they made their debut at the now legendary Doug Weston's Troubadour on Sunset Boulevard, using some old equipment from The Dillards. "When we started," Stills told *Guitar Player* magazine in 1970, "it was a Duane Eddy 500 they gave me when I was with The Buffalo Springfield. It was too heavy for me. It just wasn't the right six-string, so I took the body and filed it in a little bit on the inside because the 12-string will feed back if you don't have something solid under the bridge."

It was not an explosive start to their career: they were an unbilled extra band given the Troubadour's small front 'Folk Den' space, and they might well have been one of the first groups to play an electric set there. As luck would have it, Chris Hillman of The Byrds had dropped round to Barry Friedman's house to watch the Springfield rehearse and was in the audience at the Troubadour that Monday night. His interest and endorsement would prove crucial to the future of Buffalo Springfield. The Byrds were the real folk-rock deal at the time with two *Billboard* Hot 100 Number 1 singles to their name already and 'Eight Miles High,' their latest release, confirming their exalted status that spring. With Hillman's approval and help, by the end of the week Buffalo Springfield had found a place on the bill supporting The

Byrds and The Dillards at Swing Auditorium, National Orange Showgrounds, in San Bernardino. Their fee was a modest $125, but they were now mixing in the right circles and attracting interest from further afield.

San Bernardino radio station KMEN's British DJ John Ravenscroft (aka John Peel), who was hired to MC the event, was struck by the Springfield's friendliness and had no doubt they would do well. That impression was in stark contrast to his opinion of The Byrds, who he described as rude and "an absolutely obnoxious bunch of people" when talking to Dave Fisher of *Filler* magazine later. The gig might have been an opportunity for Stephen to meet David Crosby, who was on stage with The Byrds that day. However, Crosby's first reaction to what Stephen and Buffalo Springfield were doing would come a month later when he accompanied Chris Hillman to the Whisky a Go Go in West Hollywood to watch the band.

Chris Hillman's support–he even thought about managing them for a moment–was what got them a week-long run to show what they could do at the Whisky. Hillman talked the club's owner, Elmer Valentine, into hiring the Springfield, who would go on to make the Whisky their second home, with many more performances throughout the remainder of 1966. When asked by Dave Zimmer what he thought of the band back then, David Crosby was vaguely positive: "I don't know, man, all I can remember is Stephen and Neil cookin' real good on guitars. And I liked their harmonies. I knew they had something right away."

Tom Petty would later describe the guitar-duelling dynamic in the Springfield perfectly: "One fluid and bluesy" was how he described Stephen, and "the other fuzzy and angry," in Neil's case.

Stephen and the rest of the band were certainly enjoying themselves. "I remember that first week at the Whisky and the gigs we did with The Byrds," remembered Stephen. "We could really smoke! That band never go on record as bad and as hard as we were. Live we sounded like The Rolling Stones. It was great."

The Springfield's Whisky a Go Go appearances soon attracted queues of fans and a steady stream of music business talent scouts wanting to check out a band many felt might give The Byrds a run for their money.

A small bidding war developed to sign the band, which saw Dunhill bid $5,000, Warner Brothers $10,000, and Atlantic eventually win the day with a $12,000 advance that the band finally agreed to. Some reports suggest that Ahmet Ertegun's final Atlantic bid was as high as $22,000. Ertegun had received great reports of the Springfield. They were hot, happening, and had songs ready to record from more than one member of the band. Ertegun's initial excitement would not be misplaced and his relationship with Stephen would prove to be an incredibly enduring one in a business littered with fall-outs.

By now, Barry Friedman had enlisted the help of Dickie Davis (lighting man at the Troubadour) to manage the escalating interest in the band he and Stills had created.

As the gigs (mostly in and around L.A. and San Francisco) came thick and fast, they would share a bill with Country Joe and The Fish, The Turtles, Moby Grape, and Big Brother and The Holding Company. Most exciting of all was a support slot for the visiting Rolling Stones at the Hollywood Bowl on July 25, where 19,000 turned out to see the British band who had recently achieved their third *Billboard* Number 1 single 'Paint It Black,' coincidentally recorded in Hollywood's RCA Studios.

In the dog-eat-dog world of the music business, it was perhaps inevitable that Barry Friedman and Dickie Davis lacked the experience to handle the increasing demands on them and the band. Management of the group was soon taken over by Brian Stone and Charlie Greene, who were evidently more aggressive than Friedman or Davis. Sensational reports suggest Greene and Stone took Friedman for a limo ride, when a gun pointed on Friedman's thigh was enough for Stephen's original benefactor in L.A. to sign over his rights to the band on a hotdog napkin. Greene and Stone had previous. They had managed Sonny and Cher's meteoric rise to stardom for Atco recordings like 'I Got You Babe.' The Atco label (a subsidiary of Atlantic Records) would soon become home to Buffalo Springfield too.

In July, the process of recording the songs needed for the band's first album and single, with Greene and Stone producing, got underway. Under the watchful eye of engineer Doc Siegel, Buffalo Springfield recorded pretty much everything they had written down at Hollywood's Gold Star Studios.

Stephen's 'Go And Say Goodbye' and 'Sit Down I Think I Love You' had the upbeat quality that had single written all over them, but it was Neil's plaintive 'Nowaday's Clancy Can't Even Sing' that eventually became the band's first A-side (with 'Go And Say Goodbye' on the flip side) after distributors decided in favor of Neil's song, with Richie Furay taking lead vocal. Locally the disc would hit Number 25 in the L.A. area, but wider acceptance of the band would have to wait a few months. Another Neil A-side, 'Burned,' followed soon after, with Stephen's 'Everybody's Wrong' on the B-side. Neither single dented the *Billboard* Hot 100. The competition to see who would have the most tracks selected on their debut album was healthy and friendly at this stage. With the simply titled *Buffalo Springfield* there would be seven Stills songs and four for Young.

With high hopes for the future successful release of the album and the acclaim he craved, Stephen surveyed the music scene and was encouraged by the progress two of his peers were making. John Sebastian was enjoying his first *Billboard* Number 1 hit as the writer and leader of The Lovin' Spoonful. The band's 'Summer In The City' would be the soundtrack of the 'groovy' summer of 1966, and the other former Greenwich Village folkie friend was about to become a celebrity pop star.

Although Stephen hadn't seen Peter Tork in some time, by September he was making his TV debut and Stephen was asked by *Tiger Beat* magazine to comment on his friend's new role. "I saw the first Monkees show on TV and I liked it. Peter plays the dumby, though he's certainly not. He's the Tommy Smother's character. Now I've decided I like the show." Peter Tork would be a household name weeks later as the show drew millions of teenage fans.

"I didn't see Peter again until November 1966, and then it was a real shock. We [Buffalo Springfield] were doing a show at the Santa Monica Civic Auditorium for KBLA and, without our knowing, Peter decided he was going to introduce us. We didn't even know he was there. We were ready to go on and suddenly Peter walked on stage and there was complete bedlam! It was incredible!"

That same month something happened that would boost Stephen's career and provide Buffalo Springfield with a hit single and much critical acclaim. Stephen's new song was moody, catchy, and with a powerful message. The lyrics were written one day when he was bored and in need of a night out. Leaving his Topanga house, he headed down toward the city and describes what he saw that day that made him write 'For What It's Worth.'

"I came up over a hill in Los Angeles and went down Laurel Canyon and they were having a funeral for a bar. Now this place had been just a little bungalow in the middle of a triangular block, but it had spilled over onto the thoroughfare and that, under Los Angeles city ordinance, is a public nuisance, you know. If it's a favorite watering hole, everyone comes to say goodbye to it. It was called Pandora's Box. So the cops show up in battalion force. My sense of security said, turn the car around and go the other way. The other reason for turning the car around was I wanted to get to a guitar right then. It took me no longer to write it than it took to write the sentences on the piece of paper. It was writing itself on the way home."

Stephen has insisted that he didn't set out to write a protest song: "I don't want to be a propagandist. That's why 'For What It's Worth' is so enigmatic." That said, the song has been adopted countless times as a warning shot to be heeded by everyone when things get tough, as he explained to Dave Zimmer: "'For What It's Worth' was me going, 'Pssst. I think we're in trouble.' The troops in 'Nam took it as their marching song. It became the theme song for the entire Third Marines for a while."

But a great set of lyrics does not a great song make. It was the gentle, ominous chiming guitar that drew most people in first and enabled Buffalo Springfield to catch fire during the following months. But the process of putting everything together needed all the right help and support from the record company. Managers Brian Stone and Charlie Greene were fortunately in the office when Stephen called by, carrying his guitar to announce that he'd just written a new song. He then picked up his guitar after crucially introducing his new composition by saying, "I'll play it . . . for what it's worth."

Stone and Greene were impressed enough with what they heard to book the Columbia studio immediately, and on December 5 Buffalo Springfield recorded the as-yet-untitled song. When Stephen pointed this out, Charlie Greene reminded him that he had already given them the title when he first introduced it as … 'for what it's worth,' and Stephen went along with that.

A day later Stone and Greene played the recording down the phone line to Atlantic Records boss Ahmet Ertegun in New York, who loved what he heard. What he didn't agree with was their thinking behind the title, which he strongly felt must be the song's key lyric–'Hey What's That Sound?' He also insisted that the line 'There's a man with a gun over there' had to go. Stephen, who was present during the call, decided he wouldn't budge on either issue and, perhaps surprisingly, Ahmet Ertegun let him have his way with the proviso that his own favored title appeared in brackets before the main title. And so the track was released as '(Hey What's That Sound?) For What It's Worth,' in a compromise that would preface the incredibly respectful relationship Stills and Ertegun would enjoy throughout their working lives.

Immediately after Christmas, Buffalo Springfield completed some local TV appearances before heading to New York for a hectic week at Ondine's, preceded by one appearance at The Night Owl. Their stay in New York was blighted by the arrest on a drugs charge of the increasingly unstable Bruce Palmer, which led to him being deported back to Canada.

CHAPTER 6

There's Something Happening Here . . .

January 1967 saw the release of debut album *Buffalo Springfield* on Atco. The band were faced with the considerable inconvenience of having no bass player in the line-up to meet all the demands of the gigs they were due to play to promote the LP. As the record hit the shops the band were forced to get Dickie Davis to pretend he was playing bass for a TV appearance. The ABC-TV Hollywood Palace booking (for six appearances in total) had come about when the Springfield had impressed the show's producer, Nick Vanoff, during their recent support slot for The Rolling Stones. Stephen dressed up for the occasion in a sharp suit and huge Stetson and Davis did what he had to do to fulfil the commitment before Love bass guitarist Ken Forssi was drafted in for a one-off gig at Gazzarri's in West Hollywood.

Fortunately, they found a more permanent replacement for Bruce Palmer when Ken Koblun stepped into the breach. Koblun, who had briefly joined Stephen and Richie for a few days during their first weeks in California, was another Canadian and was recruited by Neil Young, with whom he had previously shared a stage in The Squires.

There was a good deal of nervous excitement expelled as the band waited to find out what the record-buying public thought of *Buffalo Springfield*. The seven Stills compositions showed little innovation lyrically, but it is the arrangements and the interweaving guitars of Stephen, Neil, and Richie that excited most, particularly on the up-tempo staccato country of 'Go And Say Goodbye' and 'Leave.' 'Sit Down I Think I Love You' was given a well-needed menacing injection of fuzz guitar from Neil. 'Hot Dusty Roads' was Stephen and Richie happily and harmoniously ripping off The Beatles. 'Everybody's Wrong' might have been a perfect fit for The Monkees, and maybe Stephen did offer it up at that fateful audition. 'Pay The Price' sounded like Stephen had been practising his Rolling Stones licks. 'Baby Don't Scold Me' was lyrically, like the rest, not as lucid–or as Stephen would agree–as poetic as the Neil songs on the album. Even the titles of Neil's songs indicated a certain edginess: 'Nowadays Clancy Can't Even Sing,' 'Flying On The Ground Is Wrong,' 'Burned,' 'Do I Have To Come Right Out And Say It' (featuring some wonderful prototype CSN harmonies), and 'Out Of My Mind' all sounded new and frankly a little dangerous.

In hindsight many fans, and certainly the band themselves, might have looked back on the album as an opportunity missed in one area–to convey the excitement of their live performances on disc. Stephen and Neil were still in thrall to producers Greene and Stone, who pretty much controlled things in the studio. But the results certainly came up to at least some of Stephen's expectations. He'd achieved much of what he'd attempted to set up when he departed Greenwich Village for California's rock 'n' roll gold rush, even if Buffalo Springfield weren't about to sustain their promising start. "In the end we blew it," he reflected when interviewed by the UK's *Disc and Music Echo*. "But while it lasted I suppose it was the nearest thing to an American version of The Beatles. Not in fame and acclaim, but simply in musical terms."

The Beatles influence even extended to Richie Furay and Stephen apeing the Lennon and McCartney harmonies, with Neil on the edge vocally as the Springfield's George Harrison. Like George, his guitar parts and vocal and writing skills would eventually flourish in spectacular fashion.

The Beatles also played a part indirectly in the Springfield getting some much- needed radio play. When Stephen was played an unreleased tape of The Beatles' 'A Day In The Life' by David Crosby, who'd picked it up from Paul McCartney in London, he couldn't contain his enthusiasm and told Greene and Stone. Soon after, Crosby had a visitor. "Well, these guys hired this girl to come and fuck me and swipe the tape," Crosby later told Dave Zimmer. "After that went down Greene and Stone went to KJH [L.A. Top 40 radio station] and told 'em, 'We'll give you a tape of some new Beatles stuff if you'll play The Buffalo Springfield's 'Nowadays Clancy Can't Even Sing.' I'll be damned if they didn't go for it."

Although 'Clancy' wouldn't trouble the *Billboard* Hot 100, Stephen's 'Sit Down I Think I Love You' had. When the band Stephen might have formed with Van Dyke Parks came to nothing, Parks did give Stephen a boost by recommending the song to San Francisco group The Mojo Men, who had their only Top 40 hit with it. Having already sold the rights in 1965, Stephen wouldn't get a cent more from his first hit single. But around the same time he was enjoying much greater success from a song that would elevate him to a new level entirely.

Stephen's new (and best song yet) would eventually hit Number 7. Here was a song that would resonate immediately and still get played regularly over half a century later. 'For What It's Worth' was *so* hot on release as a single that the debut album would be re-issued with it as the lead track and 'Baby Don't Scold' axed to make way. The song was a game-changer for Stephen. It was observational, strong on simplicity, but with a killer hook, musically and vocally. Who would disagree with lyricist Sir Tim Rice when he says, "'For What It's Worth' is one of the best songs ever written with just two chords."

CHAPTER 7

Ahmet The 'Elegant' Turk

The first half of 1967 would see various visits to the studio to cut new material as and when the Springfield's busy schedule would allow. A more permanent replacement for Bruce Palmer was found when The Mothers of Invention's bass player Jim Fielder was enlisted. Despite the absence of Palmer, who Stephen had grown to believe was a hugely integral part of the band, Buffalo Springfield were at this point at the height of their creativity and popularity.

With a tight schedule of gigs and an appearance on The Smothers Brothers' CBS TV show, things could have got a whole lot busier for Stephen in late February. If his old friend Peter Tork had had his way, Stephen might have been offered the chance to oversee the next Monkees album. Following the dismissal of musical supervisor Don Kirshner, Mike Nesmith turned to Turtles bass guitarist Chip Douglas for help to produce the band's first album, where they would actually get to play their instruments, with the tracks creating the soundtrack to the second TV season. It turned out that Douglas wasn't entirely confident he knew how to do the job, but financially it came with an offer he couldn't turn down. Peter Tork, who admits he was less assertive than he should have been, was disappointed his friend Stephen wasn't given the job. "I would have chosen Stephen Stills. I had considered him, then asked him, and he said, 'Yeah I'd love to do it,' and then, before I got to say that, Mike said, 'I got Chip.'"

It's clear from an interview with *Tiger Beat* magazine at the time that Stephen and Peter had a mutual appreciation society going on. When he couldn't move into his new Woodland Hills property immediately, Peter invited Stephen to stay at his place. It gave Stephen an insight into the pop star lifestyle, as he revealed to Peter's teenage fans in 1967: "It's really groovy at Peter's house. People just come over and we talk or sit around and watch color TV. We don't have any favorite programs, we just mainly like the color TV. Sometimes we mess it up so there's dots and flashes; it's like our own light show.

"I've learned some things about Peter that I didn't know before, like he likes to live in a cold house. '72 degrees is plenty warm enough,' he says. He doesn't like the heat turned up. Also, he loves Chinese food, but he doesn't cook if he can help it. He much prefers to be 'cooked for'.

"There's usually a parade of fans every afternoon up at the house. They come up to the door and whisper 'Is Peter here?' and then they run away. If he's home he'll go out and sign some autographs, but he's not home that often. He's usually working.

"We often sit around and play guitars. His favorite song right now is 'Strawberry Fields Forever.' The groups we'll listen to are The [Lovin'] Spoonful, The Beatles, of course; The Mamas & [The] Papas; and Peter digs the Springfield.

"When we're not playing music or listening to music, we're usually picking things apart—groups, ideas we hear from people, pieces of music, each other's brain.

"The quality I respect, more than anything else in Peter, is his honesty. More than any person I know, Peter gives of himself. If you have a problem you can always depend on him for some kind of answer or some kind of suggestion, no matter what it is. He doesn't worry about offending you, because he just wants to be honest. To me, that's being a true friend."

It was a rather touching, gentle interview at a time when it's easy to forget that, despite the Summer of Love vibe, America was involved, up to its neck, in a terrifying conflict on the other side of the world. By the middle of the year (on June 23 to be precise) the Vietnam War would become the longest war in American history, with more than 500,000 US military personnel deployed. Stephen's 'For What It's Worth' would become something of an anthem adopted by the young troops in Southeast Asia and anti-war protesters back home. There appeared to be no conflict of emotions by Stephen when asked for his take on the war, despite his military school background. He was solidly in favor of the growing protest movement to which many musicians were aligning themselves during this Summer of Love. "I actually quite agreed, because I'd studied a lot of history and it did not make a lick of sense," he told *Mojo*'s Sylvie Simmons in 2013. And at his draft hearing there was no need to play the insanity game well used by so many to avoid being sent to Vietnam. "I went in prepared to put on a marvelous show. But the guy said, 'You're as deaf as a post, we can't have you.' It turned out I was already deaf by then."

The regular visits to the studio began to create an impression that Buffalo Springfield were stacking up a pile of new music. Unsurprisingly, they were being cajoled into cutting new material to catch the current wave of popularity driven by the chart success of 'For What It's Worth,' and a new LP titled *Stampede* was slated for release. But the band and record company weren't quite on the same wavelength, and despite Atco printing almost 100,000 record covers for *Stampede* there was little or no music the band were happy with to fit inside the redundant sleeves.

With the band clearly trying to work at their own creative pace, more great music was imminent from Stephen, and it was about to be recorded with the control he would begin to relish over the next few years.

By this time Stephen and Neil had learned all they needed to know from Charlie Greene and Brian Stone and began to produce themselves. Under Ahmet Ertegun's benevolent and watchful eye they each took control of their own songs, and on April 4 at Sunset Sound Stephen recorded the incredibly complex but beautiful 'Bluebird.' The confidence no doubt gained creating 'For What It's Worth' had given him the ability to reach a level of song-writing sophistication that was impossible to envisage up to now. 'Bluebird' sounded more like a Stephen Stills solo song, with minimal impact from the rest of the band and expert help on a tricky banjo part added by session player Charlie Chin and bass guitar courtesy of The Monkees' session man, Bobby West.

Up to this point, Stephen hadn't actually met Ahmet Ertegun—the man he had argued with over the phone about creative differences on 'For What It's Worth.' First impressions during Ertegun's visit to the Sunset Sound studios were favorable and it would mark the beginning of the incredibly close working relationship between Stephen and the founder and chief of Atlantic Records. When interviewed by *Mojo*'s David Fricke,

Stephen remembered that first meeting well. "He was a very elegant guy. I liked him right away. He took me under his wing, right there. In later years, he admitted that I looked like Bobby Darin, whom he adored. Ahmet cared about the Springfield deeply. He recognized Neil's talent and mine."

Stephen would come to look upon the Turkish-born Ertegun, who was 21 years older, as a father figure. His respect for Ertegun was due in no small part to the music mogul's huge enthusiasm for the music he promoted and his strong business acumen. It was an incredibly rare and powerful combination of skills that Stephen would come to rely on greatly.

The debut album had begun as a band project that would quickly begin to show three individual talents flourishing separately. Their eventual follow-up album would reinforce the feeling that the three main songwriters were not going to collaborate along the lines of the Lennon and McCartney and Jagger and Richards partnerships that had certainly inspired Stephen. Neil Young was even beginning to wonder what he was doing in a rock band. The inner folk musician in him hadn't gone away, and his devotion to what started out as Stephen's project was soon to evaporate.

CHAPTER 8
Crosby, Stills, Hendrix & Young

The Buffalo Springfield touring schedule was a punishing one throughout the spring of 1967. The frequency and locations of bookings meant that a private jet was hired to enable them to fly backward and forward from L.A. to San Francisco during one intense three-day period. But tension was growing between the band members and flare-ups between Stephen and Dewey Martin and Stephen and Neil were as much to do with the lack of privacy and relentless list of gigs and interviews they were now obliged to fulfil. The lack of control over their lives was beginning to take its toll, and by the end of May, ahead of a particularly important date in the diary, Neil Young decided to opt out of the madness.

"Actually, the reason I initially left the group was because I didn't want to do the Johnny Carson *Tonight Show*,"Young told *Mojo* in 1995. "I thought it was belittling what the Buffalo Springfield was doing. That audience wouldn't have understood us. We'd have been just a f—in' curiosity to them." Dewey Martin remembers the waiting game: "What we did was we went back and had three days in Massachusetts, and the last day was the Johnny Carson show. We were hoping Neil would show up. There was no Neil and we called the office in Los Angeles and nobody had heard from him."The no-show clearly highlighted the biggest difference of opinion between Stephen and Neil at the time. Stephen saw an opportunity to raise the band's profile to a new level while Young seemed to want to lower his own personal profile. With Neil hidden away in the San Fernando Valley, Stephen was eyeing the prize, convinced that the lucrative Carson show could have led to a spot on the even more prestigious *Ed Sullivan Show*.

Neil Young would later admit that perhaps he and Stills should at least have talked about his reluctance to do the TV date. Stills' summing up? "Neil had to quit at exactly the time it meant the most."

However, Dewey Martin wasn't going to give up on the Johnny Carson booking easily. It was his idea to get Otis Redding as a last-minute replacement to perform Neil Young's 'Mr Soul' on the show. He even flew to New York to persuade Redding personally, but the singer's commitment to a concert date at the Apollo scuppered the plan.

Neil Young's reluctance to do the TV show was not the only reason he disappeared. It was the increasing speed at which everything was happening that wore him down. "My nerves couldn't handle the trip," he later revealed to *Rolling Stone*'s Cameron Crowe.

Minus Neil and with a number of prestigious appearances lined up, it seemingly never occurred to Stephen to disband the Springfield. With the Summer of Love in full swing there would be a number of changes in personnel that would hinder Stephen's ability to get Buffalo Springfield sounding like Buffalo Springfield. Soon after Neil had dropped out, Bruce Palmer somehow managed to get his act together and replace Fielder on bass. Daily Flash guitarist Doug Hastings came in to do a creditable impression of Neil's guitar-playing, but the Springfield had lost more than just a guitar player. Without Neil's song-writing contribution and stage presence, the group's acclaimed run of success would be in danger of plateauing out. The void would, at least temporarily, soon be filled by someone, like Neil, who would play an equally huge role in Stephen's life.

David Crosby was becoming increasingly frustrated with his role in The Byrds and had begun hanging out with Stephen. "He was the social gadfly and I was pretty much the shy guy–bashful" is how Stephen remembered their early encounters when interviewed by Tavis Smiley.

Both immediately found they had one important thing in common. "I remember hearing what an arrogant arsehole David was," Stephen told Dave Zimmer, "But when I met him, I found he was basically just as shy as I was, and making up for it with a lot of aggressive behaviour. I recognized the symptoms, because I was like that myself."

Both Stephen and David clearly had a ton of untapped youthful creativity and, as Stephen described later in Joe Smith's *Off The Record*, they were musically and personally compatible: "I remember David Crosby and I doing a concert for one of the free clinics. The Kingston Trio, Peter, Paul and Mary, and God knows who else was there, and we all ended up at Alan Pariser's house. I will never forget the conversation. We were all sitting around and I said, 'You know, we ought to do one of those things with a whole bunch of new rock bands.' And Alan looks at me and says,

'Where would you do it?' And I say, 'Oh, where they hold that jazz festival, in Monterey.'"

The next day Alan Pariser called up Stephen and organized a meeting with Ben Shapiro, who would become the original director of the festival. At the Hollywood meeting Stephen repeated his idea, and when asked to expand suggested a few names that might play on the bill. Pariser and Shapiro allegedly ended the meeting by saying 'We'll get back to you,' but two weeks later Stephen returned to the now- functioning Monterey Jazz Festival office to beg Andrew Loog Oldham for a place on the bill he'd suggested.

"We get to Monterey and Lou Adler is telling me maybe we'll get to play on Saturday night," Stephen continued, "But Neil's not in the group, so I get David Crosby to come and sit in with the band so at least there's somebody sitting in, and probably that was the only way that Buffalo Springfield, which was this unimportant little band, could get a spot on the bill."

How much Stephen Stills was responsible for the shape of the event or even its location is open to question, but the combination of Crosby and Stills on stage together must have sewed a few seeds in the minds of both that they could help each other in whatever future music directions they were headed.

With everyone on a high looking forward to Monterey, Stephen decided to pay his sister Talitha a visit at her Carmel High School graduation, on the night before the festival. "I had no idea he would bring the entire band of long-haired and just-a-bit-wild players to my graduation, where their rowdy vocal support got them plenty of attention. And I had no idea—of course none of us did, really—how powerful those three days would be and that they would usher in the Summer of Love."

Crosby upset his fellow Byrds at Monterey by performing a

set with them *and* their competitors Buffalo Springfield. It was the beginning of the end in terms of his status in The Byrds. The Monterey gig was also another early indication that Stephen and Crosby could work together.

One of the new songs the Springfield previewed that day was Stephen's ode to Grace Slick, 'Rock & Roll Woman,' which owed a lot to Crosby's recent time spent with Stephen. The recording of the new track would begin a few days after Monterey at Sunset Sound and the song was tagged on the release 'Inspiration: David Crosby.'

Characteristically, Stephen took full advantage of the opportunity to hang out with as many new musician friends as he could at this time.

At Peter Tork's place, he met Jimi Hendrix for the first time, the day after Monterey. Stephen remembered his new friend suffering some unhelpful criticism at the time. "He had signed on to be the opening act in The Monkees' tour, which was a big mistake because all the jerks whined about all the little white girls being exposed to this incredibly sexy gentleman of color. He was scared to death and really shy. I guess I was the southern white boy that understood him …"

With an assortment of Monterey performers still in the area, Stephen hosted jam sessions at Buffalo Springfield's rented Malibu beach house, where Jimi, David Crosby, Buddy Miles, Bruce Palmer, and Hugh Masekela all participated. "I set up my big amps, we took some acid, and just *went*" was how Stephen described the experience.

When the cops arrived to check out the noise they were so into the music that they allowed the jam to continue and remained as spectators.

"So me and Hendrix jammed with the sheriff's protection!"

Stephen confirmed later. "And that night I really learned how to play lead guitar."

Around the same time Stephen's 'Bluebird' entered the Hot 100 at Number 58, Buffalo Springfield were in New York, where Jimi Hendrix was touring with The Monkees. Stephen took another opportunity to enjoy some more guitar lessons when they met up in a Waldorf Hotel room, this time with Micky Dolenz joining in. "Jimi was my guru, man," Stephen admitted to Dave Zimmer.

Just as Stephen was forging a happy association with Jimi, Neil Young resurfaced and on August 12 was back in Buffalo Springfield. The unfortunate Doug Hastings took a call from Stephen telling him he had been fired.

The original Springfield line-up was now back in business, but for how long? The tension between Stephen and Dewey Martin would occasionally return, as it did on August 20th. Theirs was a difficult personal relationship that would eventually develop into *no* personal relationship in later years. Dewey always delighted in his ability to attract all the girl fans at gigs, and when the band headed for a couple of dates in Arizona Stephen's apparent jealously reached new heights. It all seems somewhat petty and trivial now, but these were very young men in the public eye surrounded by female adoration. When former Miss Arizona 1965 and former Miss USA runner-up, Jane Nelson, escorted by her brother, showed up at the gig in Phoenix, Dewey Martin was the center of her attention. "She walked in, he almost had a heart attack when she walked over and talked with me," said the drummer later of Stephen's reaction. "We went out later. She came to Tucson–the next gig. I think he's still jealous of me!" Dewey Martin later married his beauty queen.

With Neil apparently back in the band permanently, Buffalo

Springfield could complete work on a second album, continue some lucrative West Coast dates, and look forward to an intensive nationwide tour with The Beach Boys. Amid all the visits to Sunset Sound to complete *Buffalo Springfield Again*, Stephen found time to drop by the studio when David Crosby was producing a friend's debut album. Stephen happily joined in to play bass on Joni Mitchell's 'Night In The City' for his Laurel Canyon neighbor's LP *Song To A Seagull*.

When *Buffalo Springfield Again* was released, it showcased some terrific songs but only masqueraded as a group album. With Stephen and Neil not on the best of terms, and certainly not a song-writing team, Neil had found a new creative partner in Jack Nitzsche. In a nod to the future, Neil's heavily orchestrated 'Expecting To Fly' had been recorded with no contribution from Stephen at all. Stephen suggested that outside influences on the Beach Boys tour might have been responsible for Neil finally quitting Buffalo Springfield for good.

"The inside story on that tour was Mike Love turning into this svengali influence on Neil," Stephen is reported to have said. "It was weird. They were always off in a corner, whispering. And Mike Love is just a spooky character," he added.

On *Buffalo Springfield Again*, Stephen, Neil, and to a certain extent Richie, were all beginning to sound like confident solo artists, no longer needing the protection of a group democracy. Stephen's stand-out tracks were the biggest hit singles from the album, 'Bluebird' and, enhanced by some great Neil Young guitar work and Stephen's killer Hammond organ, 'Rock & Roll Woman.'

Fleetwood Mac's Stevie Nicks remembered how she felt as a 19-year-old listening to 'Rock & Roll Woman' when interviewed by the *Guardian* newspaper: "Hearing this for the first time was like seeing the future. [Sings] 'And she's coming, singing soft and low ...' When I heard the lyrics, I thought: 'That's me!' They probably wrote it about Janis Joplin or someone like that but I was convinced it was about me. I saw Buffalo Springfield at the Winterland Ballroom at the time, and it could not have been better."

The remainder of the album continued to be a glorious mixture of sounds. Stephen's 'Everydays' featured low-key jazz and his 'Hung Upside Down' was psychedelic. Richie's 'A Child's Claim To Fame' was a country delight, his 'Sad Memory' a rather forgettable filler, and 'Good Time Boy' seemed like a homage to James Brown. Only Neil's 'Mr Soul,' 'Expecting To Fly,' and 'Broken Arrow' seemed to mine new, exciting territory.

While the largely favorable album reviews came in, the group continued to tour until the end of the year, and with little respite until May 1968. Along the way, Bruce Palmer was replaced for the last time on bass by Jim Messina, who had already made a valuable contribution mixing and producing tracks for the new album.

When the band found themselves playing a nearby gig Stephen, accompanied by Dewey Martin, popped in to Western Recorders in Hollywood to add guitar and drums respectively on The Monkees' track 'Lady's Baby,' which, due to a delay in completion, didn't get a release until *The Birds, The Bees & The Monkees* was re-issued in 1994.

Continuing to seek out the best guitar teachers, Stephen also jammed frequently with fellow southerner Duane Allman, whose band Hour Glass had broken up unsatisfactorily and who was about to leave L.A. and return to Florida. The fragmenting elements in Stephen's group meant a similar break-up was inevitable. "I could definitely see the end coming," he admitted later, which is presumably why he continued to make contact with Jimi Hendrix whenever their schedules allowed. While recording *Electric Ladyland* in March 1968, Hendrix cut 'My Friend,' a track featuring Stephen on piano. The recording made at Sound Center NYC eventually turned up on Hendrix albums *The Cry Of Love* (1971) and *First Rays Of The New Rising Sun* (1997).

When fellow Atco label stablemates Cream were on tour in California, Stephen caught up with a third rock guitarist he revered. Eric Clapton claims he first met Stephen at The Beverly Hills Hotel. Stephen had heard that Eric had been impressed by Stephen's new song 'Bluebird' and the two must have made plans there and then to meet up after Cream's Anaheim Convention Center gig on March 18. What happened next constituted one of rock's most written-about drug busts.

Present at the get-together at Stephen's home at 1076 Old Topanga Canyon Road were Springfield members and friends and Stephen's new buddy, Eric Clapton.

"They were partying … the Marshall amps were stacked," Stephen's friend Linda Stevens told Neil Young biographer James McDonough. "Clapton and Stephen were playing so loud, the mountains were ringing. One of the neighbors didn't think it was so cool."

As a result of at least one complaint about the noise, the cops raided the house and Deputy Andrew Yobuck was quoted as saying, "When the front door opened the marijuana smoke just rolled out."

Reports at the time indicated that 15 people were arrested on marijuana possession charges, and while the Springfield's road manager, Chris Sarns, was caught disposing of a small quantity of pot in the bathroom, Stephen had just enough time to escape out of a bedroom window and run for it. Once in custody, the situation looked bleak for Eric, Neil, and Richie Furay, but Stephen had the presence of mind to phone attorneys for his friends. All those arrested were later found guilty of only disturbing the peace. Although Sarns was put on three months probation with a $300 fine, the threat of deportation for the English Eric Clapton and Canadian Neil Young never materialized.

The whole stressful affair would be a contributory factor in the demise of Buffalo Springfield.

CHAPTER 9
Last Time Around

"We had too much fame and no money" was how Stephen put it when Buffalo Springfield were no more. Their farewell gig on May 5, 1968 in front of 5,000 emotional fans at a rowdy Long Beach Arena showcased a terrific back list of songs from three talented singer-songwriters, but a group still falling short of their own expectations. "... We were trying to make it so bad and getting nowhere," added Neil Young when quizzed later by *Rolling Stone*'s Cameron Crowe. With *Buffalo Springfield Again* peaking just outside the Top 40 albums chart they had failed to make the huge breakthrough that might have made the difference. The fact that the album has now become a healthily selling classic must be some comfort to Stephen, but he, Neil, and Richie were headed for bigger things–bigger record sales, bigger reputations, and bigger pay days. Much has been made of the arguments and fall-outs, but the music and the live shows were full of invention and special energy. When they were good they were very, very good. Although Buffalo Springfield had started out as Stephen's band and he had been a strong and energetic leader, fights– sometimes violent fights–had taken place mostly because he wasn't captaining a team any more. Now outside of the band environment, he needed to regroup and rethink who he needed to work with in future and maybe–like Neil–he was already coming to the conclusion that he would never happily commit himself to the band ethic the way he had done with Buffalo Springfield. He now had the time and space and just enough money to try something new.

A couple of months after the band had ceased to be, the third Buffalo Springfield album, *Last Time Around*, was released, and like its predecessor it would again fall fractionally short of the *Billboard* Top 40. Good as they were, the three stand-out Stills songs, 'Four Days Gone,' 'Questions,' and 'Special Care,' were virtually solo recordings from earlier in the year with Jim Messina producing.

Similarly, Neil had been going it alone on most recordings and Richie's 'Kind Woman' was more Poco than Buffalo Springfield, featuring Jim Messina and Rusty Young, who would, with Richie, form the country-rock outfit in the wake of the Springfield's split. Seemingly in a hurry, Neil Young's eponymous debut album would soon hit stores but would get a 1969 remix following his unhappiness with the sound quality.

Well before *Last Time Around* was released, Stephen had been continuing to play with any musician he found interesting. As his friend and CSN tour manager Mac Holbert observed, "If you put Stephen out in the middle of the desert at midnight, within an hour he'd have a guitar, a bottle of Jack Daniel's, and someone to jam with."

This time, the new 'someone to jam with' was Al Kooper. The until recently Blood, Sweat & Tears leader wanted the freedom to record some new music with a bunch of people that he'd cherry-pick for a one-off project. The former Paul Butterfield Blues Band and Electric Flag guitarist Mike Bloomfield, bassist Harvey Brooks, keyboardist Barry Goldberg (both also Electric Flag), and drummer Eddie Hoh accepted the invitation and spent a day recording what would end up as side one of an album brim full of superb music from America's finest session men. But when Bloomfield didn't show for the next session–reportedly due to his chronic insomnia–Kooper called Stephen to tempt him down to the recording and take over where Bloomfield had left off. Keen to be involved–he already knew Hoh from seeing him play at Monterey and his work for The Monkees–Stephen immediately dropped everything and joined Kooper for what became side two of *Super Session*. One of the project's finest moments was Stephen's reworking of Donovan's 'Season Of The Witch.' Kooper's concept proved to be a winner, and following a July release, with Bloomfield, Kooper, and Stills sharing star billing, *Super Session* shot to Number 12 in the *Billboard* albums chart.

"That record had such meaning for me," Stephen acknowledged. "I should get Al Kooper on the phone and say thank you. It was my first gold record. It was a complete accident. He called on the phone and my office said, 'Al Kooper is trying to get you.' When I finally got to talk to him, he said, 'I'm making this blues album and Mike Bloomfield is on half of it but he ran away.' I said, 'How far am I down the list of people to call?' [He said], 'Actually, you're pretty close to the top.'

"It was a farce really, but somehow I managed to come out of that thing on top. I don't really know why," Stephen admitted later. "It was that cut of 'Season Of The Witch' that really did it."

The album cover, with its portraits of the three main protagonists, was reminiscent of so many of the old jazz sleeves, and the capturing on record of a temporary coming together of individual talent would encourage others to free themselves from the strict confines of the group mentality. *Super Session* had created one of the first supergroups–a phenomenon that would certainly catch on in the months and years ahead.

Stephen's stock was rising, and although he declined an offer to join Blood, Sweat & Tears as their new lead singer, he was in demand. He was fast building a reputation as an all-rounder and his guitar-playing, in particular, would see him guest on a number of well-known recordings.

His next contribution to someone's new album would, on the face of it, appear to be rather insignificant, but by the time he was adding guitar parts to Judy Collins' *Who Knows Where The Time Goes* he was hopelessly in love. His relationship with Collins would inspire Stephen to write his most personal and emotional song, 'Suite: Judy Blue Eyes.' As it turned out, Judy had made an impression on Stephen a while back. He had first fallen for her image on the cover of an album he wore out playing back in his days in Greenwich Village.

CHAPTER 10
Judy Blue Eyes

On June 11, Judy Collins flew from her New York home to L.A. to commence work on her eighth album. The folk singer's career was in the ascendency, having just enjoyed a first Top 10 on the *Billboard* Hot 100 with 'Both Sides Now.'

John Haeny was the man responsible for first introducing Stephen to Judy. Haeny, who had recently worked with some of Stephen's friends–"RCA paid me and said to earn your keep you will record The Monkees!"–was chief engineer at Elektra Records when he worked on Judy Collins' *Who Knows Where The Time Goes*. He recalls Stephen and Judy's earliest meeting by first describing the dynamics of who knew who in Laurel Canyon: "I was living in one of the side streets, at 8459 or 8259 Ridpath Lane. There were five or six of us who were the center of activity. It was a very tribal time. We all hung out with each other, got each other dope. We were stoned out of our gills and taking acid. I wouldn't say Stephen was in the midst of the tribe–he was sort of on the fringe, part of the tribe. The peace pipe was always sort of lit at my house."

Haeny rejects the notion that he was himself the center of any Laurel Canyon tribe, but he was friends with someone who was and he met David Crosby long before he encountered Stephen.

"David was the first hippie I ever met. I wasn't smoking dope then. We'd take some bongos and a guitar and go down and sit on the most beautiful beaches in the world at Santa Barbara. Crosby was a Hollywood star boy but Stephen was a country boy."

He remembers being impressed by the savvy "country boy." "Stephen was smart enough to act like he didn't know too much, so he tended to go with the tides. It wasn't unusual for him to show up at my door. I never really said the fact that he stopped by my house all the time, because we didn't work together, but I've since decided that he liked me. One day he showed up when Judy was visiting."

In her autobiography *Sweet Judy Blue Eyes*, Judy Collins' first impression of Stills was that "he was possibly the most attractive man I had ever met," and by the end of the evening "I knew I was falling in love."

It was easy to see how Judy fell so quickly for the younger Stills that day, says Haeny. "It wasn't just the rock and roll boys that were getting laid, it was the girls too. He was gorgeous. In those days Stephen was one of the prettiest rock and rollers on the face of the planet. He was a natural heart-stopper."

It's been said that Stephen was part of a band of musicians selected for Judy's new album and that Stephen was at a house party at John's to introduce everyone to Judy. John disagrees and added that his only involvement in choosing the musicians was to advise producer David Anderle that drummer Jim Keltner wasn't 'country' enough for the record and Jim Gordon was.

"I now realise that, at the time, there were two tribes of musicians. One was from Mulholland towards the ocean and then there was the tribe from Mulholland Drive to the desert, and those are all the guys that ended up at the studio in the valley– Sound City. The idea to bring Stephen in to play on the album could very easily have been Judy's. She could have said, 'Oh I met Stephen, he's really sweet, how about we get him in to play,' with the ulterior motive of getting laid! I saw the dynamics between the two of them developing."

Haeny recalls how he tapped into their love at first sight at the West Coast studio he had built for Elektra in L.A. for the record company's boss Jac Holzman. "Myself and David Anderle happened to know that something romantically and sexually was going on between Judy and Stephen. Was everyone else in the room aware that he was playing in a love duet with her? No. I certainly knew it because I'd introduced them to each other and I knew it was a very heated romance and it would certainly suit the purpose of the album."

It was a trait of Haeny's work to always get the best out of everyone in the studio and he acted quickly to capture the chemistry between the singer and the session man.

"When I clued to what was going on between Judy and Stephen Stills, I just adjusted the set up so he was sitting at her feet playing to her vagina, as it were! And he played incredibly romantic guitar. The guitarist's love call to a star."

Haeny was sure there were rehearsals going on that he didn't know about, and clearly Judy and Stephen were spending a lot of time together. But when they were in the studio Haeny and producer Anderle were determined to exploit the situation.

I had to decide where everyone was placed in the studio. They're going to be in each other's pockets, because I want that for the promotional X factor. The fact that there was something else going on between her and him was not a big thing, it's in the cracks. You can hear the way he's fitting around her singing. His playing is just exquisite and it's also some of her best singing."

According to Collins, the couple shared their first kiss in the garden of the Elektra studios, where they were working on *Who Knows Where The Time Goes*. Stephen would drive his new partner around the beaches and canyons in his prized silver Bentley, already house-hunting for the perfect Malibu beach property. And his contributions to the album inevitably became more than that of a hired session musician. Although the results from the recording sessions were already good, Stephen intuitively felt that something was missing. The missing element turned out to be one final addition to the track listing, 'Someday Soon.' It turned out to be an inspired choice. Written by the husband and wife Canadian songwriters Ian and Sylvia Tyson, 'Someday Soon' became Stills and Collins' love affair signature tune, embellished by guitar-playing from Stephen that Judy later admitted made "my heart leap."

The intensity of the love affair can be gauged from musician Neil Merryweather's memory of an incident he recalled when interviewed by journalist Ruth McCartney: "When Merryweather [the band] was living in Topanga Canyon, I remember Taj Mahal coming by the house where we were staying, and other musicians as well. It was a family oriented vibe in Topanga during those times. Chris Sarns, the road manager for Buffalo Springfield, came by a lot. He even got me a bass amp from Sun Music. He was staying at Stephen's cabin while Stephen was away in London. Chris showed me where the key was stashed, and told me that if I needed to get away to write, I should come over and let myself in. So one day I did. I picked up one of Stephen's bass guitars. It was a left-handed Fender jazz bass, but he had strung it right-handed. I picked it up and played it for a minute. I heard a noise, looked around, and there was Stephen just out of bed, wearing just a pair of underwear with a guitar strapped on. We jammed for a while. Then, Chris showed up and we all jumped into a Volkswagen bus. Stephen was driving, and we bee-lined it to the Hollywood Roosevelt Hotel. Stephen ran into the lobby and called up to Judy Collins' room and told her to come to the window. We were standing in the parking lot and Stephen was yelling up to her to come down. He was crazy about her–it was like a scene from Romeo and Juliet."

If Judy Collins was Stephen's muse and lover, his most benevolent supporter continued to be Ahmet Ertegun. "Because Steve was kind of the driving force in the group, I knew that he would come up with something great," confirmed the Atlantic Records boss after the demise of the Springfield.

Although there would be no repeat of the methods used to build Buffalo Springfield, Stephen did seek out more great players to work with and found one long-term accomplice. The Lovin' Spoonful frontman, John Sebastian, was very briefly in the frame as the drummer in his new project. "At the time Stephen was speculating as to who the rest of the instrumental band might be and I just happened to be the guy they were bouncing stuff off," John told *Mojo*'s Ross Bennett. "I stepped in on drums every now and then, just so the band could get a feel for the song. Then Stephen said, 'Wait, we don't need a real drummer. We just need a guy to thump along because really we want to accentuate all these guitars.' He said, 'You can do it, John!' After about 20 minutes of all this joking I told Stephen that Paul Rothchild had been working with this 16-year-old drummer from a Texas band called Clear Light. His name was Dallas Taylor. I was so delighted with how beautifully he played with them."

John Sebastian wasn't about to commit himself, despite Stephen offering him a song-writer and vocalist role in Crosby, Stills, and whoever else. "I had just navigated the dangerous shoals of quitting a nationally visible band," said Sebastian, "and was trying to get a solo album released."

So, recommended drummer Dallas Taylor was in and would go on to form the band bedrock for whatever was going to happen next.

Whatever that might be was still a mystery, but it wouldn't involve ex-Traffic band member Dave Mason, who Stephen actively sought out to add to his circle of playing partners. Although the British guitarist would reject Stephen's offer to work together, Mason would in future join a select band of British guitar partners on future Stills projects.

His musical partnership with local boy David Crosby would prove more enduring. Damaged egos from their respective final failures involved with the Springfield and The Byrds had not destroyed the confidence gained during the successes enjoyed in both bands.

People tend to characterize David Crosby as the cocksure Cheshire cat of Laurel Canyon. He had the best contacts, the best drugs, the best grasp of what was happening politically, but, like Stephen, he wanted a fresh start. Ignominiously, he had been ditched from The Byrds and, again, like Stephen, he was building up a collection of his own songs he needed to record.

Informally and for their mutual benefit they began playing their various new songs together. "It's funny, not a whole lot was discussed," Crosby remembers of the early days. "But the minute we started playing together again, I knew we were gonna be hot shit."

One of the first songs they played, on which the chemistry was strongest, was Crosby's 'Long Time Gone,' which he'd written on the night of Bobby Kennedy's assassination. When the duo were ready they would regularly head to friends' places like Mama Cass Elliot's or John Sebastian's and preview David's 'Guinevere' or Stephen's 'Helplessly Hoping,' before cutting demos at Wally Heider's studio. Everything was easy, self-contained, and very local, and the rumour and gossip around Laurel Canyon was that Crosby and Stills were on to something very special indeed.

CHAPTER 11
"Just Roll Tape"

Graham Nash had become increasingly unsettled in the hugely successful chart-topping band he had founded back in Manchester, England. But The Hollies were a pop band that seemingly wouldn't or couldn't evolve as Nash wished. Seduced by the possibilities he encountered on his first visit to the West Coast and his friendships with other musicians, including The Beatles, he had been inspired to begin writing new material which the rest of his bandmates didn't get. His friend and Hollies co-founder Allan Clarke put it succinctly: "Graham's idea of a good song was 'King Midas In Reverse,' our idea was 'Jennifer Eccles,' which he hated. He had no outlet for new songs like 'Marrakesh Express,' 'Teach Your Children,' 'Right Between The Eyes,' and 'Lady Of The Island' until David Crosby and Stephen got to know him and decided to 'steal him,' as they put it, away from The Hollies.

Ironically it was Clarke who had first turned Nash on to

Buffalo Springfield when Nash, as he put it, 'played the grooves off' their album while on tour with The Hollies in Canada. So when Crosby, who had first befriended Nash in London on tour with The Byrds, introduced him to Stephen at a party at Peter Tork's house, there was already a mutual appreciation society.

The chief catalyst in Stephen, David Crosby, and Graham Nash getting together was Cass Elliot.

"Cass Elliot was one of the funniest people I knew. I met her in New York and we used to sit back in the pizza house and watch the tourists go by," Stephen said, recalling her match-making skills. "She was very well read and an interesting conversationalist." And one night outside the Troubadour, a few days after they'd all seen The Hollies perform, she introduced the idea that Stephen, David, and Graham should maybe get together.

Interestingly, Nash has said he had felt intimidated when first encountering Crosby, and both Stephen and David have admitted many times that their eventual plan to 'steal' Nash from The Hollies was not based on much confidence owing to Nash's much more successful pop star status. If Crosby and Stills had been tentative about expanding their duo to a trio, that all changed with yet another Hollywood traffic jam incident–just like the one that created Buffalo Springfield. After a Hollies gig at the Whisky a Go Go in front of various members of The Mamas & The Papas, The Monkees, The Doors, The Beach Boys, The Lovin' Spoonful, and, of course, Crosby and Stills, Graham Nash left afterward with his two new friends. Everyone had been knocked out by Allan Clarke and Graham Nash's harmonies that night, and when Graham accepted a ride in Stephen's Bentley he claims Stephen stopped at a red light and turned to David and asked, 'Okay, which one of us is going to steal him?'"

As Nash would later admit to *Q* magazine, "Little did they

know, I'd totally had it with The Hollies by then. I said, 'Listen, I am not going to take much stealing.'"

That Valentine's Day three-way love-in was the earliest sign that Nash might leave The Hollies. By May the British music press was printing the rumors.

When Crosby and Stills' fantasy of stealing Nash did become reality, it was largely on the back of Nash's decision to leave everything behind in the UK for a new life in California. His new girlfriend, Joni Mitchell, would be a factor in him staying put and leaving The Hollies but, according to Stephen, she definitely didn't host the debut of Crosby, Stills and Nash singing together. The debate about the location of this euphoric moment in the band's genesis is best documented by Dave Zimmer in his *Crosby Stills & Nash: The Authorized Biography*. In it he lists all the key players, suggesting it was either at Cass Elliot's place or Joni Mitchell's, John Sebastian's or even Troubadour owner Doug Weston's home. But Stephen is adamant that it happened at Cass Elliot's home for one very good reason. He's always claimed that he would have been too intimidated to debut spontaneously in front of Joni Mitchell. While Crosby and Nash both agree he's totally wrong, Stephen maintains he can still recall the smallest of details about the first time they astonished themselves when singing Stephen's 'You Don't Have To Cry' in three-part harmony.

"A rosewood dining table in Cass Elliot's kitchen" is where he puts them on that July day, "and two days later we went to Joni's, where she lived in a lovely little bungalow where we sang round her table behind ladder-backed chairs. Cass said, 'Why don't you and David sing those things you've been working on?'" Apparently that's when Graham added his extraordinary vocal contribution. Stephen's graphic description of the trio harmonizing was summed up like this, with a large chunk of self-depreciation in his case: "The Celtic keen of [Nash's] voice, [Crosby's] cat's purr, and my cement trucker."

As Joni Mitchell put it, "Part of the thrill being around them was seeing how they were exciting themselves mutually. They'd hit a chord and go 'Whooooa!' then fall together laughing." Although it must have been clear that from this moment on they would work together, Nash was still a member of The Hollies and would remain so until the end of the year.

Characteristically, Stephen Stills wasn't wasting his time while he waited for Crosby, Stills and Nash to become a reality. Although his enthusiasm for the early August release of *Last Time Around*, the third Buffalo Springfield album, was minimal, it did contain 'Four Days Gone,' his ballad of an on-the-run draft dodger he had met, and 'Special Care.' His five songs on the album, and the Jim Messina, Neil Young, and Richie Furay-composed tracks, were really almost solo recordings and the album showcased the tip of an iceberg of inspired songs Stephen was at the time accumulating.

On August 26, 1968, his girlfriend Judy Collins recorded a new version of 'Who Knows Where The Time Goes,' for the movie soundtrack to *The Subject Was Roses*, in New York. A&R Recorders at 799 Seventh Avenue (the old Columbia studios) was where the song was cut and it was here, after lending a hand to the track, that Stills grabbed some free studio time afterward, to record a bunch of his songs that would end up on the *Crosby, Stills & Nash* album and other future releases. Stephen later confirmed: "I went to the studio straight from a Judy Collins session. I was madly in love with her and was about 23, 24 years old. At that age, with that inside you, you could blow out a lot of good music."

Stephen was under strict instructions from Judy to avoid

spending too long in the studio, as he revealed to Paul Rollo at americansongwriter.com: "I didn't write them all at one time. This was just the first crack at a tape recorder I had. Judy wanted me to play guitar, and then I took the studio after she was finished. The last thing she said was, 'Don't stay all night, 'cause I need you fresh tomorrow.' And I didn't. I stayed just as long as it took to record all those songs one time. 'Just Roll Tape' was my way of keeping my word to Judy."

These demos, recorded solo by Stephen with just and acoustic guitar or dobro, sounded so fresh and exciting that they would eventually become an album release in 2007, titled *Just Roll Tape*.

Stephen was pleasantly surprised when he got to hear the recordings again after so many years. "I thought they were pretty cool. There were a couple of things that weren't finished that I wasn't sure about putting out but Graham [Nash] insisted, so ... It's all kind of one-take stuff. I had a briefcase full of songs that I hadn't put down on tape. I'd just visited David [Crosby] on his boat in Florida and Paul Kantner was there and they had about a third of a song. I wrote two verses and that's how 'Wooden Ships' came about.

His intimate demos of 'Wooden Ships,' along with 'Helplessly Hoping' and 'Suite: Judy Blue Eyes,' would form the basis of Crosby, Stills & Nash classics on the trio's 1969 debut album. Many of the remaining tracks would find a fully formed home much later, with 'Black Queen' and 'Change Partners' turning up on Stephen's first two solo albums and 'Bumblebee (Do You Need A Place To Hide?),' which would turn into 'The Love Gangster,' and 'So Begins The Task' gracing his Manassas debut. Although 'Judy,' 'Dreaming Of Snakes,' 'The Doctor Will See You Now,' 'Know You Got To Run,' and 'All I Know Is What You Tell Me' wouldn't make it on subsequent records quite like they were cut here, there were varying elements that would. 'The Doctor Will See You Know'–later rumored to have been adapted for John Lennon, is perhaps the greatest 'lost gem.' Oddly, *Just Roll Tape*'s final track, 'Treetop Flyer,' was not recorded at this New York session.

Erroneously, *Just Roll Tape* was labeled to have been recorded on April 26, with Elektra engineer John Haeny working with Stephen. Haeny has since denied having anything to do with the session, especially as he wasn't involved on the Judy Collins rework of 'Who Knows Where The Time Goes' which preceded it.

"Phil Ramone recorded those, I didn't," said Haeny when interviewed on Skype from his home in Tasmania. "Phil Ramone recorded them at A&R Studios and Stills may or may not have given him a hundred bucks to record them. He didn't give it to me! There are a lot of people who believe I recorded Stephen Stills [*Just Roll Tape*]. I didn't do that demo."

What John Haeny and Stephen *did* do that same year was help organize a recording of a song dreamt up by Judy Collins' son Clark. Stephen had bonded well with the nine-year-old and even taught him how to play drums.

Haeny explains: "When we were trying to record 'Amazing Grace' [Judy Collins' version on Whales and Nightingales] Judy invited everybody she knew, including her son Clark Collins. Van Dyke Parks was there, Joni Mitchell was there, David Crosby, Jim Gordon, and Stephen. After it was all done she turned to Clark–who'd written a little adolescent song called 'I'm Flying'–and all of those people got involved in recording 'I'm Flying,' which I had spent 20 hours trying to make a little story out of the madness of 20 or 30 minutes of chaos."

And Haeny recalls how the Stills/Crosby and Stills/Collins

associations crossed over at one point. "There was a fairly momentous thing that happened during the recording of *Who Knows Where The Time Goes*. Stephen was a little bit at sea, Crosby was at sea–there were a number of loose ends in town and those loose ends were the roots of Crosby, Stills and Nash. I remember very specifically in the middle of one of Judy's sessions for *Who Knows Where The Time Goes* Paul Rothchild showed up, Stephen Stills, and David Crosby (and I think Graham Nash) and they were all raving about this sound they had discovered when those three voices sing together. They played for the soul of it and the joy of it. I think there was a little demo tape that Paul had produced of the three of them singing. We stopped everything and listened to their demo tape and it was truly heart-stopping. Boy! That was a moment. You don't forget those things very often."

As the long extrication of Nash from The Hollies continued, Crosby and Stills were honing the material they hoped to record with their new friend. The final death throes of Buffalo Springfield came with their final single release in October. Neil Young's 'On The Way Home,' backed by Stephen's 'Four Days Gone,' barely troubled the Hot 100 at Number 82, but despite Young's disconnected assertion that by this point "neither Steve nor I gave a shit," *Last Time Around* would go on to peak at Number 42.

Adding to his impressive list of guest appearances on other people's records, Stephen contributed guitar on the Nashville-recorded Joan Baez album *Any Day Now*, guitar on 'Talkin' To Your Toothbrush' for Mama Cass Elliot's debut solo LP *Dream A Little Dream*, and bass for Richie Havens' new album *Richard P. Havens, 1983*.

Stephen's friend, John Sebastian, was a constant presence during the slow creation of Crosby, Stills and Nash and was persistently offered a role in their project. In late 1968 he made his first record (*John B. Sebastian*) away from The Lovin' Spoonful, which saw the as yet 'unofficial' Crosby, Stills & Nash add to the sessions with Stephen on 'Baby, Don't Ya Get Crazy' and 'She's A Lady,' David (also guitar) on 'She's A Lady,' and Graham providing a high harmony vocal on 'What She Thinks About.' Their friend had already heard enough to confirm that Crosby, Stills & Nash would be hot property. In an interview with *Mojo* he later recalled hearing an early demonstration of their harmonies at Mama Cass's Laurel Canyon swimming pool: "They were under the diving board so they could get a little bounce-back on their voices, and although most of the material on that first album was still ahead of them, the first two minutes of 'Suite: Judy Blue Eyes' was already there."

Afraid that the good intentions and euphoria over their potential as a trio would evaporate when Graham Nash was back in England, Crosby and Stills decided to take no chances and follow their quarry to London.

Stephen recalls some seed money from the ever-supportive Ahmet Ertegun coming through at just the right time. "I got home one day and David [Crosby] was on the phone saying: 'Yeah, Graham, we're coming just as soon as we can get some money.' And I was able to produce 25 $100 bills from my pocket and scatter them on the floor, so David told him we'd be over the next day."

Renting a London flat at Number 16 Moscow Road in Bayswater, Crosby and Stills hunkered down and waited for Nash, who moved in with them for the first three weeks of November.

The plan they had in mind didn't always work out in the way they had hoped, as Stephen explained to Simon Harper for *Clash*:

"Well, we'll just hide in a flat somewhere and no one will be the wiser and we can really polish all these vocals and then make this album really quickly. Well, that lasted about a day, and suddenly Crosby and I are being chased by incensed fans down the street– chicks throwing stuff at us going, "You're gonna break up our Hollies!"

When Graham Nash finally did leave The Hollies in December, he departed in a blaze of glory. Two London concerts with The Hollies were performed in front of Royalty (first the Queen Mother then Princess Margaret) as the band were enjoying a lengthy stay at the top of the British albums chart with *The Hollies' Greatest Hits*.

His childhood friend and Hollies vocalist Allan Clarke described the enormity of his friend's decision: "In his mind, he'd started to leave when he met Crosby and Stills. The alternative was a [Hollies sing] Dylan album. His frustration wasn't really with the material. He thought the group was being misguided, but he didn't just leave The Hollies. He left England, he left his wife, everything …"

The fact that they were in London and the *White Album* had just come out was significant. The new Beatles release included the track 'Blackbird,' which Crosby, Stills and Nash all adored and would go on to cover, and they admired The Beatles' Apple Records initiative.

They believed Apple might be the perfect artist-friendly label for their debut album but were sadly disappointed when, after label A&R chief Peter Asher and George Harrison visited Moscow Road for a demonstration, they were turned down. According to Nash, "We really nailed it, we were on our game that afternoon," but it wasn't to be. "A few days later we got a formal reply: not for us."

Another demo in front of Simon and Garfunkel at Paul Simon's New York apartment got a similar lukewarm response.

Before the end of 1968, they squeezed in the first full Crosby, Stills and Nash recording session at New York's Record Plant. Helmed by L.A. producer Paul Rothchild, the version they recorded of 'You Don't Have To Cry' would not make the album but did have a curiosity value that saw it added to the *CSN* box set decades later. But the session was useful in that it gave them a strong feeling that Rothchild, who tended to over-produce the session, wasn't who they needed to get the true Crosby, Stills and Nash sound down on tape. They would produce themselves from now on, with Stephen taking the lion's share of the responsibility.

CHAPTER 12
Crosby, Stills, Nash & Winwood?

"We were trying to think of the name and all the animals were taken," joked Stephen Stills when quizzed about the naming of Crosby, Stills & Nash. All three had had enough of conventional groups. Their names as individuals in a string together would allow each an air of independence. What the order of those names should be would make for early arguments. A democratic two-to-one vote in favor of 'Crosby, Stills & Nash' was agreed according to Nash's recollections of the debate, as opposed to Stephen's preferred, hyphenated 'Stills-Crosby-Nash.' The biggest problem surrounding the order of names would come much later with the fiasco over their images in the wrong order on the cover artwork of their debut album.

After Christmas, back in L.A., Crosby, Stills & Nash headed east to start the year with more rehearsals and song-writing in a lakeside cabin in the snowy whaling port of Sag Harbor. The location was perfect for Stephen as it meant he could rely on frequent visits from his New York City-based girlfriend Judy Collins.

Loaned to the trio and their entourage by John Sebastian, the property had conveniently had its garage converted as a band rehearsal space, but Crosby, Stills & Nash found a variety of places to practice, as an impressed Terry Reid recalls. "I was in on the whole thing, from when Graham left The Hollies. They rehearsed up at Sag Harbor on Long Island, and Graham asked me up to watch them rehearse. They were doing 'Blackbird' in the bathroom. I heard them and said, 'I'm quitting!' Graham said, 'Oh, do you like it, then?'"

Helping them rehearse with a fuller sound at Sag Harbor were former Electric Flag bass guitarist Harvey Brooks and Paul Harris on keyboards. David Crosby has been reported as saying that Brooks didn't get the gig because he was too good. This apparently made Stephen uptight. Whatever the reason, Brooks only discovered he wasn't wanted more permanently when it seems he went to pick up his tickets to London to continue with the band but was informed there were none left for him.

When Crosby, Stills & Nash returned to L.A. to begin a schedule of recording to deliver their debut album, the only additional musicians on the final product would be Dallas Taylor and Jim Gordon. Stephen trusted them as both had contributed impressively to the *Who Knows Where The Time Goes* album sessions for Judy Collins. Taylor was not only hired by Stephen but given the impression he would enjoy royalty cheques as the fourth musician on the debut release. He would even be pictured on the album cover, at Stephen's insistence Taylor later claimed. In-demand session man Jim Gordon's only contribution would be to lay down the drum part for 'Marrakesh Express' before gaining recognition touring with Delaney & Bonnie and joining Derek and The Dominos. Aside from some guitar work by Crosby and Nash, Stephen famously played all the other instruments needed on the record and generally directed operations. Although this must have been exhausting work, Stephen was clearly in his element and recordings at Wally Heider's through February and March were producing the incredible results the three of them had hoped for. 'Suite: Judy Blue Eyes' was a shining example of Stephen's astonishingly successful control and arrangement over the project. Aside from it being three different songs and tempos, the track featured some of Stephen's best guitar work and the now perfected sublime harmonies of Crosby, Stills & Nash. Coincidentally, around the time of its recording, the subject of the song, Judy Collins, was enjoying her biggest successes. Her version of 'Both Sides Now,' from previous LP *Wildflowers*, had played out on turntables and out of radios all across America over the winter, and now in February her new album featuring Stephen, *Who Knows Where The Time Goes*, had been released, with 'Someday Soon,' its first hit single, climbing up the charts. What should have been a very satisfying period for both Stephen and Judy was overshadowed by the realization that their intense relationship was not to last. Stephen would pour his heart out in a brilliant piece of music that would be the devastatingly sad soundtrack to the end of their affair.

A month before the release of the *Crosby, Stills & Nash* debut album, Stephen visited Judy to play his now-completed composition on the restored Martin guitar he had brought her as a gift. An almost year-long romance up to this point had been interrupted by touring and recording. When Stephen previewed his new song for her in her Santa Monica Holiday Inn hotel room, she realized as soon as he put his guitar down that the song was, though brilliantly written, a painful reminder of her own struggles against alcoholism, depression, and the ongoing therapy she was enduring. "I heard for the first time, perhaps, that Stephen knew much more about my life than I had ever given him credit for," she later revealed in her autobiography.

If Stephen hadn't a clear idea that their love affair was over when he left her the song and guitar that day, he soon would. "The roller-coaster ride of emotions," as she described it, would come to a grinding halt at the end of May as Judy Collins began seeing actor Stacy Keach.

Even before all the recordings were complete, Stephen was thinking ahead as to how they might take the Crosby, Stills & Nash show out on the road. Playing every available instrument on the record was one thing, but who could they rely on to back them with, at the very least, bass and, most importantly, keyboards?

Stephen had the perfect solution. "Stevie Winwood was always my favorite blue-eyed soul sound. It had been my intention from the start to convince him to join Crosby, Stills & Nash."

So determined was he to add Winwood to the mix that he flew to England in March to track down the former Spencer Davis Group and Traffic keyboards player. Accompanied by Dallas Taylor they turned up out of the blue, rain-soaked and caked in mud, at Winwood's cottage in the Oxfordshire countryside. But Winwood's response to the invitation was a shy, polite 'no thanks.' Hitching up with another supergroup–he was already one quarter of Blind Faith at the time–was not a prospect he relished and Stills and Taylor were left rejected. Winwood would have brought the added power to proceedings that Stills wanted on keyboards, but he next turned his attention to another Blind Faith member, Eric Clapton. If he couldn't get the keyboard player he wanted, perhaps he could get guitarist Clapton, who he'd already jammed with in L.A., into his band, somehow. But despite a convivial few hours at Clapton's Surrey villa discussing their respective Ferraris and guitar collections, the timing was all wrong and Clapton, like Winwood, was already committed to Blind Faith.

Happily, the trip to England wasn't completely wasted. His mission aborted, Stills took the opportunity to jam with Clapton, Led Zeppelin's Jimmy Page, Cream's Jack Bruce, Buddy Guy, and Buddy Miles in an old carpet warehouse in the west London suburb of Staines. Billed as *Supershow*, this aggregation of British and American musicians were filmed for posterity over two days on March 25 and 26. A precious record of the times when enthusiastic musicians actually still had the control to play wherever and with whoever they wanted to, the film (now widely available) showcased three thrilling tracks featuring Stephen on 'Love Potions,' 'Crossroads,' and his own blues number, 'Black Queen.'

Before the release of their debut album, Crosby, Stills & Nash had to sort out and get help with the business side of things. They were determined to handle their own production in the studio but contracts and management were still issues that needed firm control, despite the laid-back climate of peace and love that permeated rock and roll at the time.

Despite his aspirations to manage and produce the newly formed Crosby, Stills & Nash, Paul Rothchild wasn't quite what the band needed.

Elliot Roberts and David Geffen were, as it turned out, just what they *did* need. Both had met at Hollywood talent organization the William Morris Agency and– certainly in Roberts' case–

they'd prove to be an enduring and reassuring presence in the harsh world of rock star management.

Roberts in particular was alert to the possibilities of what Crosby, Stills & Nash could achieve musically, having sensed the diminishing power of the psychedelic era and the dawning of a new age of singer-songwriters. Geffen was a tough negotiator from the start and the two young managers would make a formidable team as they mapped out their plan for music's hottest new property.

Their first job was to hunt down the best record deal for their new charges and expedite the legal issues tying each of them down. In many ways it was Stephen's Springfield contract that would prove the most difficult sticking point, and when Geffen approached Atlantic's Jerry Wexler for Stephen's release the record executive literally threw him out of his office. Wexler saw Geffen as an arrogant young upstart, but his resistance to losing Stephen wasn't matched by his partner Ahmet Ertegun, who cleverly engineered the perfect solution. Stephen would stay with Atlantic and he and Wexler would bring Crosby and Nash to join him. Ertegun's patience and belief in his young performer had won the day, but up until this point it had certainly not been inevitable that Atlantic was the obvious choice for a band of what Wexler thought were hippies. With a roster of acts like Aretha Franklin and Ray Charles, they were purveyors of some of America's finest soul and R&B music–but that was about to change with the arrival of Crosby, Stills & Nash and then Led Zeppelin.

Happy to stay with Atlantic, Stephen got involved in the process of adding his two friends by questioning Ertegun: "David isn't under contract any more but Graham Nash is signed to EMI in England and Epic in the United States. Can you sort it out?

He agreed to talk to Sir Joseph Lockwood at EMI and I started thinking about the Clive Davis/Epic part of it."

In an extraordinary move to get over the fact that he was signed to Epic, Graham Nash was swapped with Richie Furay and Poco.

"They got Poco and I went to Atlantic" was how a relieved Graham Nash put it.

"It was sort'a like a baseball deal–trading players," explained Stephen, "So we pulled that off and the details worked out."

CHAPTER 13
'Captain Manyhands'

"When they were making that first record, it was very joyful meeting and working with them. I loved the boys, the boys loved me, and the whole thing was very, very … it was really one of the most wonderful experiences I've had in the record business." So said Ahmet Ertegun of those heady days down at Wally Heider's studio in Hollywood. They were working hard–despite most of Laurel Canyon popping by to see how they were getting on–with, according to Stephen, the studio clock ticking at "two bucks a minute."

Starting at 2pm most days, they would put in anything up to a 14-hour shift before heading out to Norm's restaurant on Sunset Boulevard for breakfast. Aside from visits by local friends and supporters Cass Elliot (who added a vocal part to 'Pre-Road Downs'), John Sebastian, and Joni Mitchell, there were visits from Ertegun and Jerry Wexler, with Phil Spector and Donovan dropping by.

The sessions were supervised by an engineer who had worked with Stephen a couple of times before. Bill Halverson had engineered a demo for Stephen in late 1968 and had been hugely impressed with his technical ability in the studio. "He came in and played some acoustic guitar and did some vocals and played some bass," Halverson recalled, "and then he rented some drums from Studio Instrument Rentals—which was the big rental company out there at that time—and played those, too. The song was '49 Reasons,' before it became '49 Bye Byes'—it was an eight-track demo, and when he wanted to turn the tape over I had no idea what he was doing. Track two became track seven, and he did this backward guitar thing where he could hear the changes backward and play this part. He only did it one time, turned it over, and the guitar part just blew me away."

Stephen knew exactly how he wanted everything to sound at the Crosby, Stills & Nash sessions and set about earning the nickname 'Captain Manyhands,' bestowed on him by Crosby and Nash.

"I hadn't found anyone who could play these parts like I heard them," he later told Dave Zimmer. "And I was just trying to get the best out of everyone's songs. So they let me run with it. There were no egos. Everyone was surprisingly co-operative."

The wonderfully layered songs they were putting together needed a very particular way of recording them. They would sing all three vocal parts around one single microphone together, instead of recording separately in isolation. It was a trick employed by Bill Halverson that Stephen was familiar with. "We always sang them gathered around a big, beautiful Neumann 87 [mic]. Back when I started singing with ensemble singing groups, the mic would be at least three feet away. And you'd stand back from it, and the mic would capture the blend. I still sing at least six inches away from the mic. My voice sounds too heavy if it's miked too close. Where you stand from the mic is everything. Miking is all … Often it would sound almost right and the engineer would say, 'OK, Crosby, take one step backwards,' or 'Graham, take one giant step backwards.'"

There are some misconceptions about which of the three of them took which part of a harmony vocally. In a candid interview with Paul Rollo, Stephen revealed: "Graham doesn't have a falsetto. He just sings really high. When we sing 'Suite,' for example, I'm way on top." But it wasn't always the case. "Well, we were very clever boys. And we changed it all the time. For no reason at all. It's kind of like 'stump the band.' David was really good at finding the really cool, weird part."

As Stephen explained, "One of the secrets of singing ensemble is imitating each other," which is something Fleetwood Mac's Stevie Nicks took literally when joining Fleetwood Mac.

Would it take intense rehearsal to get the phrasing so perfect? "Lindsey [Buckingham] and I, we were the duo. So we were very influenced by the famous duos. So then when Christine [McVie] came in we had to drop that duo thing overnight and become a trio. So then we were, then we got to be Crosby, Stills & Nash. And you know, if we said it one time, it was a million times. 'I'm going to be Stephen Stills and you're going to be the [Graham] Nash. And you're going to be the David Crosby. Or, and people are like, no, no, I'm going to be, I want to be the Stephen Stills!'"

Another group who were influenced greatly by the Crosby, Stills & Nash vocals were the Grateful Dead, who learned to adapt their sound: "What happened there," explained the Dead's Bob Weir, "is that Crosby and Stills were hanging in and around San Francisco and we were amazed how they sung together. Because of that we realized we'd been neglecting one side of our music and that was singing in harmony together. So we decided to develop our vocal harmonies and that whole side of our presentation."

Some of Stephen's greatest achievements during the recording of *Crosby, Stills & Nash* weren't on his own songs. On the face of it, Crosby's 'Long Time Gone' would have seemed like a relatively straightforward song to record compared to the 11-hour session he put into his 'Suite.' But when frustration and tiredness crept into its recording one night it was Stephen, with Dallas Taylor's help, who worked through to the early morning to create the ominous, dark backing track that showcases one of Crosby's finest vocals. "I've finally found my voice," Crosby said tearfully, complimenting Stephen on the work he had done.

Even at this early stage in his career, Stephen had at his disposal a large number of instruments to choose from, as he revealed to *Vintage Guitar*'s Willie G. Moseley: "I played all of the instruments on the first album. Basically, they were sort of like Springfield tracks with new vocals. I used a standard array of Gretschs and Martins, plus a Dobro, a banjo, and pianos. I still have an old '60s Precision Bass I used back then; I call it 'Grandma.' The secret to its sound is old, flatwound strings that have been left on it for years, and it works! I'm down to my last set of pre-CBS Fender flatwounds."

The guitar parts on both 'Pre-Road Downs' and 'Marrakesh Express' was Stephen at his ingenious best. 'Pre-Road Downs' was enhanced by a unique sound that would make the song impossible to play live.

"After the basic track was laid down, Stills took the 16-track tape and flipped the reel, threading the tape through the recorder backwards," remembers Bill Halverson. "He then overdubbed on electric guitar what sounded to us like the most horrible jumble of notes. When we flipped the tape over again and listened to the playback, here was a searing electric guitar lead running backwards through the song. He literally kept the whole solo in his head and played all the notes and changes backwards."

The guitar part on 'Marrakesh Express' was equally distinctive. "I wrote out that solo like a horn chart, with two trumpets in mind, melody and harmony–it's recorded as two parts on separate tracks, a third of a tone apart."

The recordings didn't all go to plan and there were some happy accidents, as Halverson remembers. "In one part of 'Suite: Judy Blue Eyes' there's the line 'Friday evening, Sunday in the afternoon,' and then Stephen goes, 'oh, oh, oh.' That's him singing the 'oh' on three different tracks in three different spots, and they thought that was cool because it was kind of syncopated, so we left it."

Bill Halverson has an interesting theory why the sessions were so successful. "They had a rule that whoever wrote the song would have the final say, and they really stuck to that. It's a wonderful rule."

Halverson astutely kept a watchful eye on proceedings by keeping everybody out of trouble technically. "It's still a wonderful record and the warmth and fatness of the 15ips analog make it hold up today, but I didn't have any preconceived ideas as to how it should sound. There were other guys they'd done demos with who really wanted to work on that project, but I ended up being CS&N's choice because they thought I'd have less influence on what they wanted to do. And in retrospect, I think they're right."

The joy Stephen expressed at creating the sounds he'd imagined in his head must have been matched by the realization that the recording of his great stockpile of songs were now nearing completion.

Looking back later at how some of the Crosby, Stills & Nash debut tracks were created with BBC Radio One's Roger Scott, Stephen said of 'You Don't Have To Cry': "That was the first song that Graham and David and I learned together. It was a letter that happened to have bits and pieces of it fall into a song and never got sent … or it got sent through the record business rather than through the mail."

For 'Helplessly Hoping,' Stephen wrote the first line, which led him to recall an experience from his high school days in Florida, and it no doubt involved the same 'knock-out' teacher who he earlier referred to who got the football team reading poetry. "I remember specific circumstances of missing a question in English class about 'What is this?' and it was a piece of alliteration, a little piece of alliteration. I said: 'I'm going to write a song that is a study of alliteration and 'Helplessly Hoping' only blows it once. It's alliteration all the way through."

As he joked with Paul Rollo: "A lot of alliteration for a cautious cowboy. When I did the first few lines, I thought, 'How long can I keep this going?' It's basically a country song, and it sings like that. It wants brushes on the drums."

By the time he had written songs as intricate as 'Suite: Judy Blue Eyes,' Stephen had developed an organized method of working to cope with the complexity of songs like 'Bluebird' and 'Suite'. Raymond Foye, in his sleeve notes to the Special Edition re-release of the *Crosby, Stills & Nash* debut album, revealed a highly business-like approach. "Stills had developed an unusual style of writing at that time, using oversized ledger sheets divided into three columns–one for the lyrics, one for the music, and the third for the ideas relating to the arrangement."

Stephen expands on the way in which three very different emotional songs came together as one on 'Suite'. "It poured out of me over many months and filled several notebooks. I had a hell of a time trying to get the music to fit. I was left with all these pieces of song and I said, 'Let's sing them together and call it a suite,' because they were all about the same thing and led up to the same point. And the little kicker at the end about Cuba was just to liven it up because it had gone on forever and I didn't want it to just fall apart."

With the album completed and everyone waiting with baited breath to discover if the hype was justified, Stephen played scorching Hammond organ on Jefferson Airplane's *Volunteers* album up at Wally Heider's San Francisco studio. When released after Crosby, Stills & Nash's debut in November, the album would include the band's somewhat rambling version of 'Wooden Ships,' written by Crosby, Stills, and the Airplane's Paul Kantner. The Crosby, Stills & Nash original 'Wooden Ships' would be one of the electric tracks on the debut album that would resurrect the concern about how they would play live as a group. But the vibe was still very much acoustic–an aspect reflected on the album cover, picturing Crosby, Stills & Nash seated on a worn-out old sofa with Stephen clutching his acoustic guitar. This is where the issue of the order in which the three names appeared on the cover became hugely entertaining.

Former Modern Folk Quartet member–now photographer–Henry Diltz and designer Gary Burden were both friends of the band, and when the record company needed a great cover to introduce Crosby, Stills & Nash to the world they sourced the perfect location for their photoshoot at the southern-most tip of Palm Avenue, close to the intersection with Santa Monica Boulevard. The front cover photo was snapped with the three in front of a small white boarded house. Then, accompanied by

Graham Nash's then partner Joni Mitchell, they all jumped into two vehicles and headed east to the mountain territory up at Big Bear for the shot that would grace the inside gatefold of the cover. Annoyingly, when the front cover shot was processed, the trio were pictured in reverse order as Nash, Stills, and Crosby. The return visit to reshoot was a formality, but when they all piled out of their cars at the West Hollywood location again they discovered to their horror that the property had–in the few days since their last visit–been demolished. Despite the confusion it caused, everyone agreed they loved the photo, so the album was released, after a short delay, in June titled *Crosby, Stills & Nash*, but with the trio pictured as Nash, Stills, and Crosby.

There was one further twist to the saga involving the photo. In a move that angered David Geffen greatly, Stephen insisted that drummer Dallas Taylor's picture was added to the cover. According to Taylor's autobiography *Prisoner of Woodstock*, Geffen thought him a "goon" and Taylor described Geffen's reaction as, "We've already taken the cover shots. And why give up points to that country bumpkin?"

Stephen won his battle of wills with his manager this time and Taylor's somewhat menacing face was added, peering from a door on the album's back cover.

On July 5, 1969, *Crosby, Stills & Nash* entered the *Billboard* Top 40, where it would remain for 40 weeks and peak at Number 6. The music had variety, depth, and freshness, and two killer hit singles, 'Marrakesh Express' and 'Suite: Judy Blue Eyes,' boosted the trio's profile throughout the second half of the year. Even in the UK– where Stills and Buffalo Springfield had failed to chart– the album would hit Number 25 and 'Marrakesh Express' would make Number 17 in Graham Nash's homeland. Most significant of all, the trio would enjoy the accolade of 1969's Best New Artist Grammy award.

New music magazine *Rolling Stone*'s praise for Crosby, Stills & Nash was restrained but complimentary: "They are in complete control of all they do and the result is an especially satisfying work."

More pertinent was the reaction of one new young fan who bought the record. "It struck me as being very American, even though I knew Graham was English," said Glenn Frey, who would go on to form the Eagles a year or so later, "but the sound, man, it was like this massive 'ahhhhh!' coming from the heartland. And I'm telling ya, everyone who was playing in a power trio wished they could sing like those guys."

CHAPTER 14

'Why Don't You Get Neil?'

With Stephen the driving force in the masterplan to make Crosby, Stills & Nash the huge success he envisioned, both Crosby and Nash seemed relaxed about management issues. Although probably for very different reasons, Stephen and David Geffen were united in a common cause to maximize the full potential of Crosby, Stills & Nash.

Geffen was immediately proactive in getting some live shows scheduled, even before his charges were properly equipped to deliver on that front. Woodstock co-creator Michael Lang remembered his first introduction to the trio's music well. "We booked Crosby, Stills & Nash before they were a band," he revealed in Joel Makower's *Woodstock: The Oral History*. "David Geffen came into Hector's [Hector Morales] office, I remember one day, and played the record. He said, 'Wait until you hear this.' We heard it and it was fantastic. So we did a lot of interesting booking that way."

Dinner with Ahmet Ertegun at the home of the Atlantic Records chief in New York City was an occasion for Stills and Geffen to plan their strategy. That evening the three debated how to unlock the potential. Once again, Stephen highlighted the difficulties they would encounter in playing the band's new songs live on stage. It was an ongoing creative and financial restriction and an issue that needed resolving quickly following the release of *Crosby, Stills & Nash*. Stephen had already given the matter a great deal of thought and continued approaching additional musicians who he thought might compliment the Crosby, Stills & Nash sound. As he later explained in a *BAM* interview with Dave Zimmer. "I talked to a fellow in New York, Mark Naftalin, who ended up playing for [Paul] Butterfield, but I could never pin him down. I really wanted a keyboard player, but the right cat just didn't come along." It was the lateral-thinking Ertegun who believed he had the answer, as Stephen remembers it, "… and he said, 'Why don't you get Neil [Young] back in the group?' And I really wanted a musical foil. I wasn't quite confident enough in my lead guitar-playing to carry the whole thing, which, in retrospect, is kind of silly."

By this time, any old animosity from the Buffalo Springfield days had obviously evaporated as Stephen is quoted as saying in Johnny Rogan's *Neil Young: Zero To Sixty*: "Neil had turned up at one of our sessions, heard what we were doing, and liked it." But once Stills had made the first approach to Young, his former bandmate naturally wanted confirmation on his role, financial rewards, and billing, in this extension of what he saw as a folk-rock trio. A month-long debate about how he would be billed didn't detract from his admiration for what Stills had set up with Crosby and Nash. "The music was so good, I just wanted to join in–I wasn't thinking I could improve it or anything."

Initially, Graham Nash showed the greatest reluctance to change the format of the band. He and David Crosby hadn't exactly taken a back seat during attempts to hire musicians to fill out the sound they had on stage, but Nash didn't know too much about Neil Young and suddenly it looked like Stephen (prompted by Ahmet Ertegun) was adding a new band member, not just additional help on organ and guitar.

The clincher, in terms of Crosby, Stills, Nash & Young becoming reality, came when Stephen took David and Graham along to a meeting at Neil's home. According to Crosby, by this time there was little debate about whether or not Neil should be a fourth member. "There was never any thought about billing him any less than us," he later insisted to writer Johnny Rogan.

The little doubt about whether to push on with Stephen's plan must have disappeared completely when Neil concluded the meeting by picking up his guitar and previewed a few new songs, including the plaintive ballad 'Helpless' that would wind up on the quartet's first album together. Stephen had got his way, but Neil made sure he had negotiated a move to Crosby, Stills, Nash & Young on his terms, with the proviso that he could continue a solo career on the Reprise label.

Crosby, Stills, Nash & Young still weren't a group who could record live or perform successfully without a bass player. Whether he was beginning a round of auditions or whether it was more a case of thinking he'd found the solution already is unclear, but Stephen called on another former Buffalo Springfield member, Bruce Palmer.

The new bass player was very quickly put to work, and in June, Crosby, Stills, Nash, Young, Taylor, and Palmer entered L.A.'s Sunwest Studios, where a new recording of Stephen's 'Helplessly Hoping' was made. The recording wasn't much of a test of how they might beef up their sound on stage. Stephen playing a Chet Atkins Country Gentleman guitar turned the track into a country cousin of the recording on the *Crosby, Stills & Nash* album. "I couldn't find a real steel player, so I had to make do with my little volume pedal and my Gretsch with the tone bar," he revealed.

Palmer sounded pretty good too on 'Horses Through A Rainstorm,' a demo the six-piece band cut at Stephen's house of the very Hollies-like song Nash had written with his old friend Terry Reid.

Despite Palmer gelling with his former bandmates Stills and Young and getting on fine with Dallas Taylor, subsequent band rehearsals at Peter Tork's Studio City house were strained from the outset. Crosby and Nash didn't take to Palmer and the feeling was mutual. Crosby later described him as "unstable," but Stephen, according to Palmer, was adamant he should be added to the line-up. "At one point Stephen stood up and declared that he would leave unless everybody in the room was in the band."

It may have been another example of Stephen's loyalty and generosity with friends and musicians he had shared his increasing success with, but even he must have realized that beginning with an unhappy band of brothers wasn't going to work. Crosby and Nash weren't budging on the issue and Palmer wasn't going to stay where he wasn't appreciated. Palmer was out of the band before they'd even set foot on stage, although he did feature in some early group publicity photos at the time.

The ongoing problem of adding a bass player was solved successfully, at least for a time, by Crosby and Nash before Stephen could act. Their brief couldn't have been simpler. Find someone who wouldn't be likely to get ideas above his station, who just did his job, played bass, and wasn't an erratic liability.

The answer, they discovered, was teenage Motown session musician Greg Reeves.

Talking to Dolf van Stijgeren's website *4WaySite*, Reeves recalled how the pair quickly enlisted him, having tracked him down to L.A. musician Rick James's home. "David and Graham drove up to the apartment where we lived on Olive Drive at the time, right behind the Playboy Club on Sunset Boulevard. From the pool I saw them knock on the door, and Rick yelled for me. They asked Rick James who I was and Rick came, got me, and brought me out front to the limousine that Graham Nash and David Crosby were in and asked me in front of them, would I mind going with them to jam. I asked Rick James, 'Aren't you coming too?' He said, 'They want you to come alone.' I went back to the house, grabbed my Fender Precision Bass guitar and Gibson acoustic guitar, climbed into the limousine and never came back to Rick's house again. They would not let me go. From the first time jamming with me, they would not let me leave. I stayed with Stephen Stills, Dallas Taylor, and Graham Nash at Peter Tork's mansion in Studio City. To this day I don't how Graham and David knew where Rick and I lived."

Rehearsals integrating Greg Reeves into the band for their first concert tour were reconvened at the Shady Oak house in Studio City Stephen had acquired from Peter Tork. His friend had originally bought the property with the fortune he had quickly accumulated from his role in The Monkees, but his generosity in offering free board and lodging to half of Laurel Canyon's hippie tribe had cost him dearly. Over time he struggled to pay the bills and even began to collect $75 a week unemployment benefit, accepting David Crosby's hospitality by moving into his downstairs apartment. When Stephen took over the place the open-door policy was immediately ended and the sentry gate shut. It was an impressive base. Once the home of the comic actor Wally Cox, the property was set on the side of a steep hill and comprised 14 bedrooms, a wet bar, pool, sauna, and permanently set-up drum kit. Stephen's house was an "all-purpose hippie haven," according to Nash. The legendary pool was nicknamed the Naked Party Pool, and perhaps the only visitor not availing himself of the unwritten nude bathing rule was manager David Geffen. "Strutting around like a dandy peacock," as Nash described him, in expensive crisp white shirt and slacks, he was ceremoniously picked up and chucked fully clothed into the pool one day by Stephen and David Crosby.

Stephen's rather different 'open house' policy at Shady Oak was mostly restricted to rock royalty. When they flew into L.A., The Who, Jimi Hendrix, and Eric Clapton would drop by and The Rolling Stones would hang out there on vacation. Stephen would even join in a Stones recording session, adding his uncredited contribution to the Mick Taylor-penned 'I'm Going Down,' a track eventually released on the band's 1975 album *Metamorphosis*. Standing in for Keith Richards, who wasn't present that day, Stephen sang and played guitar alongside Mick Jagger, Mick Taylor, Charlie Watts, Bobby Keys, Bill Plummer, and Rocky Dijon.

Meanwhile, Crosby, Stills, Nash, Young, Reeves, and Taylor worked hard on the louder electric numbers they were rehearsing indoors and outdoors at Shady Oak. The two Buffalo Springfield sparring partners were enjoying working out their guitar solo trading that would become such a feature in the concerts to come. Not quite so easy was the integration of Neil's fourth vocal part. "Neil and I had sung great two-part–I know Neil's voice and I can sort of follow it; it's got so much character but it wanders a bit and ordinary rules don't apply," Stephen told *Mojo*'s Sylvie

Simmons. "So you've got that beautiful Celtic keen of Graham's and David's cat's purr, and my cement mixer, and you add that cat that stepped on someone's tail," he added, in a variation of his often used description.

Amid all that was positive during the summer of '69 there was one setback that probably rankled with Stephen the most. When actors Peter Fonda, Dennis Hopper, and a whole bunch of other people had discussed the possibility of Crosby, Stills & Nash contributing to a movie score earlier in the year, Stephen had jumped on the opportunity. At the request of Hopper, Stephen wrote 'Find The Cost Of Freedom' for Hopper and Fonda's movie, but in July, when *Easy Rider* was released, the song was not included. Hopper, who admitted falling out with Stephen, described the incident that led up to his decision: "We were driving back to my office in his limo and I said, 'Stephen, this simply isn't going to work.' He asked why and I shouted, 'Because I've never been in a limo before and anyone who drives around town in a limo can't understand my movie!' Stephen's recollection of the rejection was a little more subdued: "I wrote it at the request of Dennis Hopper for the final scene in *Easy Rider*, where the dude gets blown away as his motorcycle burns and the camera pans way up in the sky. I played it for Dennis but he was in a fog and just didn't get it. I was depressed about that for years."

Peter Fonda had an interesting take on the whole West Coast music and movies scene. "All the actors I know want to be singers. All the singers I know want to be actors. It's so far out. Right? Stephen Stills would give his right nut … or David Crosby, to get a great acting role. And I'd give my right nut, if I could sing and phrase like Stills. Just not doing the coke …" he joked, "you know?"

Stephen's *Easy Rider* disappointment would not distract him from the upcoming live debut of Crosby, Stills, Nash & Young. On August 16, while the huge Woodstock festival got underway in New York state, they took to the stage for the first time at the Chicago Auditorium, with Joni Mitchell for support. For a newly formed group they had a hefty back catalog between them already and proceeded to deliver three hours of acoustic and then electric rock music. It was the perfect warm-up for the most astonishing event in popular music history.

CHAPTER 15

Woodstock Good, Altamont Bad

"This is the second time we've ever played in front of people, man. We're scared shitless!" Stephen's famous appraisal of how Crosby, Stills, Nash, and Young felt that night at Woodstock was more about the pressure to deliver in front of his music peers than the thousands of fans spread out before them.

Crosby, Stills, Nash, and Young's appearance at Woodstock, not least because they played a major part in the subsequent movie, was well received and gave their profile an astonishing boost. But according to organizer Bill Belmont, Stephen had reservations about making the festival at all.

"Wednesday or Thursday before the show I get this phone call and somebody hands me the phone and says, 'Here, talk to Steve Stills. He doesn't want to come.' So as I'm talking to Steve Stills, they're playing 'Suite: Judy Blue Eyes,' testing the sound system. I stuck the phone out of the window of the trailer and he says,

'Wow, man. Really–it's going to be OK? It's going to be alright? I'm not going to get killed, man?' I said, 'Sure, it's going to be fine.'"

Although Stephen's worst fears about the danger involved with such a unique event weren't realized, there were moments when the band must have wondered whether they were doing the right thing. With the freeways choked with abandoned cars, arriving at Max Yasgur's Farm in upstate New York could only be achieved by air drops, and although the helicopter transporting Stephen, Neil, and David touched down without a problem, the chopper carrying Graham Nash and Dallas Taylor was not so lucky. Fifty feet from the ground the tail rotor blade failed and the helicopter went into a spin and had to land very abruptly. Fortunately, the pilot crash-landed safely before any damage could be done and Nash and Taylor jumped out without any injury.

With the schedule overrunning and their equipment still missing, the portents did not look good for Crosby, Stills, Nash, and Young to make much of an impression. Earlier rain had thinned a large proportion of the estimated 300,000 to 500,000 crowd. By the time they introduced themselves on stage it was dark, cold, and 3.30am. They played 16 numbers and acquitted themselves well. Stephen made the most memorable impression of all, squatting on his stool, hunched over his guitar in a striking black and white poncho to keep the cold at bay. 'Suite: Judy Blues Eyes' was particularly well received by the remaining 30,000, who though curious to see this new supergroup had braved the elements to see Jimi Hendrix close the event. It was so chilly when they hit the stage that the guitars were going out of tune, a fact borne out by Stills playing along while frantically gesticulating and retuning as the song unfolded. But it was some well-chosen words that endeared him most to those out there in the darkness.

"I just gotta say that you people have gotta be the strongest bunch of people I ever saw! ... Three days, man! ... Three days! We just love ya!"

His blissed-out homage to the endurance of the fans, along with his earlier "scared shitless!" admission, gave the Woodstock movie, released a year later, some of its best soundbites.

When Greil Marcus filed his *Rolling Stone* review of Crosby, Stills, Nash, and Young's contribution to Woodstock, he homed in on the moment their set really took off. "Then they hit it. Right into 'Long Time Gone,' a song for a season if there ever was one: Stills on organ, shooting out the choruses; Neil snapping out lead; Crosby aiming his electric twelve-string out over the edge of the stage, biting off his words and stretching them out–lyrics as strong as any we are likely to hear."

As 'new boys,' Crosby, Stills, Nash, and Young would bank just $5,000 appearance money for Woodstock, but the event would prove priceless in their development.

"Woodstock? A complete accident that the organizer handled rather adroitly," was how Stephen later summed up the experience when talking to Tavis Smiley.

On the Monday after the festival weekend, the world's media were all over the event and clamoring for interviews with anyone associated with the event. ABC's *The Dick Cavett Show* had judiciously already booked Joni Mitchell and Jefferson Airplane to appear in front of a TV audience hungry to hear and see more about the revolutionary nature of the people and music behind Woodstock. For the purposes of his 'Woodstock show,' the host was dressed specially for the occasion and was clearly uncomfortable wearing a silk scarf in a misguided attempt to be a little groovier than usual. Joni had been denied the opportunity to attend the festival as there was no guarantee should could get away from Woodstock in time to make the show, and had to be content with following events on TV. Halfway through Cavett's show, he had some surprise guests who had played the festival. "We have two people who just happen to be passing through the studio looking for a pay phone that works in New York and they are Stephen Stills and David Crosby of Crosby, Stills, Nash & Young," said Cavett, followed by the kind of applause reserved for armed forces personnel returning somehow unscathed from a particularly grueling battlefield.

"I still have my mud," said Stephen, displaying his spattered jeans. Considering the sleep deprivation he must have suffered over the previous days, he then launched into a beautiful, crystal-clear version of his new song '4+20' for the young studio audience and viewers at home.

Though Crosby, Stills, Nash, and Young had begun their concert career on a historic high, their young management duo were mindful of the hazards of overworking them. "CSN&Y took a minimum of gigs. We discussed certain exposure points and took the ones that were important," Elliot Roberts told Dave Zimmer. "We knew the money would be there down the line, so that never came into play."

But the lure of the stage was powerful, and a series of post-Woodstock concert dates in their home base of L.A. were too good to miss, especially as they would perform at a venue not renowned for hosting rock and roll. The week-long residence took place at the Greek Theatre, an amphitheater in Griffith Park, on August 25 and once again it was a booking confidentially made months earlier, before the release of any record. The sold-out run of concerts (again with Joni Mitchell opening for them) would see 30,000 tickets sell out and a real buzz around their appearances.

David Geffen and Elliot Roberts must have been busy that late summer picking and choosing potential gigs, but in September there were two massive no-shows. With England hungry to experience the Woodstock vibe, a free festival in London's Hyde Park was scheduled for September 6. Supergroup Blind Faith and The Rolling Stones had played two huge events earlier that summer, and now it was Crosby, Stills, Nash & Young, Jefferson Airplane, and the Grateful Dead's turn. This West Coast extravaganza was subject to a late cancellation and a second high-profile appearance, this time back home on the *Hollywood Palace* TV show, was nixed in favor of a seemingly low-key affair on the California cliff tops at Big Sur.

With little or no security and performers mingling freely with the 5,000 music fans, the Big Sur Folk Festival was staged on the weekend of September 13 and 14 at the Esalen Estate, off Highway 1. Without a stage, Crosby, Stills, Nash & Young, Joni Mitchell, Joan Baez, John Sebastian, and a host of other folk-rock artists performed around the cramped confines of the swimming pool. The close proximity of the audience led to one extraordinary incident involving Stephen and a crazy-looking guy from the crowd, who lost control and heckled Stephen and his friends for compromising their principles with the trappings of fame and money. Stephen approached the man and appeared to try to smile him down and even give him a hug before something snapped and he lost control and began to fight. Stephen clearly looked in no mood to allow the guy to get the better of him and it was fortunate that despite the lack of any security Stephen's friends were able to pull him away from a full-on fist fight. All the action was captured in the movie *Celebration at Big Sur*, including the contemplative introduction he gives to his solo rendering of '4+20.'

"You know we think about that shit that that guy was saying and we look at these fur coats and pretty guitars and fancy cars and say, 'Wow, man what am I doing?' you know? So when somebody gets up and freaks out like that, you know, it kinda strikes a nerve and ya end up right back in that old trap. And where that guy is at is in that same trap, and that's getting mad about something. And that ain't nothing, ya know. I had some guys to love me out of it and I was lucky. We gotta just let it all be. Coz it all will be, however it's gonna."

The gig might have been a folk festival, but the movie footage of the Crosby, Stills, Nash & Young numbers show just how exciting the electric Stills/Young guitar sparring was becoming at this time. 'Down By The River' is a particularly good example, with Joan Baez lost in the music performing a particularly groovy dance while Stephen and Neil trade power chords with each other.

While Crosby, Stills, Nash & Young were making their strategic first steps as a live band, recording sessions for the first album as a quartet were spread out mostly over the second half of the year in L.A and San Francisco.

Unsurprisingly, the studio hours on the new project, *Déjà Vu,* eclipsed those made on *Crosby, Stills & Nash*. If the time spent on the trio's debut was joyous, the 800 hours spent getting this one right sounded more like an endurance test at times. "Like pulling teeth" was how Stephen put it.

The debut album had been created by three men very much in love. Stephen was still seeing Judy Collins, Graham was blissfully happy with Joni Mitchell, and David Crosby was in love with Christine Hinton. The *Déjà Vu* sessions saw the three of them all saddened by the loss of their partners. Sadness was an understatement in Crosby's case. Hinton had been killed in an auto accident when she was on her way to the vet with their pet cat, midway through work on the album. It was a devastating blow which saw Crosby in the depths of despair as he attempted to complete recordings of some of his finest songs. Even the weather was miserable when they headed north to Wally Heider's San Francisco studio, according to Stephen: "It was very cold in San Francisco with that nasty marine layer," he later recalled to *Mojo*'s Sylvie Simmons, "and the studio was in the Tenderloin. I was living in a horrid little hotel just up the way."

Stephen kept working through the difficulties. Not for the first time he grafted away, mixing and remixing the day's work with Bill Halverson until five in the morning.

The tracks that finally made it onto *Déjà Vu* saw the writing spread fairly evenly, with three credited to Stephen: 'Carry On,' '4+20,' and 'Everybody I Love You' (a rare collaboration with Neil). Graham Nash contributed the two catchiest numbers: 'Our House' was the story of the Laurel Canyon home he shared with Joni Mitchell, and 'Teach Your Children' featured astonishing pedal steel guitar by the Grateful Dead's Jerry Garcia–astonishing because Garcia was a novice on the instrument at the time. "We just sat down and fiddled awhile," Stephen explained to *Rolling Stone*, and promised "the opening lick will just curl your whiskers."

Crosby was in powerful form, rocking out on his 'Almost Cut My Hair.' The track created the perfect space for some heavy guitar interplay by Stephen and Neil, but Stephen thought Crosby's vocal was too raw, and at one stage wanted the song dropped from the album. The deleted 'Almost Cut My Hair' would have created one big void to fill, but thankfully Stephen let

Crosby fly his 'freak flag' and the number went on to become a concert set list mainstay.

Crosby's 'Déjà Vu,' with its complex timings and great harmonica part from John Sebastian, took an estimated 100 takes according to Stephen, who contributed nothing to Neil's 'Country Girl' and, like the rest of the band, encountered a particularly drawn-out session on Neil's other contribution, 'Helpless.' The band delayed pushing the 'record' button until after the copious amounts of cocaine some of them had been consuming had worn off. Desperately trying to slow down their playing to the optimum speed, it was 2am before they managed to get the wistful ballad completed for the final take. Stephen's beautifully played tumbling piano and some razor-sharp Crosby, Stills, and Nash harmonies demonstrated perfectly how Neil's 'Helpless' was enhanced by the group experience.

The standout track where everything seemed to come together perfectly was on Joni Mitchell's 'Woodstock,' where Crosby, Stills, Nash & Young rock out on the song that she had written about the festival she had not attended. The gentle, spiritual vocal inflections on Mitchell's and the Matthews' Southern Comfort version were dispensed with here as Stephen served up one of his most strident CSN&Y vocals.

Stephen's sophistication and quieter side as a songwriter was most evident on '4+20,' the story of an 84-year-old's desperately sad life, with echoes of the tragic emptiness expressed in The Beatles' 'Eleanor Rigby.' It was a solo vocal and guitar recording that Stephen believed would be squirreled away for a future solo album, but Crosby, Nash, and Young insisted it be included on *Déjà Vu* with no input from any of them.

'Carry On'–a combination with earlier song 'Questions'–would appear to have been written to order by Stephen when

Graham decided that the tracks they were collecting for *Déjà Vu* lacked an opener. Graham saw it as the missing link in making the album kick off successfully, in the same way 'Suite: Judy Blue Eyes' had done for the Crosby, Stills, and Nash debut. 'Carry On' apparently needed very little fine tuning and was written, recorded, and committed to master tape in just eight hours. It wouldn't be the last thing they would complete on the album, but it did give the feeling that a release was imminent.

There were at least two noteworthy tracks that would fail to make the cut, however. A cover of The Beatles' 'Blackbird' had been an early contender, with Stephen's keening lead in the harmonies, and Graham and Terry Reid's collaboration 'Horses Through A Rainstorm' (aka 'Without Expression') was also discarded, as the disappointed Reid recalled. "It got all messed up, though, because Stephen Stills didn't want to put it out. He was short of a song on the LP, and so he wanted another of his put on instead. But they recorded it, I heard it. Graham's got a tape of it. When he played it to me, you can imagine the shock of hearing them doing that, in four-part harmony. I'm going, perhaps there is a God after all! It sounded great, unbelievable."

Stephen may have been right to overlook the song. It might have fitted better on the more upbeat *Crosby, Still & Nash* debut. 'Horses Through A Rainstorm,' enhanced by Stephen's scorching Hammond organ, would finally see the light of day on the *CSN* box set in 1991, along with the ditched 'Blackbird.'

In spite of the circumstances surrounding the recording of *Déjà Vu*, the end result would prove to be more than just a successful follow-up to *Crosby, Stills & Nash*. Neil Young had clearly forgotten how exciting it was to play electric guitar in a band with his former Springfield adversary, and his songs added a touch more depth to proceedings. Everyone was on darker, more contemplative, and dramatic form on *Déjà Vu*. At times it might not have been a true group album, with little collaborative writing and even sometimes little recording all together, but the result was stunning and it would go on to more than double the sales of the trio's predecessor.

Crosby's participation in the *DéjàVu* sessions was understandably affected by Christine Hinton's death. The inevitable down time allowed everyone to get away from what must have seemed like a claustrophobic studio atmosphere at times.

On one such window of opportunity, Stephen hitched up once again with Jimi Hendrix for an all-night jam session at the Record Plant in New York City.

Organized by Jimi's producer Alan Douglas, the sessions saw Stephen play guitar, organ, and sing, supported by Jimi on bass and guitar, John Sebastian (guitar and harmonica), and Buddy Miles and Mitch Mitchell on drums. A lengthy jam, based on Joni Mitchell's newly written 'Woodstock,' formed the basis for 'Live And Let Live,' a track that would feature on 1970's *You Can Be Anyone This Time Around* by Timothy Leary. The album, on which the controversial psychologist and advocate of LSD narrated to an accompanying psychedelic soundtrack, was part of his campaign strategy in an unsuccessful bid for candidacy to be Governor of California.

The recording of *Déjà Vu* may have been a strain at times, but Crosby, Stills, Nash, and Young weren't ignoring their growing army of fans. There were some significant live shows during the fall through to the end of the year. They'd perfected a performance format which began with an acoustic set, then each individual's solo spot, and finally a full-on electric climax. The fan's loved it and certainly got their money's worth. Crosby, Stills, Nash &

Young shows were developing into some of the longest rock gigs around.

But 1969 would end on a sour note. Altamont was the gig that everyone cites as the end of the bright dawn of optimism started by flower power, the hippie movement, and culminating in Woodstock. It neatly and horrifically book-ended the Sixties' optimism with a show of aggression none thought possible at the large music gatherings, which by this time had become the norm. If the intention of those booked to appear at northern California's Altamont Speedway venue was to squeeze in 'another Woodstock' before the decade ended, that notion backfired spectacularly. Perhaps the headlining Rolling Stones felt they had missed out on that vibe, but the outcome was a tense affair, with a 300,000 crowd pressing up close to a stage ridiculously constructed at just knee height and protected by a security ring of local chapters of the Hells Angels.

Crosby, Stills, Nash & Young were on the bill due to an invitation from the Grateful Dead's Jerry Garcia to David Crosby, and their short set consisted of just four numbers: 'Black Queen,' 'Pre-Road Downs,' 'Long Time Gone,' and 'Down By The River.' The irony of the invitation was that when their time came to perform, the Dead abandoned their appearance after the Hells Angels had attacked lead singer Marty Balin during the Jefferson Airplane set, following an angry exchange of words.

Stephen appeared most wound-up by the intimidating atmosphere, which later led to the stabbing to death of 18-year-old student Meredith Hunter. "I was literally flinching on stage and had a horrible feeling someone was going to shoot Mick [Jagger]," he later told Dave Zimmer.

Crosby, Stills, Nash, and Young didn't hang around for The Rolling Stones' set.

They were away in a helicopter, before Keith Richards ripped into the opening chords of 'Jumpin' Jack Flash,' to make another appearance that night. Three-hundred-and-thirty miles south of the mayhem, at UCLA's Pauley Pavilion, Stephen fainted from exhaustion. "… that night the tension caught up with me and I got the whirlies on the way to the dressing room," he later admitted.

CHAPTER 16
Solo In England

The new decade began far more auspiciously for Crosby, Stills, Nash & Young. Six days in and they made their European debut with a memorable concert at London's Royal Albert Hall.

It was also Stephen's first performance in front of a British audience, which included Paul McCartney. "An outstanding concert by an extremely talented group" was how Richard Green reviewed the gig for top UK music paper the *New Musical Express*. Green's report made special mention of the hugely impressive lighting and sound system Crosby, Stills, Nash & Young employed to deliver their show. "The stage looked like a junior Cape Kennedy, with all sorts of projections, booms, and 12,500 watts' worth of equipment!" The now familiar CSNY acoustic encore–Stephen's 'Find The Cost Of Freedom'–"went down a storm," according to Green.

In the run-up to the sold-out performance they passed the time by doing interviews, sightseeing, and celebrating Stephen's 25th birthday while based in five flats rented for them above the shops near South Kensington London Underground station. When the four held court in front of the British media, Stephen gave a somewhat confusing assessment of his first impressions after a few days in London. "England is the most advanced, cultured country in the world–yet it's so far behind, it's frightening," he said.

Paul McCartney's attendance at the Albert Hall, where Stephen pulled off an impressive vocal on McCartney's 'Blackbird,' came a couple of days after The Beatles' final studio work on the song 'Let It Be' had been completed at Abbey Road, with George Harrison and Ringo Starr. The three Beatles (Lennon was out of the country in Denmark with Yoko) left Abbey Road in the early hours of Monday January 5– having completed their final album. Sensing the end of an era, David Crosby took the opportunity to lay into The Beatles to provoke them into playing live again during Crosby, Stills, Nash & Young's UK visit, but there would be no more stage shows and no more recording until the *Anthology*/'Free As A Bird' sessions in the 1990s.

The band completed two further concerts in Sweden and Denmark in January before all four took a break from CSNY. A confident sailor, Crosby steered his sailboat, the Mayan, with Nash a novice crew member, from Fort Lauderdale to San Francisco via the Panama Canal, while Neil Young hitched up with his old buddies, Crazy Horse. Stephen, by contrast, headed back to England and made his home there. He had been the unknown quantity in Crosby, Stills, Nash & Young on arrival in London, but the British press had obviously been impressed with what they had seen and heard of him since his arrival. "Unquestionably one of pop's most important musicians along with McCartney and Clapton," was how *Melody Maker* described him, and he was certainly moving and shaking with the cream of the capital's rock royalty.

"CSN[&Y] got to England and I just went, 'I'm staying! I don't have a girlfriend back home. I'm gonna stay here and just muck about. It'll work out.' Over the course of the next few weeks I ran into Jimi [Hendrix] and I had my assistant with me who was from New Orleans, and he just gravitated to us. He was just dying for an American face. So we became chums."

"We were like two lonely Americans in England," Stephen told Max Bell for *Classic Rock*, "no different to the English in Los Angeles, who sit around all day talkin' about bloody Arsenal."

So the London-based Hendrix was Stephen's regular companion: "We would just get in a limo and drive all over London, take over every club in town. Hendrix taught me that you'd got to get switched on and stay switched on till you dropped."

Those visits to the London clubs would include a lengthy jam session one night playing with Jimi under the watchful gaze of Australian-born feminist and *OZ* writer Germaine Greer.

After some of these exhilarating but exhausting sessions, Stephen and Jimi would be too wired for sleep: "[Jimi] would come over and get out of the clubs and take a few minutes to recover from whatever people had been shoving down his throat and have some coffee, and then we would sit and talk music and talk playing and talk philosophy for hours, and in the process he began to show me certain things about playing lead guitar," Stephen added.

Stephen later expanded on this friendship in Joe Smith's *Off The Record: An Oral History Of Popular Music:* "In England Jimi had a hard time relating to anyone, but he could talk to me. We formed a deep bond. We would play clubs. I would play bass or rhythm guitar, and he would play lead guitar. I sort of followed him around like a little puppy dog waiting to learn how to play guitar. He always thought that was silly because he was actually learning acoustic guitar from me. But he was so shy, so impossibly shy. If you weren't playing real close attention, you would swear he didn't like anybody."

Stephen also made friends quickly with the English guitarists, partying with Ronnie Wood and catching up with Eric Clapton, who was helping out on a George Harrison project for The Beatles' Apple label. He felt an affinity toward them, as he later admitted to Tavis Smiley. "The three English boys, Jeff Beck, Jimmy Page, and Eric Clapton, 'the Surrey Boys' I call them, we were all listening to the same records at the same time."

Stephen soon found himself drawn into the Apple sessions for the Doris Troy album that George Harrison was overseeing. Stephen, Eric, Ringo Starr, Klaus Voormann, Billy Preston, Peter Frampton, Delaney and Bonnie, and Leon Russell would all drop by the R&B singer's sessions in London.

Doris Troy recalled the process as a happy collaborative period when talking to Richie Unterberger for his book *Unknown Legends of Rock 'n' Roll*. "Some of the stuff we did in the studio, I'd be messing around on the piano and somebody would walk over and say, 'What is that?' I'd say, 'This what I got so far.' And they'd go, 'Okay, try this, try this,' and that's how come on the [songwriting credits] you see Ringo [Starr] on some of it, Stephen Stills on some of it, and George [Harrison]. Nobody stopped to say, well, you can't do this or you're signed to this company or you're signed to that company. We were all just doing it."

The soul/rock fusion of the sessions–Stephen's old Springfield song 'Special Care' was covered by Doris–might have relaunched the singer's career, but The Beatles' sad, public break-up and the mismanagement of Apple didn't give her album the expected boost it deserved.

Working with George Harrison, Stephen admitted, wasn't always easy, as he later explained to *Classic Rock*: "George was friendly at first and then we played together. I'll never forget this, we had a session with Ringo, and George would start a solo as the playback was going by and then make a mistake and start over again, even though the changes were different, which drove me absolutely out of my mind. I finally had to put my guitar down and say, 'When you're done …' I don't know how he took it, apparently it was like, 'Oh okay, everyone has their own way.' I just had to let it go. I didn't say, 'You're driving me mad'–it's George fucking Harrison already–but it was. It was driving me absolutely mad. So I just waited and when he was done, I went zoop zoop zoop and did my bit. I played something neat. I didn't work on it that long. Then he came and heard a couple of things, but it was not really his thing, big long jam at the end and stuff … but a lovely guy. He's what everybody said. He was much more opinionated than anyone knows. He could be tough."

Stephen meeting Ringo Starr–either at the Doris Troy sessions or in a London discotheque–for a first chat was fortuitous. He'd been staying in the Dorchester Hotel and a small apartment, but when the opportunity to rent a property in the country presented itself Stephen jumped on the offer to move into Ringo's 15th-century house and estate in Surrey. As it turned out, Ringo and wife Maureen had tired of commuting up from Surrey to London and were moving into John and Yoko's Tittenhurst Park.

"Well, [Ringo] was the first friend I made over there … but Maureen, his first wife, was always good at setting everyone at ease," he told *Classic Rock*. "When I first went over to visit he was living in Hampstead Heath and Mo [Maurice] Gibb was down the street, and Klaus [Voormann]. We had kind of a hootenanny. It qualified as a hootenanny, just hacking away. It was mostly friends."

"[Ringo] had me up to his house and we started talking about his place in Elstead. And Maureen ... she took me down to see it and I said, 'I'll take it.' I settled on a price with Ringo, then bought it eight months later. When I sold it, I turned it over for 100 percent profit. So, I still haven't lost my real estate chops," he later reflected.

Brookfield would prove to be a fertile base for Stephen's song-writing to grow, and provide a beautiful home for his two horses. "Living in Britain in the early 1970s was my salvation. That's when my creativity in song-writing exploded," he revealed. The rambling oak-beamed house, complete with stables, cinema, and a Japanese deer pond with waterfowl, had been owned, before the Starrs, by Peter Sellers when the actor had been married to Britt Ekland. "Brookfield was a magical place," Stephen admitted. "There were ghosts and I had wonderful bursts of creativity there."

Those bursts of creativity would see him writing and recording his first solo album, commuting back and forth between Brookfield and London's Island Studios.

Stephen clearly felt at home in England, although he did appear to be escaping from several issues that bothered him back in the US. The political situation in America was troubling. He went as far as damning the government for creating a totalitarian state and a police state. At the forefront of his disapprobation was the scourge of the anti-war movement back home, Vice President Spiro Agnew and, of course, President Richard Nixon. Was he on some kind of government blacklist? At the time, his manager David Geffen didn't think so, although David Crosby reportedly had told Geffen he thought he might be. Geffen's rather chastening summing up was that "I don't think Nixon cares very much. He probably doesn't know who David Crosby is."

Perhaps the previously much-traveled Stills wanted a new environment again, with new musicians to shake him up a little. Paranoia about what was going on back home was one thing, but another fear was that he was "getting cosy," as he put it.

Despite his happiness at settling in the Surrey countryside, he was conscious that popular opinion might be against him living in a beautiful old country estate costing hundreds of thousands of dollars. Living and working at Brookfield, training his horses, driving fast cars, and drinking cups of tea might make "those idiots who say they've got their finger on the pulse" think his wealth should be used more altruistically, he was prone to ponder.

Stephen's debut solo album took 25 nightshifts in London's Island Studios during March. The sessions were so successful that he ended up recording enough material for his debut, with some left over for the follow-up.

Established by Island Records founder Chris Blackwell, Island Studios had only been open for business a few months when Stephen block-booked his lengthy stay. The former church on Basing Street had been kitted out with the latest Helios desks and the facility would attract a who's who of rock stars in the coming months and years.

Early demand for the studios was high and Stephen's March booking scuppered the plans of Love's Arthur Lee, who needed just a day there himself to record a potentially explosive project with Jimi Hendrix. A night out at the Speakeasy led to Lee persuading Hendrix to record something with him, but apparently Stephen wasn't giving up any of his precious studio time and Lee reluctantly headed across London to Olympic Studios, where Hendrix jammed with Love on what became known as the *Blue Thumb Acetate* recording.

It wasn't just the Island Studios set-up that appealed to Stephen. The methods of recording were different and, he felt, more adventurous. "… the equipment in England was ex-government or from the BBC," he told Max Bell, "… y'know, all the tricks that mother hen George Martin used on The Beatles? 'As long as you don't set the studio on fire!'"

With the location for his recordings booked, Stephen turned his attention to assembling the best musicians to play on his solo project. Young bass guitarist Calvin 'Fuzzy' Samuels was enlisted by Stephen after the two had met at either the Bag O' Nails or even a club up the Edgware Road or Harrow Road, where Samuels performed with his band One. The bowler-hatted Samuels, it turned out, had actually attended Crosby, Stills, Nash & Young's Royal Albert Hall concert earlier in the year as a fan, but after waiting for two hours at the stage door couldn't get in without a ticket and had to walk home.

Other musicians helping out on the eponymously titled album would include some of the biggest names in rock and, of course, Stephen himself would play guitar, percussion, organ, piano, and direct the string arrangements.

The recording process that he enjoyed so much on the *Crosby, Stills & Nash* debut album was used to good effect again here. Layering the sounds, he would start by creating a basic rhythm track, then add lead guitar and keyboard parts, and then finish with the vocals. As Stephen would recognize, it was a DIY method also employed by another famous band member striking out on his own: Paul McCartney's eponymous post-Beatles solo debut album was just being completed across London as Stephen was beginning work on his. David Crosby endorsed his friend's ability when talking to *Rolling Stone*'s Ben Fong-Torres after the *Stephen Stills* album had been released. "If you want to hear a cat go in and do the I-can-make-a-record-by-myself trip, check out Stephen Stills, 'cause he happens to be better at it than Paul McCartney or Eric Clapton or anybody else."

Working with Ringo Starr on the Doris Troy sessions had the benefit of securing The Beatles' drummer for Stephen's solo album. In fact Ringo was returning a favor as Stephen had already helped out on a first attempt at cutting Ringo's terrific new song, 'It Don't Come Easy,' at Abbey Road on February 18. George Martin was producing, with George Harrison playing acoustic guitar and directing the other musicians–namely Ringo on drums, Klaus Voormann on bass, and Stephen on piano. What would ultimately become the final version of Ringo's biggest hit began at Trident Studios on March 8. This time Harrison produced the sessions and played guitar, as did Stephen, with Beatles assistant Mal Evans on tambourine and Ron Cattermole contributing saxophone and trumpet.

Ringo's contributions to Stephen's Island Studios solo sessions on both 'To A Flame' and 'We Are Not Helpless'–later credited as by 'Richie' on the album–went like clockwork. Like any great drummer, his time-keeping was excellent–literally–as Stephen explained to Ritchie Yorke in an interview with *Hit Parader*. "We set the time 7pm and we rolled up about half an hour late, expecting Ringo to turn up later in the evening. But there he was, a smile on his face, telling us he'd been there since 6.45. The stuff he did was great. Besides being very good period, Richie is very good at playing to earphones. He just belts it out with a beautiful sort of feeling."

With all the right connections, and perfect timing, Stephen was in his element and reveled in being able to a call on the world's two best rock guitar players to enhance his album. "We're all a big community, I figure," said Stills at the time, referring to his friends Hendrix and Clapton. "Wasn't it some American poet who said something like we shall hang together, or we shall hang separately? It's like I'm willing to help anybody whose music I dig, and I figure that if I do, these people will help me and that's sort of the way it's been."

Eric Clapton's contribution to Stephen's blues rock on 'Go Back Home' was simply some of the Englishman's finest electric guitar work. "... and that was his rehearsal take," Stephen revealed later.

Eric, it would seem, wasn't in the Ringo Starr league when it came to enthusiastic time-keeping: "Well, Eric was a pretty hard man to pin down at that time. I usually had to drive over to his house and drag him out to get him to play," Stephen said when talking to Dave Zimmer for *BAM*.

Both Surrey-based neighbors benefited from the fact that they were creating debut solo albums in the same studios. Stephen only had to walk up the corridor to return the guest guitarist favor by adding a beautiful solo in the middle of Eric's 'Let It Rain,' on *Eric Clapton*.

When Jimi Hendrix dropped by Island Studios to play on Stephen's sessions, his guitar work, like Clapton's, showed a musician at the top of his game. Jimi's explosive guitar part for Stephen's 'Old Times Good Times' could have led to a whole album's worth of material following on from it, but they postponed further sessions for another time. The only surviving recording–later released on Stephen's box set– was the 'No-Name-Jam,' although Jimi did lay down a guitar part on perhaps the stand-out track on the album, 'Love The One You're With.' There are reports that those who heard it thought it sounded great, but for whatever reason Stephen later recorded over it with steel drums, which he later claimed was his favorite part. Could it have been Jimi's last recorded solo? Some believe it might have been.

"He did play on ['Old Times Good Times']; that one and the coherent one were going to be the start of our album, and then–circumstances being what they were–he said, 'You go ahead and put that out and we'll get back to it.' Then we said our goodbyes and I think that's the last time I talked to him."

'Love The One You're With,' which would end up being the big hit single from the album, "has been very good to me," Stephen admitted in the notes he submitted for the *CSN* box set. "The title came from a party with Billy Preston. I asked him if I could pinch this line he had, and he said, 'Sure.' So I took the phrase and wrote a song around it. It's a good-time song, just a bit of fun."

After the party at Brookfield, the writing of 'Love The One You're With' obviously just flowed. "That song is actually multi-layered—the line about 'the rose in the fisted glove' refers to an English icon, a chainmail glove with a rose in it. It comes from the [15th century] War of the Roses." On another occasion he offered another great English iconic moment as inspiration: "That's the Battle of Hastings–1066." Either way, David Crosby was moved to describe 'Love The One You're With' as having "the best chorus that anyone ever wrote."

"I clearly recall Eric [Clapton] telling me that Stephen would go to heaven for writing that song," George Terry, who played with both guitarists, said later.

As Stephen's future publisher and personal manager, Ken Weiss pointed out that songs like 'Love The One You're With' were setting him apart from his peers. "Let's face it, he was the one who had a lucrative solo career, who had solo albums that were gold and platinum, whose song–a Gold Hill song of course–'Love The One You're With' that was not only a smash hit record by Stills but had over 100 cover recordings, including by Joe Cocker, Aretha Franklin, Bob Seger, The Isley Brothers, Luther Vandross, and many others. Neil Young certainly has had a fine solo career, but at that time Stills was the one who drove all those ships."

As a contrast to the infectious driving rhythms of 'Love The One You're With,' the eerie, serene 'To A Flame' would be selected as the single's B-side. The song was like nothing Stephen had ever created before. Incredibly atmospheric, and with an unusually restrained vocal, the cool vibe was enhanced by vibraphone and sweeping strings. Vice President of Atlantic Records, Arif Mardin, was present when Stephen made one of his most ambitious recordings: "One of my great experiences was doing that ballad ... with Stephen Stills in London," he told Robert Greenfield for the biography of Ahmet Ertegun. "I had heard the song and arrived with an outline for a score. Stephen and I sat down at the piano and he just started. He had the whole thing, virtually note for note in his head. We worked for hours making sure he had recalled the range of the various instruments correctly, and there were a very few instances where I filled in the blanks, but even those he corrected over the course of the session. Every note of it was his."

Encouraged by the assembled musicians among a 22-piece

orchestra, Stephen described the 'To A Flame' session as "the biggest 'wow' moment of my career."

In complete contrast to the lush, spaced-out, meticulously recorded 'To A Flame' was 'Black Queen.' This was Stephen Stills at his rawest, and the album cover note is revealing: "Was recorded live & the performance is courtesy of Jose Cuervo Gold Label Tequila." The five minutes and twenty-eight seconds of blues wailing were recorded at the end of a long day in the studio with Eric Clapton, when the two had recorded 'Go Back Home' and Eric's 'Let It Rain,' followed by a lengthy tequila-fueled jam. The two-hour session and drinking competition ended when Eric reportedly disappeared, unable to continue further, but Stephen stayed put and recorded Robert Johnson's 'Crossroads' and his own blues number, 'Black Queen.'

As Bill Halverson revealed later, Stephen had instructed him to switch off all the lights while he summoned up the spirit of the song. "It's recorded live, with Stephen working the mics as if he's giving a performance. My job was simple: know when to press 'play,'" he told Max Bell.

"I was real drunk when I cut ['Black Queen']," Stephen admitted to Dave Zimmer. "And that was just meant to be a demo for me and Eric or me and Jimi to work from and play electrically later. But everybody loved me doing it solo acoustic so much, I put it on the record."

CHAPTER 17
The Chart-Topping Déjà Vu

With the Island sessions over, further work would be added to the solo record in the months ahead, but for now all the press attention around Stephen was focused on the release of Crosby, Stills, Nash & Young's *Déjà Vu* on March 23, 1970, and the opening of *Woodstock* the movie a few days later. With pre-orders of two million and sales eventually topping 13 million, *Déjà Vu* would become the biggest commercial success for any of the quartet, collectively or individually, and was responsible for displacing Simon & Garfunkel's *Bridge Over Troubled Water* at the top of the *Billboard* 200 in May. Of its release, *Billboard* were gushing in their praise of *Déjà Vu*: "Last year's phenomenon is this year's super-group," read the review, "and the awesome performing talents of Crosby, Stills, Nash, and Young are etched into their second album with a skill and sensitivity bound to be the measure of excellence in rock for 1970."

Melody Maker was equally positive. Reflecting on the success of the "huge world-wide hit" the year before for *Crosby, Stills & Nash*, the British music paper asked: "Question: how the hell do you follow that? The answer comes from Atlantic Records in a couple of weeks, when they release the group's second, and even better (would you believe?) album."

Langdon Winner's *Rolling Stone* review was mostly negative, and he answered his own question when he wrote, "... are there any truly first-rate songs here? If there are, I don't hear them." Winner's biggest moan was directed at the cover, and "the absurdity of its pretensions."

Curiously, on release the chart-topping album name-checked more than the quartet on the extravagantly designed cover Winner loathed so much. "Crosby, Stills, Nash, & Young–Dallas Taylor & Greg Reeves" proclaimed the gothic-style lettering in an apparent nod to keep the rhythm section happy. All six group members were painstakingly and rather beautifully photographed as if in a snapshot from the 19th century, with the sepia print fixed to a mock leather photo album background. Unsurprisingly, Stephen elected to wear the confederate gray soldier's uniform when the band raided a local costume store, before convening in the garden of David Crosby's rented property in Novato for the photoshoot.

The March release of *Déjà Vu*, and an invitation from Neil Young to add some guest vocals to tracks he was recording for his *After The Gold Rush* album, saw Stephen leave England and join up with CSN&Y to finalize touring plans. Shortly after adding a vocal part to Neil's 'Only Love Can Break Your Heart,' Stephen's ability to play guitar was ended temporarily when he broke his left wrist when driving near his L.A. home. Distracted by a police car he spotted in his rear-view mirror, he crashed into a parked vehicle and needed time out to let the injury heal.

What Stephen didn't know at the time was that while he was out of action, vacationing in Hawaii with his friend and photographer Henry Diltz, Jimi Hendrix was searching for him.

"I did not find this out for years," Stephen told Simon Harper for *Clash*. "It was in [Mitch] Mitchell's book–we'd talked about doing something, you know? I had a commitment and he had a commitment and we were gonna get together, but there was a time there in between when I was back in California and had an accident and broke the little bones in my left hand. So I'm in a cast and calling into the office every day. And apparently, according to Mitchell, at that time, Jimi's office was desperately trying to find me, and David Geffen just stalled them endlessly. 'I don't know where he is. I'll pass on the message.' And so Jimi did something else. I would have gladly put down the guitar and played bass for him."

So the "Stephen Stills joins The Jimi Hendrix Experience" headlines never got printed, and amid frantic preparations for the new Crosby, Stills, Nash & Young tour, Stephen literally fell victim to another painful injury.

Out riding, he fell from his horse and tore a knee ligament, which necessitated the use of a crutch. Amazingly, the injury wasn't serious enough for the tour to be canceled, but there were other factors at work that would stretch the patience of everyone involved.

"Cocaine madness," as Graham Nash described it, was beginning to affect the dynamic of the band, particularly in Stephen's case. More immediately unsettling was the dissent in the ranks from Dallas Taylor and Greg Reeves, who now felt that they wanted to be acknowledged as songwriters and perform their own material on forthcoming tours. The insistent Reeves was unsurprisingly fired, and a ready-made replacement in Calvin 'Fuzzy' Samuels, from Stephen's London solo sessions, was quickly installed on bass ahead of the tour opener in Denver, Colorado.

The Stills/Samuels axis would prove to be the best-rehearsed section of the band and Stephen tended to dominate proceedings in the Denver concert. Graham Nash didn't hide his frustrations. "I don't mind being guided, but he was being preposterous," he admitted to Dave Zimmer. Stephen, naturally, saw the situation quite differently. "They were not into being arranged," reasoned Stephen. "So I had to cop out. It wasn't me trying to dominate anything. I was just trying to act like a pro and carry on in the middle of a difficult situation."

While they had been happy for 'Captain Manyhands' to take command previously, now Crosby and Nash clearly felt that Stephen was taking authority too far. It might have been Stephen jesting that Crosby and Nash were glorified backing singers that began the simmering tension.

The "difficult situation" Stephen referred to became much worse by the end of the Denver gig when Neil Young issued an ultimatum: "Either Dallas goes or I go" was what the drummer said he overheard Neil say at one point, and Stephen knew which way that would have to be resolved.

Great drummer that he was, Taylor's style was not the 'less is more' type of drumming that Neil Young thrived on, but it was more his destructive behavior that had led to Neil's ultimatum.

Dallas Taylor had been Stephen's recruit, but he didn't want to lose Neil. He could see the band he had worked so hard to create falling apart at the seams.

Between the Denver and Chicago tour dates the squabbles took their toll. With disharmony reigning and the quality of performances threatened, the Crosby, Stills, Nash & Young juggernaut ground to a halt.

With Stephen still in plaster and only mobile with the aid of a crutch, an unrehearsed band, a new bass player, and no drummer, Crosby, Stills, Nash & Young were in terrible shape to exploit the terrific exposure their new album was giving them.

Despite Stephen's protestations and drive to continue, they had to take some time out to see if there might be the faintest hope that they could resurrect the special relationship they had developed when first joining forces. It was a fracture in the band's togetherness that Stephen would reflect on later. His quest to create a great band that would challenge the world's best was over, at least for the time being. "If a voice of reason could have cleared that fog, we would have realized our full potential and CSN&Y would be mentioned in the same breath as The Beatles and the Stones," he later suggested to Dave Zimmer. "We lost it all right there, that day to indulgence. We lost it all."

Maybe he was right. Nothing would ever be quite the same again. Had there ever been a band with four such egotistical talents before? Why would anyone expect them not to uncouple at the first sign of tension? Neil Young was beginning to exercise his right to challenge his bandmates and it was clear that neither Stephen's dictatorship, nor a four-way democracy, were a recipe for harmony.

Hastily recruited to replace Dallas Taylor, drummer Johny Barbata had an interesting take on things when he reminisced about the time he joined CSN&Y with Dolf van Stijgeren: "Neil's role was to write, sing, and play guitar. But as with the Eagles, Glenn Frey was the leader, but in the end he was passed up by Don Henley. The same thing happened with Stephen and Neil. Neil got bigger." Crosby, and to a lesser degree Nash, were instrumental in the former Turtles drummer, Barbata, replacing Taylor. Stephen's influence over his bandmates was waning.

Despite the tour hiatus, new boys Calvin Samuels and Johny Barbata weren't left kicking their heels for long. Both were summoned to L.A.'s Record Plant Studio 3 for a very special recording on May 21, 1970, when Crosby, Stills, Nash & Young cut the quickest protest record of all time.

When four Kent State students were shot dead by the National Guard for protesting against plans to ramp up the invasion of Cambodia, CSN&Y's response was instant. 'Ohio,' with its ominous 'tin soldiers and Nixon coming' opening lyric, was the product of David Crosby's indignation and Neil Young's killer lyrics. The song-writing came about in a moment shared by the two while they enjoyed the afternoon sun one day, relaxing on the porch of road manager Leo Makota's California home in Pescadero. When Crosby showed Neil Young a copy of the May 15th issue of *Life* magazine, featuring photographer John Filo's horrific image of 20-year-old student Jeffrey Miller lying dead from shots fired by the National Guard, he immediately reacted by writing 'Ohio.'

The B-side was equally poignant and had been quickly written. Stephen's mournful 'Find The Cost Of Freedom' had been completed in under 30 minutes, but until now never found its way onto a record release. Here it contrasted perfectly with Neil's indignant 'Ohio.' Crosby, Stills, Nash, and Young sat in a square facing each other on four chairs around a mic at Record Plant's Studio 3, with just the doubling of their voices before the master track was done. None of the *Déjà Vu* sessions had seen them record as a band like this. 'Ohio' had galvanized them as a unit. The fragile state of the nation back in 1970 meant that when CSN&Y spoke out about drugs, politics, the war in Vietnam, or social injustice, America's teenagers listened. The relevance of four powerful musicians as spokespersons for their generation must have been a cause of some considerable irritation to President 'Tricky Dicky' Nixon, as he would be labeled. As rock promoter Bill Graham put it, they were "the leaders of a whole socioeconomic movement." Of the four of them, Neil Young was the least likely to preach politics on stage, while Crosby and Nash, who had a new song, 'Chicago,' about the violent detention of political activist Bobby Seale, would speak out forcefully between songs. At this point Stephen was equally outspoken, but realized their power to change the system had its limits. "Everybody was looking for a political message in everything I wrote, like I was running for the senate at 24. I said, 'Hang on, wait a minute. I do not know the rules of the Senate."

Like it or not, all four of them were being labeled as outspoken, politically cute rock stars. In Stephen's case, he was uncomfortably embracing the responsibility.

The unplanned nature of the recording of 'Ohio' was a headache for Atlantic Records. Ahmet Ertegun was in two minds about what to do next. With the *Déjà Vu* track 'Teach Your Children' still riding high in the charts, he knew it wasn't best business practice to be releasing another CSN&Y single at the same time. But this was no business decision. Released on June 27, just a week after it had been conceived, written, and recorded, 'Ohio' hung around the charts for nine weeks, peaking at Number 14 on the Hot 100.

Reinvigorated by the reception for 'Ohio,' Crosby, Stills, Nash & Young returned to their aborted tour on May 29 with new drummer Johny Barbata, who this time, sensibly, had been thoroughly put through his paces at rehearsals on the Warner Brothers Studios' sound stage. The huge, cavernous structure had been booked by the band immediately after it had been used for the filming of the movie *They Shoot Horses, Don't They?*

With the group's personnel now settled again, the tour

continued with a few more bumps in the road. The Stills/Young guitar wars threatened to derail things during numbers like 'Southern Man,' and their overblown sparring would alienate Crosby and Nash at times. Frustration and anger would usually involve one of the four seemingly trying to out-do the others. But there were strong contractual reasons why they couldn't just walk away. They had an obligation to fulfil the dates and were estimated to be earning up to $100,000 a night, and on the plus side there were some incredible highs and a unique empathy between CSN&Y and their audiences. And CSN&Y weren't at each other's throats continuously: even a tiff between Stephen and Graham at the Fillmore East, when Bob Dylan was present in the audience and Stills extended his solo section of the gig by a couple of numbers, blew over before the night was out. Tensions inevitably rose to the surface, but CSN&Y held things together–just.

Relatively unscathed by the close of the tour in Minneapolis on July 9, they then went their four separate ways after marking the end with a huge poker game and civilized dinner together. "The first prerequisite of being in a Stephen Stills band is that you must be able to play poker," Stephen confided later to Tavis Smiley.

For Stephen it was a time to take stock and reflect on his disappointment at Crosby, Stills, Nash & Young dissolving. His expectations had been matched in one sense. The band he had created were big business, but could he or others handle the madness that accompanied the music?

He was in philosophical mood when he pondered the state of the music scene in an interview for *Guitar World* that summer: "What movie stars used to have in the way of public appeal, the rock and roll bands have taken over. It isn't so much what the rock musicians are doing, it's what the kids are doing with the pop musicians. The larger-than-life thing. It's like John Lennon is much more important than Vanessa Redgrave, whereas Paul Whiteman was never more important than Gary Cooper. And therefore, the more all the little pieces of bullshit that go on with the superstar, the less important your music becomes and the less people seem to realize what you are doing musically."

CHAPTER 18
Lovely Rita

Having left the band Traffic, Dave Mason's debut solo album *Alone Together* had been released with some important help from Stephen, and significantly featured guest vocals from singer Rita Coolidge. Mason remembered his collaboration with Stephen on 'Only You Know And I Know,' which was the hit single from the album. "I personally spent a good deal of time with Stephen socially and in the studio and he is certainly a unique talent. In fact my song 'Only You Know And I Know' would probably not have been written without Stephen showing me some different guitar tunings."

Delaney and Bonnie, who would have an even bigger hit with the song in 1971, would work with Stephen much later, but it was Rita Coolidge from the Dave Mason sessions who would make a really big impression as Stephen began to complete recordings for his debut solo album in L.A.

Stephen enlisted the honey-toned vocal backing of Coolidge

and her sister Priscilla (wife of Booker T. Jones) for the completion of his recording work, and a relationship developed with Rita which inspired him to write the track 'Cherokee' for *Stephen Stills*. Significantly, Graham Nash was also a guest vocalist on the album. His love affair with Joni Mitchell had ended by this time, and Nash was also attracted to the raven-haired 'Delta Lady,' immortalized in Leon Russell's song. Ironically, all three protagonists in this love triangle (Stills, Coolidge, and Nash) would contribute to the album's lead track, 'Love The One You're With.'

The daughter of a Cherokee father and mother from Cherokee-Scottish lineage, Rita Coolidge was still to hit the heights of her solo singing career when she answered the call as a session singer for Stephen's album. The July evening vocal session for 'Love The One You're With,' at Wally Heider's Studio 3 in Hollywood, completed the original work begun at London's Island Studios back in March. Gathered round two microphones, sisters Rita and Priscilla were joined by Stephen, John Sebastian, Cass Elliot, possibly Claudia Lennear, Crosby, Nash, and the later uncredited Peter Tork.

What happened next would have a dramatic effect on Stephen, Rita, and Graham, and seriously compromise the future harmony of CSN&Y.

As Graham Nash explained in his autobiography *Wild Tales*, "He [Stephen] was coming on to Rita all session long, but I beat him to the punch. I invited her to go to a concert with me the next day at five o'clock."

Undeterred, Stephen put a devious battle plan into action to make sure he and not Nash would get the date. According to Rita's own memoir *Delta Lady*, when she rang the number Graham had given her at Stephen's house where he was staying overnight, Stephen answered the phone and told her Graham had made other arrangements (or was sick, according to Nash) and that he, Stephen, would pick her up. This he duly did, in his Mercedes sports car, according to Coolidge, who also recalled the remarkable coincidence on that first date that made Stephen stop the car and pull over. Chatting about their respective star signs had led her to reveal her May 1 birthday–the exact same birthday of his former lover Judy Collins.

Without a clue as to what had happened and why he hadn't had a call from Rita, the duped and unhappy Graham Nash simply ignored Rita and she and Stephen went on to see each other over a period of weeks. But Nash hadn't lost interest in pursuing Rita and she clearly hadn't forgotten him. "Made of the stuff women really fall in love with–tall, good-looking, kind, sweet and polite" is how she later described him in her autobiography.

Sensing that Rita wasn't fully committed to the relationship with Stephen, Nash made his move and they "fell for each other hard," as he put it. Ever the gentleman, Nash decided to settle things properly and called on Stephen. Unsurprisingly, the meeting to inform Stephen of Graham and Rita's love for each other did not go well, and according to the tearful Rita a fight ensued and somebody was forced to separate Nash and Stephen.

The bitterness left behind from Nash then moving into Rita's home in Beachwood Canyon would rumble on, and decades later Nash would admit, "I'm not so sure he has forgiven me to this day."

Graham Nash and Rita Coolidge would share a happy year-long relationship together. Nash's debut solo album *Songs For Beginners* would be conceived and written with the support of his new lover at Beachwood Canyon, a romantic echo of his time with Joni Mitchell. He would also write 'Wounded Bird' for the album, a song about the fallout from Stephen's love affair with Judy Collins. When Nash's *Songs For Beginners* was recorded (again at Wally Heider's Studio 3), there were guest appearances by Coolidge and David Crosby, but there was no contribution from Stephen Stills.

The heartbreak Stills had suffered after losing Judy Collins was being repeated all over again, and despite the brief nature of the affair with Rita Coolidge there would be songs written and references made in lyrics to his 'dark-eyed Cherokee,' 'the raven,' 'the lady from Tennessee,' his 'Sugar Babe.' There's a touching fondness for Stephen written as a footnote to Rita's autobiography: "I probably don't need to ask, but please never lose that delightful, mischievous spirit that keeps you so young, like Peter Pan," she wrote.

Losing Rita Coolidge to his friend hit Stephen hard. His state of mind was so appallingly skewed after the event that he wound up being arrested for possession of cocaine and barbiturates. The cops were called to a La Jolla motel, where an ambulance was summoned to assist him with what Stephen later admitted was a case of "OD-ing on pills." The incident left a dark impression during a hugely successful year for him musically, and it wasn't until the following April that the charge was reduced to 'a misdemeanor' and a $1,000 fine with probation.

CHAPTER 19
Jimi's Dead

When the old telephone on the wall of Stephen's Colorado cabin rang on September 18, 1970 it was a call to deliver the dreadful news that Jimi Hendrix was dead. With work finished on his debut album, Stephen had escaped from his unhappy experience in La Jolla for a vacation at his Gold Hill mountain retreat. Accompanied by his personal assistant Dan Campbell, friend and photographer Henry Diltz, and Calvin 'Fuzzy' Samuels, he would pick at his guitar most nights and explore his Rocky Mountain surroundings by day.

The afternoon phone call about Jimi Hendrix left Stephen shaken and devastated. "I sat on a mountain and cried for two hours when I heard he'd died," he told *Sounds*' Penny Valentine.

The circumstances behind his friend's death–choking on his own vomit following an overdose of barbituratcs–must have resonated. There was also the feeling that Jimi's rather squalid end might have been prevented if he'd been in London. "He was running with a strange crowd then," was how Stephen remembers the situation from the last time he was in England with his friend.

There was just enough time for Stephen to get Atlantic to print a dedication to 'James Marshall Hendrix' on the new album sleeve, especially as they still didn't have a cover picture. That problem was solved when Stephen and Henry woke up one morning to find a thick covering of snow outside the cabin–a perfect backdrop for an iconic photo by Henry of Stephen playing his acoustic guitar in two feet of virgin snow.

Henry and Stephen had only just begun their photo session when Stephen crunched through the snow and back into the cabin. He returned moments later clutching a pink-spotted papier mâché giraffe. Perching the giraffe in front of him, he lit a cigarette, picked up his guitar, squatted cross-legged on a wooden seat, and resumed the session.

Speculation that the inclusion of the giraffe in the photo was a coded message to a former girlfriend proved correct when Stephen later admitted that the giraffe was indeed a present from Rita Coolidge. Initially, Henry Diltz wasn't satisfied that Stephen's addition to the photo was a good idea.But the photographer eventually grew to appreciate the cover photo, as he told the *Phoenix New Times* in 2001: "That giraffe really offended my sensibilities. It wasn't organic. But I've looked at that picture on the walls in these gallery shows and thought without that giraffe it wouldn't be much of a picture. Just some guy playing guitar in the snow."

Henry Diltz was spending a good deal of time with Stephen during the fall of 1970. The pair traveled to England, and from there flew over to Europe on the trail of Chip Monck, who Stephen wanted to hire for future concerts. Monck had been

Above: As a student in Costa Rica, the 17-year-old Stephen Stills made his first recording.

Left: The Buffalo Springfield debut album was hastily re-issued in 1967 to include Stephen's hit song 'For What It's Worth.'

Late Springfield: From the left, Bruce Palmer, Neil Young, Dewey Martin, Richie Furay, and Stephen Stills. (Pictorial Press/Alamy) Below: Stills and Dewey Martin performing on the CBS TV show *The Smothers Brothers Comedy Hour* in February 1967. (CBS Photo Archive/Getty)

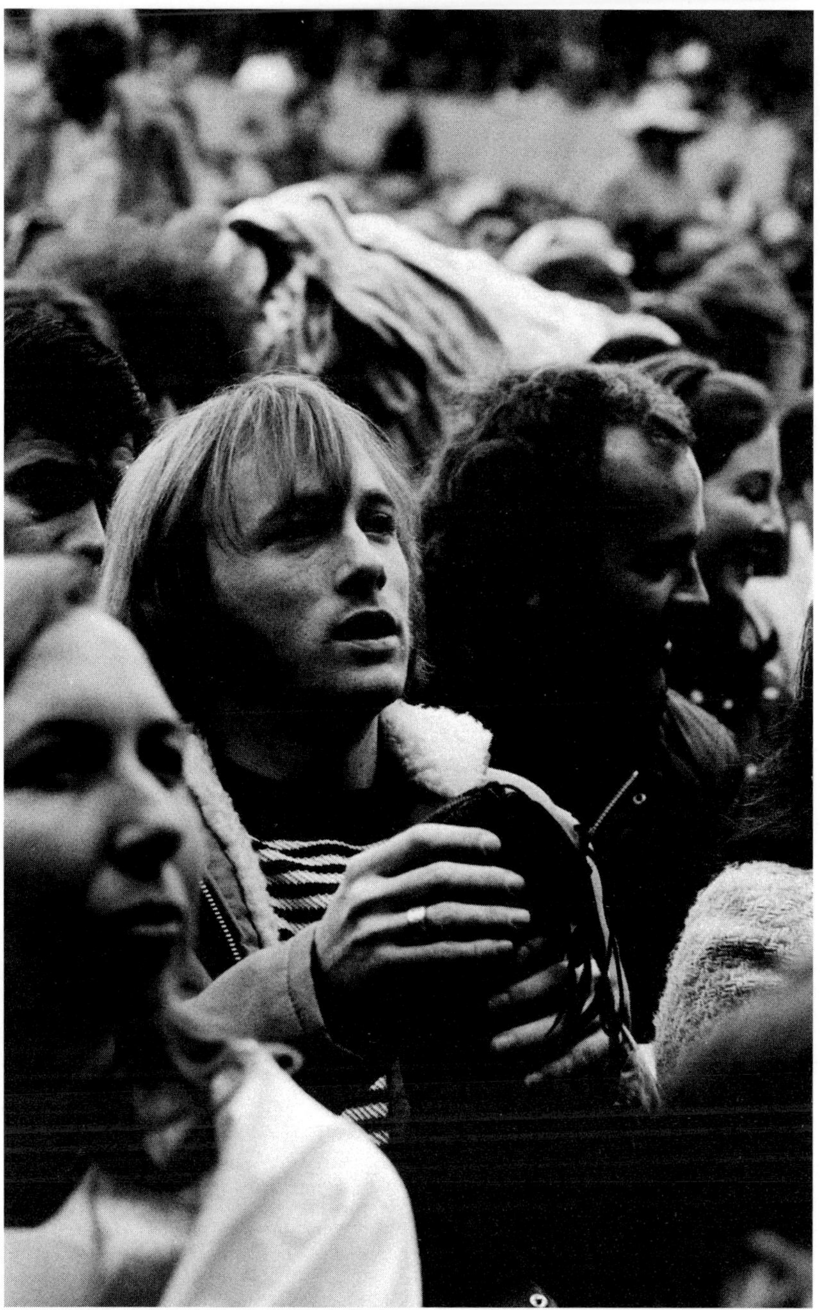

An enthusiastic performer and spectator at the Monterey Pop Festival in June 1967, Stills also had a hand in the creation of the event. (Michael Ochs Archives/Getty Images)

Stephen Stills was captivated by "Judy Blue Eyes," even before he met her. The *Judy Collins 3* LP cover was his introduction to the girl with "cornflower eyes," as he described her. (Interfoto/Alamy)

Above: Crosby, Nash, and Stills engage in some of their hallmark three-part harmony. (Tom Copi, Michael Ochs Archives/Getty Images)
Left: Stills' Colorado cabin was the setting for the picture used on the front cover of his debut album. The addition of the giraffe–a gift from Rita Coolidge– was a spur-of-the-moment decision by Stephen. It was during this stay at his mountainside home that he got a phone call to tell him that his good friend Jimi Hendrix had died in London.

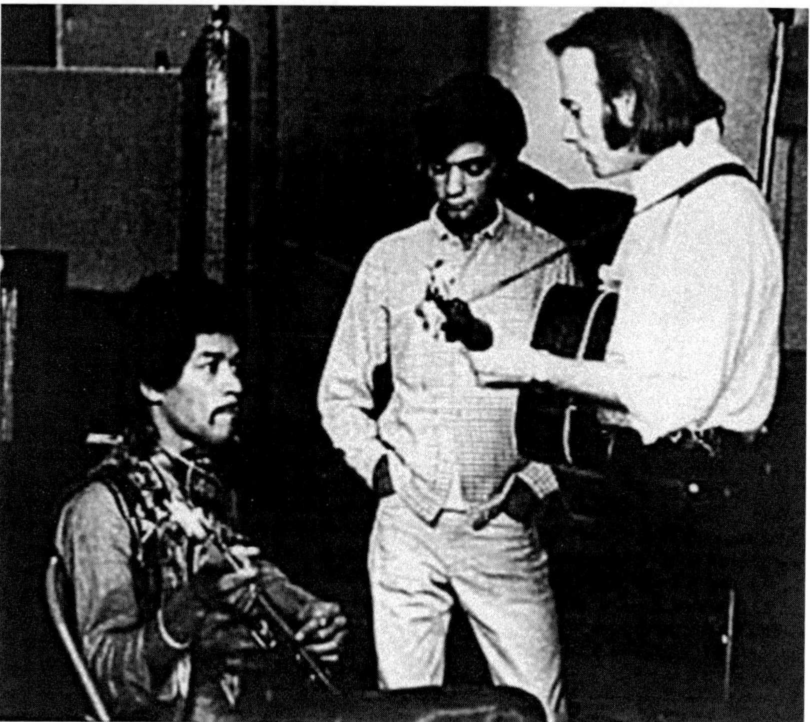

Top: Stephen playing bass with George Harrison during the *Doris Troy* album sessions for Apple Records, at London's Olympic Studios, in February 1970. Above: "We were like two lonely Americans in England" was how Stephen described his friendship with Jimi Hendrix.

"Why don't you get Neil?" suggested Atlantic Records boss Ahmet Ertegun to Stephen, and CS&N became CSN&Y, just in time for Woodstock. Nash, Crosby, Stills, and Dallas Taylor with 'new boy' Neil Young. (Pictorial Press/Alamy)

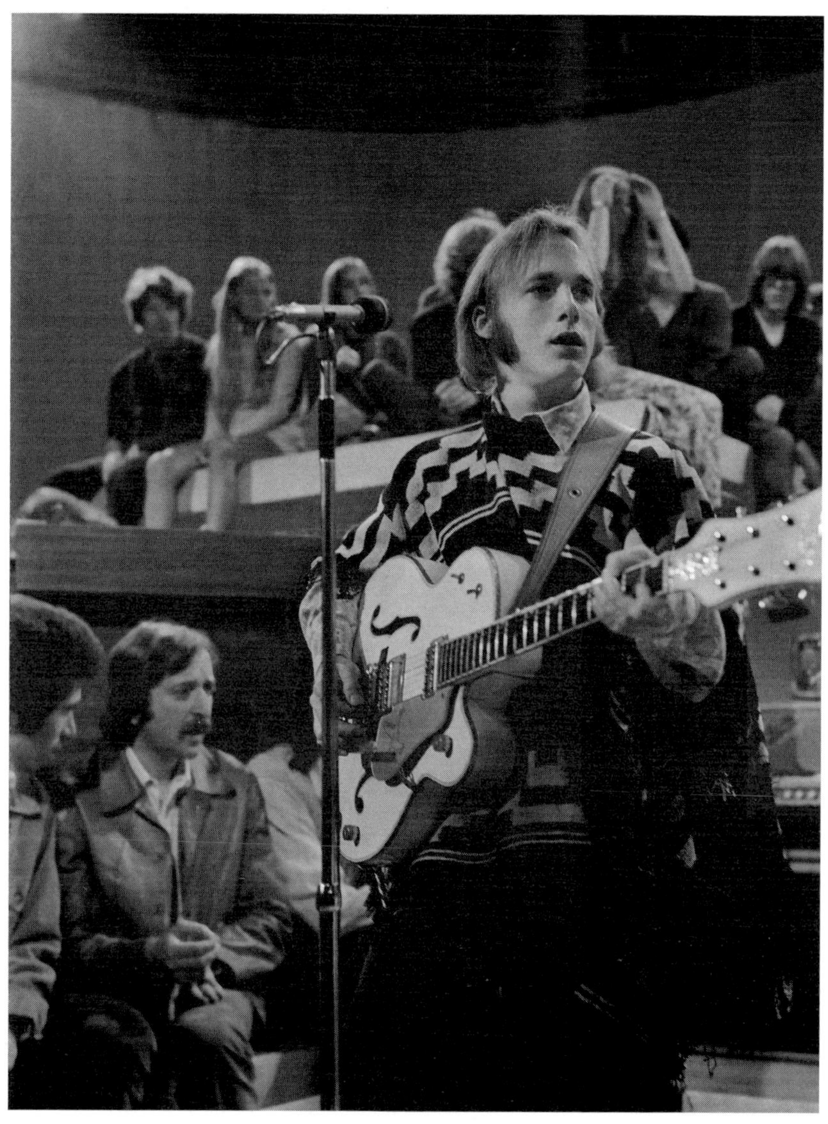

Wearing the famous poncho he wore at Woodstock, Stills rehearses for a Crosby, Stills, Nash & Young *Music Scene* TV appearance where the band's managers, David Geffen and Elliot Roberts, joined the studio audience. (Michael Ochs Archives/Getty Images)

Stephen pictured in Amsterdam at the start of his Manassas adventure in 1971. (Gijsbert Hanekroot/Redferns/Getty Images)

Above: Manassas, comprising Paul Harris, Chris Hillman, Calvin "Fuzzy" Samuels, Al Perkins, Joe Lala, Dallas Taylor, and the 'fragile' Stills, smile or grimace for a publicity shot in the garage of Stephen's Brookfield home in Surrey, England. Left: Atlantic Records promote the band's first tour.

When Stephen Stills straps on his Gibson Firebird it generally means the audience are about to witness something loud. (Steve Morley/Redferns/Getty Images) Below: The moment in the 1974 CSN&Y setlist where Stills cuts loose, watched by Neil Young, to play his electric blues number 'Black Queen.' (Gijsbert Hanekroot/Redferns/Getty)

Top: Oakland Coliseum, July 1974: Cigarette clamped firmly in his mouth, Stills watches intently as Neil Young brings another number to an end. (Gijsbert Hanekroot/Redferns/Getty) Above: The 1974 CSN&Y stadium tour's London, Wembley Stadium concert saw Stephen bring his five-month-old son Christopher on stage when accompanying Nash and Crosby on The Beatles' 'Blackbird.' (Pictorial Press/Alamy)

By Cameron Crowe
SOUTH AFRICA
The Dark Side of Paradise
By Jan Morris
TWYLA THARP
Something in the Way She Moves

Front page news: Inexplicably, in the midst of the punk movement, the 1977 reunion of Crosby, Stills & Nash produced *CSN*, an album that gave the trio their highest *Billboard* album and singles chart positions.

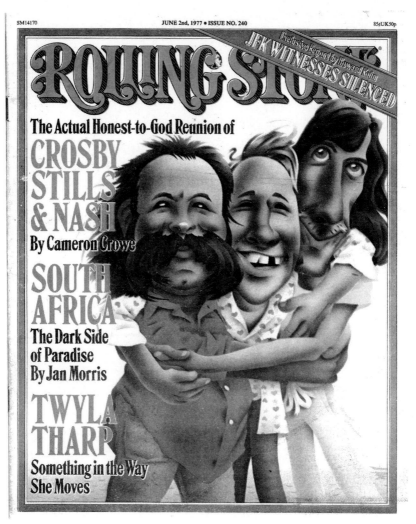

SM14170
JUNE 2nd, 1977 • ISSUE NO. 240
85¢UK50p
ROLLING STONE
Exclusive Report by Howard Kohn
JFK WITNESSES SILENCED
The Actual Honest-to-God Reunion of

Stills lifts both Rock and Roll Hall of Fame induction awards he bagged in the same night in 1997–the first musician to achieve the feat. (Reuters/Alamy)

Above: Stills and Bonnie Raitt join forces in a Musicians United for Safe Energy benefit concert in 2011. (Zuma Press/Alamy) Below: Jack Black, Stephen and Kristen Stills harmonize ahead of the couple's first Light Up The Blues concert in aid of Autism Speaks, in 2013. (Zuma Press/Alamy)

Above: Stills takes center stage during a CS&N gig at Switzerland's 2010 Paleo Festival. (Agron Dragaj/ZumaPress.com) Left: Crosby, Stills, Nash & Young share a moment of togetherness during a press conference to announce their CSNY2K tour. (Reuters/Alamy)

Dressed for every eventuality: Stills plays England's Glastonbury Festival with Crosby and Nash in 2009. (Rune Hellestad/Corbis/Getty)

the Woodstock stage and lighting director deputized by Michael Lang to do those legendary booming stage announcements. Now he was stage-managing The Rolling Stones on their current tour through Europe. Nothing much came of the plan to hire Monck, but Stephen did get to hang out with the Stones and even play piano on stage with them. The opportunity occurred during a Stones gig at the Amsterdam RAI Exhibition & Convention Centre, on October 9. Stephen and Henry were standing in the wings when Mick Jagger beckoned Stephen to join them. While the camera-ready Henry snapped away, Jagger, Richards, Watts, Wyman, Taylor, and Stills rocked the audience with 'Dead Flowers.'

"I wish they still had that tape, because it was absolutely amazing the noise that we made between us," Stephen recalled. "We were just batting around. You know the old joke: blues musicians play three notes for ten-thousand people and jazz musicians play a thousand notes for three people."

Another adventure around this time saw Stephen go on another abortive trip, this time in search of movie star Steve McQueen, who was on location filming *Le Mans* in France. The protracted journey, by car and ferry across the channel, turned out to be a complete waste of time and waste of tens of thousands of dollars. On arriving in France, he eventually discovered that McQueen had already left and gone home. A trip "I'm still paying for" is how the disgruntled rock star summed up this anti-climax.

Back home at his English base, Brookfield, Stephen awaited the release of his debut album while riding his horses and planning his next move. With the inactivity of CSN&Y and the satisfaction of creating what he hoped would be a well-received debut record, he began to imagine what he might do differently on a follow-up solo release.

But when Crosby and Nash flew to the UK and were filmed performing for the prestigious BBC *In Concert* series, they dropped in on Stephen at Brookfield. Crosby, Stills & Nash were briefly reformed, long enough at least for the three of them to sing together on a new song Stephen had been working on called 'As I Come Of Age.'

Another visitor to Brookfield at this time was Peter Sellers. The actor, who had previously owned the Surrey estate before Ringo and Maureen Starr, was curious to revisit the home he had once shared with Britt Ekland. Once again, Henry Diltz was there to record the event with his camera and Stephen later recalled in a *Classic Rock* interview: "His children really wanted to see his old house, so his office calls up and says, 'Mr Sellers would like to come and visit you,' and I said, 'Of course.' So he came out and we were rehearsing. They had a little walk around and then the children went off to play and Peter comes in and starts playing drums with his hands. We didn't really say very much. I never really sat down and had a conversation with him."

On November 16, 1970, *Stephen Stills* was released in US music stores, and a couple of weeks later in the UK.

When a reviewer tries to backtrack a little by adding the words "I'm not saying I don't like this album," you know the general endorsement isn't going to be a ringing one.

Stills' debut solo album didn't get a pasting from *Rolling Stone*–Ed Ward even went as far as saying that "'Love The One You're With' will make a killer single"–but the dismissive closing words "But when it's over, I put something meatier on" suggested *Stephen Stills* was a collection of samey pop songs.

This would be the first, but certainly not be the last time Stills the solo artist would suffer less than enthusiastic *Rolling Stone* reviews.

As for the rest of us, we pretty much all liked *Stephen Stills* greatly. As already detailed, the songs were good, the guest performers were the cream of contemporary rock, blues, and R&B, and the single 'Love The One You're With' would be a radio and chart smash hit, not only in the US but also in Stephen's adopted UK home.

Billboard was gushing in its praise and described Stephen as "a genius for absorbing influences and surpassing them through his own powerful creativity." The all-star support and "brilliant arrangements," it added, "takes rock to new musical heights on 'Love The One You're With,' 'Go Back Home,' and 'Cherokee.'"

Over the winter of 1970/71, the album peaked at Number 3 in the US (Number 8 in the UK) and 'Love The One You're With' made Number 14 in the US (Number 37 in the UK). Stephen wasn't satisfied, as he told *Creem*: "My first album would have been a Number 1 record if George Harrison hadn't come out right behind me with *All Things Must Pass*."

He did beat his old rival Neil Young though. Young's *After The Gold Rush* stalled at Number 8 on the *Billboard* albums chart, although this was the point at which Neil's career would begin to outstrip Stephen's, and David and Graham's for that matter. Neil's chart-topping *Harvest* was up next in 1972, and by then he would wield considerably more power in the will-they-won't-they reformations of Crosby, Stills, Nash & Young.

CHAPTER 20
Stills 2 and 4 Way Street

For Stephen, there was a reminder of a love lost in early 1971 when Rita Coolidge's eponymously titled debut album hit the stores. Stills and Nash (whose relationship with the singer was still ongoing) both appeared on the February release, with Stills playing his trademark chiming acoustic guitar on 'Second Story Window' and electric guitar on her version of Van Morrison's 'Crazy Love.'

By May, both Crosby and Nash had completed and released their own solo efforts. Neither Crosby's *If I Could Only Remember My Name* (peak position US Number 12) nor Nash's *Songs For Beginners* (peak position US Number 15) would include any contribution from Stephen.

Atlantic Records were busy marketing Crosby, Stills, and Nash solo LPs, but what they wanted most of all was a new band record to follow up the chart-topping *Déjà Vu*. With little sign that the three or four of them were going to get back together, let alone enter a studio, Atlantic released a selection of some of the best live performances from the previous year's touring, under the highly appropriate title *4 Way Street*. If Atlantic wanted to keep the dissolved band in the public eye as long as possible, their strategy certainly worked. Released in April, the double album shot to Number 1 just over a month later, toppling Janis Joplin's posthumously released *Pearl* from the chart summit. *Rolling Stone* and Stephen Stills were once again not in agreement when it came to reviewing the album.

Bizarrely, this time the *Rolling Stone* review was largely favorable, but Stephen had doubts that the record should have been released at all in the form it did. "I hated *4 Way Street*," he admitted to the music paper. "I mean you've got to be good to get a live album and not have to overdub and do some cheating."

The album, warts and all, with some off-key harmonies, did however capture the electricity between the band and its audience. It was a shrewd move by Atlantic to leave the recordings untouched and "pure," as David Crosby remarked. *4 Way Street* would encourage fans who hadn't seen the band yet to clamor for future concert tickets and purchase the album for Christmas. But while Atlantic, Crosby, Nash, and Young were all enjoying the plaudits connected to the various solo releases and the huge success of *4 Way Street*, Stephen had already spent the first part of the year beavering away on solo album number two.

It was Ahmet Ertegun who suggested Miami's Criteria Studios to Stephen as a base for recording his second solo album. Starting in February, *Stephen Stills 2* was created over a period of five months, with a summer release. Would the change of scene from the London winter of its predecessor to the warmer climes of Florida help create something different?

Like London's Island Studios, Criteria was a long way from

everyone else and another bolt hole for Stephen. Here in Miami, an enduring working relationship would be formed between the Criteria engineers Ron and Howard Albert and Stephen that would see him return on numerous occasions. The Albert brothers had already worked with The Allman Brothers, James Brown, Otis Redding, and Aretha Franklin and were putting in some overtime on their current project when Stephen showed up. "We were working on a Johnny and Edgar Winter live LP," recalled Howard Albert. "Ahmet Ertegun told him to look us up. It was about one or two in the morning."

It was just as well that Ron and Howard were round-the-clock engineers. That very first day saw Stephen persuade them to help him record an acoustic version of 'Relaxing Town.' Stephen's famous work ethic would set a pattern of more than just late nights. "Usually, a two- or three-day session" was how Howard remembered it. "Ron and I would tag team. I would work 10 or 12 hours and then Ron would come in for another 10 or 12."

The album would include a number of tracks left over from the London Island Studios sessions for *Stephen Stills*. Eric Clapton's second guest appearance–another powerful lead guitar contribution–came on the swirling 'Fishes And Scorpions.' The rather lyrically lightweight 'Marianne' was another track cut in London that was a surprise departure for Stephen's song-writing. Certainly catchy, and released as the album's second single, the song looked like an attempt to create a simple hit to emulate 'Love The One You're With,' but 'Marianne' even failed that audition.

The first single nominated turned out to be a Stills classic: 'Change Partners.' The song swayed and rolled to the accompaniment of some beautiful Crosby and Nash vocals, augmented by friends Henry Diltz and Fred Neil. "Ostensibly it was about growing up in the south, attending the debutante balls, although Graham likes to refer to it as the Crosby, Stills & Nash theme song, which I suppose it is," remarked Stephen.

This London recording of 'Change Partners' got the nod on the album, but many Stills fans would argue that a second version, with an exquisite pedal steel guitar part by Jerry Garcia and some neat piano by Nils Lofgren, made and mixed at Wally Heider's Studio 3 and then Criteria, was superior. Decades later, this version of 'Change Partners' would get an airing on Stephen's box set, *Carry On*. Garcia echoed the sentiments of the Howard brothers when recalling his sessions with Stephen on 'Change Partners' and 'So Begins The Task,' a track that would wait another year or so for its release. "Sometimes they were very weird experiences," the Grateful Dead guitarist told writer Ken Hunt. "Like, for [*Stephen Stills 2* and *Manassas*] I didn't know what records they were for or anything. The way Stills worked at the time was he just accumulated endless tracks. He worked on dozens of tunes. He actually flew me into Florida for a week, me and Ramrod, my equipment guy, with my pedal steel and guitars. I went down there and did sessions at the weirdest hours! Stills had two teams of engineers, two shifts. The way he worked in the studio was totally crazy. At the time he was really happenin', really doing well, could afford it easily. They were not only studies in over-indulgence, but there was some pretty OK music too!"

There was plenty of light and shade on *Stephen Stills 2*. If 'Change Partners' and 'Marianne' were the lighter side of Stills, 'Word Game' was the dark side. This was Stephen at his angriest. For four minutes, accompanied by just his acoustic guitar, he railed at an injustice he'd witnessed while watching TV one evening at Brookfield. On the BBC *Sounding Out* program, coincidentally also recorded at Brookfield (a year later), Stephen described to Charlie Gillett what drove him to write the song.

Being raised in the southern states of America and growing up with black people and learning the blues, he'd been subjected to abuse and labeled a "n****r-lover." He'd felt that his generation had the will to overcome racial hatred peacefully and that the Black Panther movement was not the answer. But then he saw the BBC documentary–a film smuggled out of racially segregated South Africa by a group of students–which angered him to such a point he could understand how violent protest could be justified. 'Word Game' was how he articulated those feelings.

Contrast this with yet another love and relationship song. 'Sugar Babe' seemed out of place next to 'Word Game,' but was picked up quickly by Tim Rice, who, having 'discovered' Yvonne Elliman, nabbed the song for his *Jesus Christ Superstar* prodigy's debut album.

Maybe the mix on *Stephen Stills 2* was too varied. One element that left a strong impression was the session work from The Memphis Horns, already famous for their soul recordings for Stax Records. 'Open Secret,' the track that closed side one, is almost completely blown away by the Horns at its climactic ending. The edge they bring to the record is something Stephen obviously thought worth pursuing as he quickly booked them to accompany him and his band on a summer tour covering all the major US cities.

Midway through work on his new album, Stephen contributed one of his best-known sessions when he played on a future smash hit for Bill Withers. His guitar part on 'Ain't No Sunshine' was recorded at Sunset Sound, in Hollywood, produced by Booker T. Jones. The date of the recording is sketchy, but there's nothing sketchy about where Stephen was on May 12, 1971.

On that bright sunny day he found himself in the south of

France, a guest at the wedding of Mick Jagger and Bianca Macias, at St. Anne's Church, St. Tropez.

Most of the rock royalty attending the service and celebrations flew out from Gatwick Airport–a short drive from Stephen's Surrey home. On board the flight that day with Stephen were Paul and Linda McCartney, Ringo Starr and wife Maureen, French film director Roger Vadim, photographer Lord Patrick Lichfield, Eric Clapton, Ronnie Wood, Nicky Hopkins, Glyn Johns, Doris Troy, PP Arnold, Terry Reid, and assorted Rolling Stones and members of The Faces.

Terry Reid remembered getting the call from Mick Jagger very late: "I was playing down at the Marquee and someone came down and said Mick wanted us to do the wedding. I said 'When is it?' and he said 'We've got to leave tomorrow.' We jumped on the plane, flew out there, took a bus down to St. Tropez, and of course everyone was there at the hotel, it was just nuts, great party. Everybody got up and jammed, Stills, Ronnie Wood, all going bananas."

Hours later, at the Café des Arts, Mick Jagger was up on stage performing soul standards with P.P. Arnold and Doris Troy in a 25-minute set organized by Stephen, Bobby Keys, Nicky Hopkins, Michael Shrieve, and David Brown of Santana. Brigitte Bardot and Julie Christie were among those watching and boogieing the night away.

Stephen Stills 2 was released on June 30th. A week before, Joni Mitchell's *Blue* had hit record stores. The Canadian's fourth album featured Stephen's bass and guitar parts on the deliciously upbeat 'Carey,' which the two of them had recorded earlier at Hollywood's A&M Studios. The *Rolling Stone* reviews of both albums could not have made a bigger contrast. While Joni's latest offering, rightly, had the music paper's Timothy Crouse saying, "She has given us some of the most beautiful moments in recent popular music," Stephen got a savaging from *Rolling Stone*'s John Ned Mendelsohn. "The words to *Stills 2*," said Mendelsohn, "are alternately trivial, cloyingly self-important, and downright offensive, the music is decidedly lacklustre and undistinguished, and the production of the whole shebang is so distant from up to snuff that one is hard pressed to get much impression at all of the playing of the latter."

In addition to finding the cover "singularly undistinguished," Mendelsohn didn't mince his words in summation when describing his victim's solo output as "fifth-rate self-indulgence."

Not all reviewers agreed with Mendelsohn. The necessarily upbeat *Billboard* review advised record buyers that "Stills has outdone himself with his second LP" and that "this LP is destined for the number one spot in the nation."

The fact that it would go on to hit Number 8 in the *Billboard* albums chart would have been of little consolation to Stephen as he prepared for his first big solo tour that summer in support of his two hit albums.

In addition to The Memphis Horns, Stephen's touring band that summer included the trusty rhythm section of Dallas Taylor and Calvin 'Fuzzy' Samuels. Also enlisted was keyboard player Paul Harris and Steven Fromholz, an outlaw country music singer-songwriter friend of Stephen's.

"I went to work for Stephen Stills during 1971," Fromholz remembered when talking to the website *No Depression*. "I had met Stills in 1969, I guess. We made the Frummox record *Here To There*. It was released in 1969 and included my 'Song For Stephen Stills.' I sent a copy of the album to him and he called me one night in May 1971 and said, 'Come to my house. I want to talk to you.' So I did."

Having joined Stephen's band, he entered the whole world of drink, drugs, and excess. "I went off to play rock and roll. It was an amazing experience. I went as far into that as you can go into the rock and roll experience, and still survive. I loved it."

Preparing for the 27-city American tour necessitated a good deal of practice with Fromholz's new bandmates. "We went to England on June 1, 1971 and stayed there three weeks and rehearsed. Came back, and went to Memphis for ten days and rehearsed. Then we went out on the road. I was playing rhythm guitar and singing second vocals. Originally, we had a five-piece band. When [percussionist] Joe Lala joined us, we started doing a six-piece rock and roll set. Stephen and I did an acoustic thing together with two guitars, and after a while I started to do two or three songs on my own during the set."

A typical show would go something like this, according to Fromholz: "Stephen would come out and do a big piano thing–'America's Children' and stuff. Then the [Memphis] Horns came out and we ended with a 13-piece on stage, and we really kicked ass. We were great, when we were great. We were awful, when we were awful. We had some great nights though."

Stephen's confidence, however, had taken another blow before the tour had hardly begun. The band's first date was in Seattle, a city with some recent mass unemployment problems, which, as he explained later to Dave Zimmer, impacted hugely on the success of the opening night. "I was booked into the city three months after Boeing was closed. So when I played this 15,000-seat auditorium, 3,000 people showed up. I was mortified. So I got blind drunk and was suitably horrid."

There would be a number of shows where alcohol would play a part, as he later admitted to *Rolling Stone*: "For a few years of my solo career the bourbon king showed up and it was just messy."

Reports suggest that there were more successes than disasters on this tour, although the prestigious Madison Square Garden date proved to be another downer for Stephen, despite drawing a capacity crowd.

"[The Concert For] Bangladesh happened three days later and all of the New York critics were living in George Harrison's hallway. My show didn't even get reviewed. And when I donated all my stage, sound and lighting system, and my production manager to George [Harrison], he didn't just not invite me to play, he didn't mention my name. I never got a thank-you note."

What he did next was symptomatic of his state of mind during various moments on the tour. "I got so upset, I went to Ringo's room, got real drunk, and just sat there barking at everyone."

With "more extraneous crew members than Madonna had dancers," Stephen later joked, the tour proved to be overblown and financially draining.

Around the time the tour was coming to a close there was an oddly interesting story about Stephen related by The Who's Pete Townshend. It appeared that Stephen may have unwittingly contributed something to plans for a new Who movie at their Track Records offices in London, without even being present. According to Townshend in his autobiography *Who I Am*, The Who's manager Chris Stamp and music critic Nik Cohn were brainstorming ideas for the movie one afternoon when Townshend arrived. On a school-style blackboard was scrawled, presumably for inspiration, a Stephen Stills lyric fragment. What the lyric was and whether this was in any way connected to the build-up to a script for *Tommy* the movie is unclear. Pete Townshend said that he felt disconnected from the discussions Cohn and Stamp were having at the time, and this bizarre diversion ended in a dead end.

Typically, even on the tour with The Memphis Horns, Stephen had been planning his next move and a new and different kind of sound for the fresh start afterward. Atlantic's Jerry Wexler had suggested he make a return to Criteria Studios in Miami. Steven Fromholz, Dallas Taylor, Fuzzy Samuels, and Paul Harris were all in the frame for the band he was forming, as was Joe Lala. Fromholz, however, would quit during rehearsals for the new project, but a lucky meeting with Chris Hillman when the Stills tour rolled into Cleveland enabled Stephen to expand his repertoire musically in a completely new direction.

CHAPTER 21
Manassas

Chris Hillman and ace pedal steel guitarist Al Perkins were on tour with The Flying Burrito Brothers, playing the university circuit. "We met Stephen after his Cleveland, Ohio, concert with The Memphis Horns," recalled Perkins. "At his hotel, he asked Chris and I if we would consider coming to Criteria Studios in North Miami Beach and work on the 'country' side of his double-album project."

Another musician invited into Stephen's new project was fiddle player Byron Berline, who was also playing with The Flying Burrito Brothers at that time. "Stephen was into bluegrass but I don't think had played or studied it very much, but he liked it. Chris Hillman played the mandolin and Al Perkins played the banjo a little bit, so I remember us trying to sound like a bluegrass band and sometimes we did. We didn't record any of that but had fun playing some bluegrass tunes together."

The whole notion of playing country music had been introduced to Stephen from discussions with his old school friend Michael O'Hara Garcia, who had recently returned from Vietnam. Garcia clearly thought that the genre would be a good fit for Stephen, who identified why it appealed to him at this time. "We knew we were on the cutting edge of something. It took what The Flying Burrito Brothers and all of them were supposed to be and made it more of a marriage between Rolling Stones rock 'n' roll and country. It widened the tent, if you will."

Clearly influenced by former Flying Burrito Brothers main man Gram Parsons' association with The Rolling Stones and the resulting 'Wild Horses,' Stephen was going back to some roots. But as Berline pointed out, this was a type of music he hadn't played much. With Garcia and Michael John Bowen's help, he took the plunge and surrounded himself with–in Hillman, Perkins, and Berline–some of the best country pickers and players around.

Before Stephen had time to properly begin his new project, there was a surprise opportunity to briefly reunite Crosby, Stills, Nash & Young. During sessions for his album *Harvest*, Neil Young enlisted the help of all three of his ex-bandmates. Stephen and David Crosby added vocal parts to 'Alabama' and Stephen and Graham Nash did the same on 'Words.'

By early fall, unofficially at least, they were all back together on stage. By this time Crosby and Nash were touring as a duo, and at dates at the Boston Music Hall and New York's Carnegie Hall, Stephen showed up and guested on the second half of the shows. Stephen's appearances weren't coincidental or casual. There had been an invitation from Crosby and Nash to Stephen to fly up from Florida and make a guest appearance with them in a bid to show the world that "things were groovy between the three of us," as Stephen put it. 'Things' were so groovy that Young later joined in too, and no doubt rumors began to circulate that a more permanent reunion of all three or even four might be imminent.

The pressure the four were under to record or even play together must have been immense. Was Atlantic's Ahmet Ertegun behind the unofficial get-togethers? If that were true, at least the moves brokered an outbreak of peace. Full on commitment to CSN&Y, though, was not something the participants wanted or needed at this point.

Stephen's attention still seemed to be thoroughly focused on his newly assembled band down in Miami. His trusty rhythm section, plus some of the best country musicians in the business, were now all assembled at Criteria Studios, with Ron and Howard Albert, once more, at the helm.

Quite when Stephen's third solo album turned into a new band (Manassas) is hard to pin down, but Chris Hillman, Joe Lala, Al Perkins, Paul Harris, Fuzzy Samuels, and Dallas Taylor were now a team, with Stephen, Chris, and Dallas taking production credits in the studio. Specialist extra help came in to add fiddle (Byron Berline), harmonica (Sydney George), acoustic bass (Roger Bush), Clavenette (Jerry Aiello), and bass (Bill Wyman). But the seven-piece band was together and as tight as any band unit Stephen had ever played in, or recruited, before.

In percussionist Joe Lala, Stephen enjoyed the company of someone who remembered school days back in the south. "Lala went to the Italian/Cuban school and I went to this rich Jewish/Wasp school, on the other side of town. I was a poor member of the rich school and Lala a rich member of the poor school," Stephen joked. "He was this short, dumpy kid who played in the school band, and I was a little undersized kid in the band. So we immediately started telling stories about Tampa and stories about Tampa and Baker's Pool Hall and stuff like that."

When Lala got the call to join Stephen he was a little sceptical, as he told *Examiner.com*: "After I left Blues Image, I was with a band called PG & E. They did a song called 'Are You Ready' and we did a record for CBS. I worked as a session guy around L.A. and then I got a phone call. I was house-sitting for somebody. The phone rang and the conversation went like this, 'Hi, this is Stephen, I'm thinking of putting a band together.' I said, 'Stephen who?' 'Stills.' I said, 'Yeah right.' 'We met at the cigarette machine at the Whisky a Go Go with Dallas, we talked for a minute. I've got this idea about putting a band together. Come to my house in Colorado and let's see what happens.'"

Joe Lala's earlier childhood memories of the Stills family might not have been entirely accurate, though. "We did not know each other in Tampa. He went to Plant high school. He loved the Latin influence of Blues Image though. His dad worked for the CIA, and had a seafood plant in Costa Rica."

Evidently, aside from a great sense of humor, Lala brought an element to Stephen's music that he had long tried to perfect. "Joe Lala was an answer to a prayer. I desperately wanted to find a 'Spanglish,' a Latin-Cuban player, 'cause I was going absolutely crazy trying to play that kind of music with those turkey-white drummers. No matter how good they were, no white drummers could cut it, and my songs were getting more and more Spanish-flavored."

Lala would cut an imposing, tall figure on stage too, in his shades, with his afro, rocking away behind his congas.

Everyone on the project seemed to agree that the first few days in the studio were an incredible experience. Chris Hillman, Al

Perkins, and Byron Berline came under starter's orders, and by all accounts tore through their terrific repertoire of Burritos numbers and some old bluegrass classics, with Stephen and the rest of the band desperately trying to keep up. Although 'Panhandle Rag,' 'Uncle Pen,' and 'Dim Lights, Thick Smoke (And Loud, Loud Music)' didn't make it on to the eventual double album, they would get a well-deserved airing on the album of Manassas outtakes, *Pieces*, in 2009.

Stephen was incredibly impressed by what was rapidly turning into a trademark band sound, thanks to Al Perkins. "That was actually supposed to have gone back to more of a Springfield sound, he admitted to *Vintage Guitar*'s Willie G. Moseley, "but to me it's all been kind of seamless. Manassas had a pedal steel guitar player, as well as Chris Hillman, who could play the shit out of a mandolin, so the band did have a bit more of a traditional country approach, but the pedal steel guy could also play rock and roll on his instrument, which scared me to death!"

The likeable Al Perkins explained the unique fat sound he was creating perfectly: "It may be interesting to note I had not steadfastly followed the groups I was indirectly a part of [Chris in The Byrds and Stephen in Buffalo Springfield]. However, my sound was a peculiar mix of influences and I felt right at home playing a 'fuzz tone' or rock styles on the pedal steel and electric guitar. I also loved the full, warm sound of Tom Brumley's pedal steel in The Stone Canyon Band. Thus, the 'fat sound' mentioned came about. Thankfully, Stephen also loved these same styles and had begun a very diverse album in which he invited Chris and I the freedom to express our musical tastes."

Stephen's admiration for what the country boys brought to the mix is obvious. "When I heard the tapes of me playing bluegrass with Byron Berline, Al Perkins, and Chris Hillman, I said I can't keep this to myself. I couldn't believe I could keep up with those guys, doing all those Lester Flatt runs and stuff. I was guessing. What a fabulous musician Chris is. Or 'Curly,' as Byron called him. He hates that, by the way!"

Inventing a new sound might be putting it too strongly, but clearly the country influence on some of Stephen's best rock guitar gave the recordings an exciting and powerful country-rock fusion.

The sessions capturing the sound they wanted might have been lengthy, but they certainly weren't painstakingly pieced together. They involved an unusual recording regime which certainly didn't faze Al Perkins. "Who could forget the all-night sessions, which usually began after dinner each evening. Stephen liked to record in the 'wee' hours in order to get raw instinct from each player: the idea being to capture actual live performances with as few overdubs as possible. The number of recordings allowed for each song would not exceed five-seven takes. While being an unusual method of recording, the idea seemed to have worked very well."

There was clearly camaraderie about this band that augured well. "We did socialize," Howard Albert remembered. "Criteria had a house that the groups stayed at. Stephen would sometimes cook for everyone when Geri and Cindy (the girls from [caterers] Home at Last) didn't cook or he just felt like cooking. We did become close to the band of musicians. After all we did spend hours with all of them."

Happily, the relaxed atmosphere was a huge tonic that affected everyone and filtered through to the music that they were creating. Stephen, who was paying for everything, including the Coconut Grove house where they all stayed, bossed the project. He described his Manassas role as a "benevolent dictator" in a "quasi-democracy." The fact that nearly everyone had come into the project on a downer–Stephen's frustration over his tour, Chris Hillman's boredom with The Flying Burrito Brothers–meant Manassas was a breath of fresh air.

As Stephen summed up later: "It's kind of indicative of where this band is at in that it's finally gotten to the point where after all this time–I've been in this for eight years, Dallas has been with me for four, Fuzzy's been with me two, Chris goes all the way back to The Byrds and got us the Buffalo Springfield, our first job. It's a question of, 'OK fellas, let's get real. Let's do it right and make up for our mistakes.'"

"The chemistry in that band was perfect," remembered Joe Lala. "When Stephen was on, he was on! He was really good. The rest of us got along great. We had a lot of fun together. It was a great bunch of guys and we got along and we enjoyed being together."

October saw the band begin to record the incredibly accomplished six tracks that would eventually make up side one of the double LP. The limited number of takes that Al Perkins alluded to were evident in a breathless, seemingly non-stop run through 'Song Of Love,' 'Rock & Roll Crazies,' 'Cuban Bluegrass,' the lumbering blues of 'Jet Set (Sigh),' the pacey 'Anyway,' and culminating in the wistful, ethereal 'Both Of Us (Bound To Lose),' which highlighted just how good a song-writing team, and vocal duo, Hillman and Stills could be.

Early January 1972 saw Stephen cut three of the best tracks on the album. 'Johnny's Garden' (recorded on January 7) was a gentle, swaying acoustic homage to a very special Englishman. "Written for my gardener, John, at Brookfield House in Elstead, England," explained Stephen when submitting notes for the *CSN* box set. "He had soul. He was a herbalist and used to make incredible herbal teas."

Stephen wasn't the only occupant of Brookfield to be profoundly affected by the pipe-smoking gardener and guardian of the 'green and quiet' estate. Peter Sellers would later base his character Chance The Gardener on John in the 1979 movie *Being There*.

The next day an older song Stephen had written, 'So Begins The Task,' was revisited for the new album, with a wonderful pedal steel part from Al Perkins and a little vocal support from Fred Neil.

On January 9, 'It Doesn't Matter' (co-written by Stephen and Chris Hillman) had the entire band (minus the absent bassist Fuzzy Samuels) faultlessly weaving some liquid guitar arrangements. Understandably, when they were hot Stephen had no intention of pulling the plug on some very long sessions. "The longest session was 106 straight hours," confirmed Howard Albert, and the engineer remembered Stephen apologizing, but insistent when waking everyone up after one exhausting session to get them all back in the studio again, as he had an idea he needed to get taped before he forgot it.

A whole raft of country numbers would make up another complete side on the album. Of those six tracks that made the final cut, nearly all were autobiographical. The hopeful, bouncy 'Colorado' extolled the virtues of Stephen's defiant, solitary cabin life up in the Rockies and 'Don't Look At My Shadow' was a journey through his past playing for pennies, to the present where he's playing to the L.A. Forum Sports Arena in front of 20,000 fans. Those country songs were where Byron Berline got to make his huge contribution to the sessions.

"'Sing To The Fallen Eagle' was the most memorable song for me," admitted Berline, "as it featured the fiddle a lot and I really liked the song as my band Country Gazette recorded it later. Stephen was an interesting guy; not your typical good ole boy from the south. He liked to give things to people to show his friendship I guess. I remember when he gave Chris Hillman the Gibson Lloyd Loar mandolin; we were in the studio when he gave it to him and I thought, boy, that was nice. Those mandolins are, and were then, very collectable and today worth a lot of money. I am sure he gave it to Chris to persuade him to join up with his band. I remember Al Perkins got a 20-dollar gold piece."

The tracks that would close the album comprised three rockers: the urgent 'What To Do,' 'Right Now,' and 'The Treasure (Take One).' The latter track included another loner lyric from Stephen: 'Alone with my guitar, living on a mountain … ' it began, before heading off into one of rock's great jams. As an end to proceedings there was 'Blues Man,' an acoustic solo Stills wail, remembering lost legends Jimi Hendrix, Al Wilson (the Canned Heat leader), and Duane Allman. The accompanying album cover dedication to the three aggravated some critics, who labeled it pretentious. It's a charge that Stephen found hard to handle. "Everybody thought that was really jive," he told Barbara Charone later. "Isn't that incredible? That really broke my heart a little bit because they didn't understand where I was coming from. The facts I was dealing with broke my heart."

Outside influences on the Manassas project were few, but when Rolling Stone Bill Wyman popped into Criteria to play bass on a jam one night, the session eventually became another track logged for the album. 'Love Gangster,' with some particularly snakey wah-wah from Stephen, had enough of a creative contribution from Wyman to give him a writing credit and, according to Dallas Taylor, The Rolling Stones' participation in Manassas might have been far greater had Stephen only known then what Dallas later discovered. "Years later," he wrote in his autobiography *Prisoner Of Woodstock*, "Bill confided in me that he had been really disappointed that day when we didn't ask him to join Manassas. As comical as it sounds, Bill had been feeling fed up with the Stones and was ready for a change."

Having recorded most of the album (which became a double album due to the large stock of great material), the band reportedly didn't have a name or a title for the LP. If everyone had assumed it would get a release as Stephen's third solo album they were in for a surprise. Naming both the band and the record only happened after the seven of them lined up for the cover photograph.

"I was looking for a train station and the photographer [Ira Wexler] called me and said I've found this great place Manassas," Stephen explained shortly afterward. "I said Manassas? That's the first and second battle of Bull Run."

"Being a civil war buff, Stephen wanted to evoke that dreary, wintry appearance," recounts Al Perkins. "So we all flew from Miami to Washington, D.C., where we rented clothes for the shoot. The next day, at the Manassas, Virginia, train station, an old luggage cart was loaded with our cases and brought out while the pavement was wetted around the side of the building. It didn't take long. We were lined up, and before we knew it they had the shot."

Only when he pored over the resulting photos with Wexler later did Stephen decide to incorporate the railroad station sign above all their heads and name the band Manassas.

According to Perkins, that same week the locals got a sneak preview of what Manassas were up to when the band made their unofficial debut. "One night while in D.C. for the album shoot, Manassas played several songs on stage at the Cellar Door. Chris and I had played there with The Flying Burrito Brothers earlier in '71 and had met Emmylou Harris. We were able to contact her and she came and sat in with us."

Sadly for Stephen, the Manassas momentum stalled at the end of 1971 when he was admitted to hospital for treatment on his leg. When a knee operation quickly followed he found himself needing to rest up a while and recuperated at his estate, Brookfield in England.

With a tour and promotion for the forthcoming album release on the horizon, Stephen decided to fly over every member of the band for rehearsals at Brookfield.

"The only customs detention I've experienced was after I arrived in London for our rehearsals in January of '72," Al Perkins remembered. "I arrived at the Elstead manor before my instruments and gear. It seems they were curious about the numerous packs of Carefree sugarless cinnamon gum stashed all through my cases and gear. They were delayed several days until proof was provided that all the chewing gum was for my personal use during the three-month stay in England!"

Leaving behind the California sun for a damp, cold British winter in the Surrey countryside might not have appealed greatly to his new bandmates, but Stephen made sure they were well looked after.

Al Perkins has an almost photographic memory of Brookfield: "During Manassas' residence, in the early months of 1972, it was amazing that lodging was also available for all the band and crew. The multi-car garage was a newer structure built separately to include a cinema, complete with a bathroom. The crewmen lived there and the cinema seats were replaced by bunks, similar to military barracks. Our flight cases were stowed in the garage below, where one of the Manassas promo shots was taken. For rehearsals, we turned the recreation room (near the pool) into a makeshift sound stage."

The old house was well equipped to cater for everyone's needs, as Al continues: "Most evenings, Stephen employed a chef to prepare proper dinners for the band and family. Johnny [The Gardener] would stoke the fireplaces and it became a very serene experience. At times, cars would leave for Guildford or other points of interest and schedules were flexible."

Dining arrangements were flexible to, Al remembers. "For morning meals, the early risers could be found in the kitchen for tea and biscuits or Ribena and Weetabix. Just across the stone walkway from the kitchen entrance was a sauna and wine cellar. Both of which received a lot of patrons, ha! Yes, as I recall, the 'spartan' breakfast scene was due to everyone's differing sleep habits. Occasionally there would be a brave soul who'd march in and prepare a nice meal for any early risers, ha! Being a teetotaler, I understood later that those who frequented the wine cellar ran the tab up quite handily during those three months."

One 'brave soul' who did his fair share of home catering was Joe Lala. "I cooked for Jerry Wexler and for the band. I made homemade sausage balls, Chateaubriand, and these baby potatoes. We kept a low profile while we were there."

He was also quoted in the *Examiner* as discovering some property belonging to a previous owner of Brookfield. "When I first moved in I found a stethoscope and a blood pressure monitor next to my bed. Peter Sellers was married to Britt Ekland at the time. She was insatiable. I found out that he would check himself with the blood pressure monitor after having sex with her," claimed Joe.

But Lala's memory might not have been that reliable. It was the percussionist's love of Brookfield's wine cellar that cost Stephen an "arm and a leg," as he explained to Dave Zimmer: "I was supporting everybody. Joe Lala himself drank almost $10,000 worth of wine. He drank a case of 1947 Cheval Blanc without knowing how expensive it was."

Despite rarely venturing out to the Surrey village pubs and restaurants, the band weren't exactly imprisoned in Brookfield. On one occasion, several band members decided to enjoy some midwinter hiking in the local countryside and were confronted by a jeep carrying British Army personnel. The three or four musicians were promptly searched and asked for their ID before being allowed to continue their ramble. IRA terrorist bombings were occurring regularly at that time and security levels were on high alert.

Very little rehearsing seems to have taken place during this English winter, but when Stephen's knee was up to it, he headed into London and dropped in at Olympic Studios, where the Eagles had been recording their debut album. Stephen may have already heard the result of their efforts, as on one afternoon Eagles guitarist Bernie Leadon visited Chris Hillman and Al Perkins at Brookfield to play them recordings from the forthcoming release.

While visiting Olympic Studios, Stephen met Steve Marriott and guested on three Humble Pie tracks for the band's album *Smokin'*. He added organ and harmonies to '30 Days In The Hole,' Hammond organ on 'Road Runner 'G' Jam,' and over-dubbed vocals on 'Hot 'n' Nasty.'

"I thought Steve Marriott was a dear and it was tragic, the circumstances of his passing," Stephen told *Classic Rock* years later. "My children told me that they ran across one of his children and said, 'My dad used to work with your dad.' I was like, 'Wow, that was working together?' We were just careening about Olympic Studios. I just remember him being really fun, a good soul. A great guy. Yeah, we did some things and it's all a blur. That time is a bit of a blur, for various reasons."

With just four or five rehearsals under their belts since Christmas, Manassas nevertheless appeared ready to meet the rigorous demands of a European tour and TV, radio, and press appearances. Disappointingly, Byron Berline (who hadn't traveled to Brookfield) couldn't be persuaded by Stephen to join his team. "He asked me to travel with the Manassas band to Europe but I declined because I was wanting to play with my band Country Gazette as we were just getting a deal with United Artists," explained the fiddle player.

Stephen had already raised awareness of his profile in an earnest interview for BBC2's *Sounding Out*, conducted at Brookfield. Now Manassas would road test their music in a few concert dates and TV appearances over on the continent.

Their concert debut was to be an eagerly anticipated date in Holland on March 22. A day before that, though, they would record a fantastically tight set of numbers from the new album for German TV's *Beat Club* in Bremen.

The first Manassas gig, in Amsterdam's Concertgebouw, made the front page of British music paper *New Musical Express*. "STILLS DUTCH TREAT" declared the headline. "The initial frantic rush of photographers produced ludicrous scenes, the like of which I have not experienced since Dylan at the Isle of Wight" was how the paper reported the exciting moment the band took to the stage.

The gig proved to be a triumph for Stephen and Manassas, who eschewed almost any numbers connected to CSN or CSN&Y.

There was no sign of 'Suite: Judy Blue Eyes,' and the 30 songs were drawn mostly from the newly recorded *Manassas* album. The audience certainly weren't complaining during the three lengthy sets of rock, acoustic, and rock music again. To a roar of approval a few numbers in, Stephen proclaimed, "We'll be here for the next four hours, so don't go away!"

And when it was all supposed to finish, the band found it impossible to stop. A ten-minute encore greeted the band's new guitar jam vehicle 'The Treasure' before lights dimmed and they huddled round a single microphone to sing 'Find The Cost Of Freedom' acapella.

A day later and Manassas performed at Jahrhunderthalle in Frankfurt, before a sightseeing day off in Paris and a concert at the Olympia on March 26.

"We were first scheduled for the Nationale Theater in Paris on the 27th," Al Perkins pointed out, "but were moved back a day to the Olympia [appropriately an old train station] to give us French press and prep time back in England on the 28th."

Then the entire Manassas entourage flew out from London on a bizarre trip to Australia to play one gig. "It began a world tour, so to speak, but also provided a back way to some warm Hawaiian beaches before the first U.S. tour," explained Al.

The Rock Isle Mulwala Festival in New South Wales was held over the Easter weekend (March 31–April 2, 1972) and featured a whole bunch of Australian bands, with Canned Heat and Manassas headlining.

The Australian security at Melbourne Airport was not the friendliest, as Al Perkins remembered. "Canned Heat had arrived from the U.S. just prior to us when customs inspectors found illegal recreational substance or substances in Canned Heat's luggage. So, after we deplaned, Australian customs performed luggage searches on our group. Afterward, there became a little friendly contention between Stephen and Bob Hite."

In a revealing TV interview on arrival in Australia, a seemingly jet-lagged Stephen talked about the soon-to-be-released album. "Instrumentally, it outstrips anything I've ever done. This is the best band I've ever done. The last two albums that I've done have been searching for it, trying different things. You could make one good album out of picking the best of both of *Stephen Stills 1 and 2*. Ultimately I was just searching, which is a musician's right."

Stephen had this to say about the reasoning behind the Australian trip: "The European jobs, successful as they were … when you go to Europe you figure how much money can I afford to lose and the people here have just been great. They've made up the majority of the losses that I took in taking the group to Europe. It's a beautiful place. I'm a diver and we'd like to do a little scuba diving if we can find a place that's safe."

Scheduled to headline both the Sunday and Monday at the Mulwala Festival, Manassas didn't perform on the final day when heavy rain led to a wash-out. Even so, Stephen and the band were reported to have pocketed $35,000 for their appearance.

The American headliners went down well with the wildly enthusiastic crowd, according to Greg Quill of Country Radio. "Stills and Canned Heat were given star treatment, and didn't fraternize with the local talent. They came and went. I was impressed by Manassas–very organized guitar band with great percussion, a touch of African rhythm, and excellent harmonies. Very big band, I remember. And Stills appeared cranky, detached all the time on stage, maybe scared. It was probably the most primitive audience he'd ever seen."

Al Perkins concurs: "I remember the audience being a bit raucous but very responsive. Lots of beer consumed … enough that when we loaded out the next morning there was a mountain of cans pushed to the center of the site by bulldozer."

Equally primitive was the rock star accommodation, according to Al. "Being in the outback, our accommodation could be described as very spartan. As I recall, they were attached wooden rooms with few conveniences and little or no insulation. Something the Australian cowboys might stay in, yet near enough to the Mulwala Festival site.

"Our Melbourne hotel base was very nice and our transportation over the Australian continental divide was made in larger American cars and were considered limousines. Reviewing some amateur film we took, on the way back from Mulwala one of our cars had a flat. We had some fun by placing coins on the adjacent railroad track and collecting them after the train rolled over them."

With their short Aussie rock 'n' roll adventure behind them, the band took a break ahead of the demanding US and European dates booked for the summer and fall.

The release of *Manassas* on April 12 would encourage positive reviews and, for a double album, some very satisfying sales figures. The release would eventually hit Number 4 on the *Billboard* chart (UK Number 30).

Most interesting of all the reviews, perhaps, was Andrew Weiner's for *Cream*. Weiner gave the impression that Stephen's work hadn't added up to anything special up to this point. "Stills," he wrote, "perhaps the most maligned superstar in recent rock history, has finally–and against all the odds–got it on.

"And Stills has written too many good songs here even try to count them," he added.

Those 23 songs were unusually released in four separate

sections (or sides) on the double album and each with their own title. Side One: The Raven was the breathless introductory run through some great rock, salsa, and blues. Side Two: The Wilderness featured the country tracks. Side Three: Consider made you do just that. This was a mix of sounds, which included the somewhat out-of-place swirling synthesizer on 'Move Around' and perhaps the album's most radio-friendly number, the sublime 'It Doesn't Matter,' which Stephen maintained was the song that kicked everything off and cemented the Manassas partnership with its co-writer Chris Hillman. Side Four: Rock & Roll Is Here To Stay really did prove that particular point, before coming to a close on the downbeat, acoustic 'Blues Man.'

It's not often engineers get credited so highly on a record, but on either side of the album cover's gatefold inside picture of the band there's a picture of Ron Albert and Howard Albert. Howard's appreciation of what had been achieved at Criteria was glowing. "I tell ya, Manassas was one of the greatest and most under-rated bands of the Seventies. That double album, along with Eric Clapton's *Layla*–which me and my brother both worked on–stand as the most important and best albums we've ever been part of."

To tour and promote the album took a lot of cash and hard work, but the enjoyment for Stephen far outweighed the expense and the organizational hassles. In short, this was a more rewarding experience than Crosby, Stills, Nash & Young. "I was fed up with having the responsibility of being the leader in a group that would rebel at the first sign of leadership," he said.

And he had some reliable help when it came to taking Manassas on the road. In John Michael Bowen he had a manager and a friend who was incredibly focused on hiring charter planes and getting the band from A to B as efficiently as possible. Bowen had been a sergeant who had served in the Vietnam War and his military training was a real advantage in the day-to-day running of a seven-piece rock band.

After almost a month on the road, the U.S. tour arrived back on home territory at California's Berkeley Community Theater. On the second date of a three-night run (July 21-23), Manassas were joined on stage briefly by guests Graham Nash, Neil Young, and Chris Hillman's former Byrds bandmate Roger McGuinn.

Then they were off on a return visit to Europe, where British fans got their first opportunity to see Stephen Stills' Manassas play in his adopted country. First up was a date at Manchester's Hardrock Concert Theatre in Stretford on September 15. Then came two exceptional performances in one day, at the Rainbow Theatre on September 17 at London's Finsbury Park. The London appearance coincided with the taping of a BBC TV appearance titled *Stephen Stills Manassas: In Concert*, where the now well-oiled machine ran through a dozen numbers: not one of them borrowed from his CSN&Y or Buffalo Springfield back catalogues. The TV show and Rainbow concerts proved, yet again, that Stephen Stills didn't need the security of the Crosby, Stills, Nash & Young supergroup to make his mark.

More gigs followed on the continent, at Kungliga Tennis Hall in Stockholm, Sweden, then in Hamburg, Frankfurt, Munich, Amsterdam, and Paris.

The day after the late scheduling of a concert at the Olympia Theatre (on October 5) was when Stephen met, and began to fall for French singer-songwriter Véronique Sanson. It was her boyfriend and musical partner Michel Berger who'd persuaded her to attend the concert.

When Stills and Sanson met at the Warner record company

offices in Paris the next day, they hit it off immediately. Prophetically, in November, Joni Mitchell's *For The Roses* album was released, which included Stephen's contribution to the track 'Blonde In The Bleachers.' Here he played the entire rock band of instruments as the song–all about the dangers of falling in love with a rock and roll star–came to a climax.

Having fallen in love in Paris, and with the Manassas tour reaching an exciting conclusion, Stephen, if he ever stayed still long enough to take stock of his career, must have felt thoroughly satisfied.

The business side of his life reached a fork in the road at this time when he and David Geffen parted company. "Geffen made his reputation with that incredible deal for Laura Nyro," Stephen told *Rolling Stone*'s Judith Sims at the time, "and he wanted to make the same kind of deal with me, but I said 'no.' I didn't want to be dealing in stocks and papers, I wanted to take a crack at getting my own publishing company built up. Geffen was really incensed, but I wasn't about to be manipulated like that, it's not in my nature."

Helping Stephen take control of his music was 22-year-old Ken Weiss, who was keen to leave the protective cocoon of Warner Music and become independently active in the music publishing business. Weiss remembers how he first encountered the man with whom he would share an enduring friendship. "I met Stephen after meeting Chris Hillman, who was working on what was the final Byrds album for Elektra Records, a full reunion of the five original members, including David Crosby. Chris wanted to control the rights to the two songs he wrote on that album and formed Bar None Music for that purpose. We entered into an agreement to take over Bar None, a company of two songs, but with it an opportunity to begin making worldwide deals for the songs, effectively operating as an independent publisher for the first time. Stephen became interested in that particular kind of business arrangement for his songs–so I was the guy who could manage the publishing rights without the contractual burden of a major company–including his earning far more in income than would be likely from a traditional major company deal."

In time, Weiss would, in addition to handling all future publishing rights, extend the association to become Stephen's personal manager.

CHAPTER 22
Marriage and Mountain Music

When the successful but strenuous Manassas tour ended, Stephen made for his Colorado home that winter. There was a real buzz about the area he called home at that time. High up in the Rockies, the local Caribou Ranch recording studios were a hive of activity and a real draw for visiting musicians.

Stephen flew in and out of Boulder County on a Learjet, named his publishing company Gold Hill Music (set up with Ken Weiss) after the local town, drove around in his Mercedes snow plow, and occasionally helped out the local fire department as a volunteer. While the offices for Gold Hill Enterprises were located in Boulder, Stephen's home was 40 miles away in Rollinsville. His neighbors, who included his old friend Michael John Bowen, were a familiar bunch. Chris Hillman purchased a property in Golden, while Joe Lala and Richie Furay both had homes in Boulder.

Completing this magnificent mountain music mafia was Joe

Walsh. Drummer Joe Vitale had also moved out to the Rockies when he got the call from guitarist Walsh to form a band there. "We all moved to Colorado and Stephen was already living there," he told *Classic Rock Revisted*'s Jeb Wright. "He came and sat in with us on one of our sessions. He had heard about this new band from back east that had Joe Walsh from The James Gang in it. Stephen came to the studio and watched us do some of the work for the *Smoker* ... album. He was there when Joe did the vocal on 'Rocky Mountain Way.' We were just hanging out and we all became friends."

He enjoyed his anonymity 9,000 feet up in the Rockies enormously, Stephen told *Colorado Rocks!* author G. Brown. "Basically, nobody up on that mountain gave a shit who I was or what I did."

The Rollinsville cabin soon provided a home for Stephen and his new bride. After they had both left the offices at Warner Music in Paris together, during their first meeting, Stephen had rung Véronique Sanson every day thereafter. At times it must have been a difficult long-distance courtship, but on March 14, 1973, Stephen and Véronique were married at Guildford registry office in England, a short drive from his Brookfield home, in Surrey. In charge of proceedings, according to Véronique, was a woman who looked like Groucho Marx's double! Among the guests at the wedding were Harry Nilsson, Marianne Faithfull, Marc Bolan, and, indicating that the hostilities over Rita Coolidge had by now cooled a little, Graham Nash. The groom wore a tweed three-piece suit and was now sporting a beard.

It's worth noting that the family Stephen was marrying into were no ordinary family. Both her parents, René and Colette, had met while playing prominent roles in the French Resistance movement during World War II. Colette had at one point escaped imprisonment when sentenced to death by France's occupying forces and René became a minister in Charles de Gaulle's post-war government. Stephen may have felt a trifle intimidated by all as he moved things forward in the old-fashioned way. After he had formally met with Véronique's father to ask for her hand in marriage, Véronique made a clean break and flew to New York to be with Stephen.

Leaving Michel Berger had not been an easy decision to make for Sanson. She later described the incredible changes that occurred in a 2005 TV interview. "My life was very peaceful with Michel. And with Stephen it was an amusing hurricane." Aside from Veronique and Michel's personal relationship, Berger had produced Sanson's critically acclaimed *Amoureuse* album that year, a release which included a title track that would be covered successfully by Kiki Dee, Helen Reddy, Olivia Newton-John, and many others. "When I first heard 'Amoureuse,' I had the impression that every female singer, including myself, was left far behind," reflected French singing star and actress Françoise Hardy.

Stephen and Véronique's wedding celebrations were extended at a reception dinner a few days after the Surrey ceremony at New York's Hotel Carlyle. The party was thrown by Atlantic Records boss Ahmet Ertegun. Helping the couple celebrate that night were Mr and Mrs Ertegun, Jerry Wexler, Jac Holzman, Donny Hathaway, Herbie Mann, and Vinegar Joe.

Back at work with Manassas, Stephen readied a new album and fulfilled more live appearances. The overflow of material from the band's first album had led everyone to think that quickly recording a second album was a good idea. But the project seemed hamstrung from the start. The fact that Criteria in Miami,

Caribou Ranch in Colorado, and the Record Plant in L.A. were all involved this time around indicated a more fragmented, less successful process. Democratically, the Manassas follow-up had a greater spread of songs by different band members. Irrespective of the quality of the music at that stage, Ahmet Ertegun felt that Stephen should have a greater presence on the record and demanded more from his protégé. In adding more of his songs and rushing to meet deadlines, Stephen didn't get close to the high standards of the previous record. Worst of all, the trust between the Albert brothers, so important on the double album, was broken during studio disagreements on the quality of what they were engineering. "I short-circuited there for a while," Stephen confessed to Dave Zimmer. "I got a little crazed. Too much drinkin', too many drugs. What can I say?"

The spring release of *Down The Road* was generally greeted with disappointment and went on to peak at Number 26 and Number 33 in the US and UK, respectively. It may not have been the "turkey" Stephen later described it as, but it lacked the exuberant confidence of its predecessor. Although Stephen's opener, 'Isn't It About Time', was a powerhouse wall of sound that kicked things off nicely, the best of the rest were a brace of Chris Hillman songs–'Lies,' with Al Perkins exceling himself on power pedal steel, and 'So Many Times' (co-written with Stephen). The Latin urgency of 'Pensamiento' provided some lively contrast, but the remaining tracks left little impression, despite some stellar support from Joe Walsh, Bobby Whitlock, P.P. Arnold, and the return of Byron Berline. 'Do You Remember The Americans' would have graced the first album's country side, but its quality owed mostly to some exquisite mandolin picking from Chris Hillman and wonderful Al Perkins banjo.

Although now happily based in Colorado with wife Véronique, in the first half of 1973 Stephen wasn't in great shape musically. And despite the 'household name status' he had been accorded through the worldwide success of *Harvest* and his hit single 'Heart Of Gold,' Neil Young was struggling too. The death of his long-time friend and Crazy Horse guitarist Danny Whitten from a heroin overdose had hit him hard. Meanwhile, Crosby and Nash were successfully touring and recording together, although both were suffering bereavement–Crosby with the death of his mother and Nash with the incredibly harrowing murder of his girlfriend, Amy Gossage, at the hands of her brother.

When Neil found himself struggling, vocally and practically, on his tour with The Stray Gators, he sent a call out to Crosby and Nash to join him, which they did for the remaining 19 dates. The best that can be said is that their arrival at least held things together until the end of a tour which was both filmed and recorded for posterity as *Time Fades Away*.

Why the available Stephen wasn't also involved is a mystery, but three did eventually become four in June when Neil rented a large wooden beach house by Mala Wharf, on the island of Maui, and invited Crosby (with Debbie Donovan), Stills (with Véronique), and Nash on his own, to join him and Carrie Snodgress to vacation together. How much of the plan was to vacation and how much to rekindle the spirit of CSN&Y was difficult to establish, but the surroundings were idyllic and the vibe initially good. The quartet's own expectations about creating a new album might not have been the highest priority, but the pressure was still there, nevertheless, from Atlantic Records for another number one album. Work distractions were many– David's sailboat was anchored nearby and Hawaii's beautiful beaches beckoned–but begin work they did. On paper, some of the songs stockpiled around this time for the soon-to-be-aborted project *Human Highway* looked like making a great album. Stephen had two songs, 'See The Changes' and 'As I Come Of Age,' that were a perfect fit for the CSN&Y harmonies; Neil brought 'Human Highway,' 'Through My Sails,' and 'Pardon My Heart'; David donated 'Homeward Through The Haze' and Graham contributed 'Wind On The Water' and 'Prison Song.'

Significantly, Stephen was positive enough about the project to even nominate a photograph as the album cover for *Human Highway*. All four of them were snapped in the last frame of a roll of film when Graham snatched up Stephen's Hasselblad camera. "I got everyone together, focused the camera, set the time exposure–with no meter–placed the camera in the sand, and ran into the picture," Graham told Dave Zimmer.

The sunset portrait of four incredibly relaxed and tanned friends sharing an idyllic moment encouraged further thought that *Human Highway* was a reality. "The new CSN&Y album cover!" Stephen instantly proclaimed.

But when they all returned to Neil's Broken Arrow Ranch in California to record the material, with bassist Tim Drummond and drummer Johny Barbata, something soon must have gone horribly wrong and the album "just turned into a piece of shit," as Neil put it.

All was still not lost though. Could they eradicate the problems they'd encountered in the studio by simply touring together? It seemed they might, until a fall tour together was nixed when Neil dropped out.

The nearest CSN&Y fans came to witnessing something of the *Human Highway* vibe that year was at what turned out to be a very special Manassas gig in October.

"I remember the second-to-last Manassas show at Winterland, in San Francisco, in 1973," recalls Ken Weiss. "A great performance by a fantastic band about to, sadly, sail off into the sunset. Following the first set's intermission, four stools appeared in front of the stage, shortly to be occupied by David, Graham, Stephen, and Neil, an extraordinary event for a foursome that had not sung together for some time, and, given their enormous status, never to be in a relatively small room like Winterland. They performed a short acoustic set to a delirious crowd–a set that turned out to be something of an advance look for the CSN&Y stadium tour the following year, one that was the biggest tour in music history. The Winterland show finished with the second Manassas set, and not for a second was it upstaged by the CSN&Y extra treat that had just been performed. It was truly a great night."

As Ken Weiss recounted, Manassas had come to the end of the road, and, despite the triumphant gig at Winterland, cracks had started to appear in the previously so solid group dynamic.

Live appearances that year had been hampered by Dallas Taylor's drug addiction. Stephen insisted that Dallas enter into a detox program. This he duly did, with Stephen footing the bill. Within a month Taylor was sober, but within a day of leaving the program he'd scored some coke and shot up in a bathroom. Believing his first high in a month had gone undetected, he was horrified when he discovered Stephen watching him from a doorway. Expecting the usual explosion of anger from Stephen, this time Dallas saw only tears, and described the incident as something of a final chance blown in his autobiography *Prisoner Of Woodstock*. "He was worried and in pain and he hugged me and I cried with him knowing that I'd crossed a line and that now he was every bit as lost to me as my mother."

This sad drama led to drummer Johnny Barbata substituting for

Dallas on the remainder of the Manassas gigs. Meanwhile, Kenny Passarelli had become bass guitarist when Fuzzy Samuels "wanted to develop something else on his own," according to Stephen's reading of the situation. Passarelli had greatly impressed Stephen drumming with Joe Walsh's Barnstorm as support for Manassas, then sitting in with Manassas. Stephen's Colorado neighbor, Joe Walsh, had also caught his eye. "I've never put anyone on in front of me, but Joe Walsh, yeah," said Stephen in an interview with *Rolling Stone*. "He's about three times the guitar player I am."

Dallas Taylor would eventually reinvent himself as a substance-abuse interventionist, helping others to stay sober.

Stephen may have hoped that Manassas could continue in the same on/off vein that Crosby, Stills, Nash & Young had intended, but Chris Hillman and the rest of the group sensed that Stephen would soon be dragged back to the CSN&Y 'mothership.' Encouraged by David Geffen, Chris Hillman formed Souther-Hillman-Furay with J.D. Souther and Stephen's Buffalo Springfield bandmate Richie Furay. The group was a home from home for Manassas members, with Al Perkins, Paul Harris, and Joe Lala all contributing greatly.

If Manassas was finished, the band had left an important legacy. "Manassas was, if not the first, the best version of what Nashville rock is now," Stephen suggested later.

Sustaining the energy, drive, invention, and sheer exuberance of the music had been too much, but it would prove to be a significant high point in Stephen's career.

Having shed Manassas, Stephen also made a clean break by selling Brookfield, in England, for a reported £180,000–double what he bought it for when he'd purchased it from Ringo and Maureen Starr. It was also time to build a new band.

Joe Lala was the first name on the team sheet when Stephen recruited the new group to tour solo in February 1974. In addition to his old friend, he brought in Kenny Passarelli (bass), Jerry Aiello (keyboards), Russ Kunkel (drums), and young guitarist Donnie Dacus. The guitarist had proved his worth working in Véronique Sanson's band and clearly provided a completely different foil to Stephen's former vocal/guitar partners Chris Hillman and Neil Young. The tour–in keeping with the new line-up–offered Stills fans a brand new set list, with little or no Manassas material. Older favorites 'For What It's Worth,' '49 Bye-Byes,' and 'Bluebird' made a welcome return, along with his take on Joe Walsh's ode to Colorado living, 'Rocky Mountain Way.' The solo acoustic sections of the shows were particularly impressive, as *Melody Maker*'s Chris Charlesworth recalled in his review of New York's Carnegie Hall appearance. "It's not until Stills actually performs on his own like this that you understand how skilled he really is. He's casual in the extreme, lighting cigarettes during numbers and just tapping his foot to retain the time signature, and he creates an aura of respectful silence all along. He is undoubtedly one of the best guitar players rock has produced, equally at home on either the acoustic or electric instrument."

Stephen's support act for the tour was new singing sensation Maria Muldaur. She had an interesting insight into how the press often branded Stephen with a less than favorable reputation. "Sometimes I'd get mad at the critics that would rave about me and then pan Stills when he played well," she told Barbara Charone. "Things like that taught me a lot. I'm glad I was able to observe that particular showbiz phenomena. Stills had already made it so he was an open target. I was on the way up so everyone was enthusiastic."

The tour's two Chicago Auditorium performances on March

8 and 9 were recorded, with the results winding up on a live album release in early 1975. The music that night was extra-specially good, but it was one announcement to the crowd that got the biggest reaction. "Folks," he began. "CSN&Y are getting back together this summer for a big tour, and we'll make another album in the fall."

Stephen's prediction–well at least the first part–would prove no idle boast. The big tour would be the most ambitious in rock history so far, and the dates scheduled would take in all the largest stadiums across America. There was exciting news for the quartet's British fans too, when it was announced that London's Wembley Stadium would host the band's final show of the tour, in September. Even before that announcement, headline news in the UK's *New Musical Express* revealed the enormity of the plan: "Crosby, Stills, Nash & Young are together again. And that's official. One of the hottest-selling properties in international rock when first launched–they have not played together as a foursome for almost four year–CSN&Y are reuniting for a major US concert tour this summer."

CHAPTER 23
The 'Excessive Excess' Tour

"I'm basically a blues singer and blues singers are supposed to suffer. I almost feel guilty" is how Stephen joked about his new-found contentment in an interview with Cameron Crowe for *Crawdaddy*. "Ever since I got married, life is such a gas," he added.

A new album, *As I Come Of Age* (later retitled *Stills*), was taking shape and he was enjoying the benefits of being a husband and father, with son Christopher born in Boulder, Colorado, on April 19, 1974.

"I'm still arrogant," he admitted to Crowe. "I can be an absolute bastard. I have a bad habit of starting things bluntly. I'm not known for my tact. But look, I can see I got really carried away with myself."

The signs were that Stephen's new-found emotional security would help in the run-up to the huge concert tour with Crosby, Stills, Nash & Young. Was there a hint in this comment to Dave

Zimmer, though, that the forthcoming tour might be for the money this time? "My financial situation was starting to get a little strange," he admitted. "I'd been thinking about getting a band together with Eric [Clapton], but no solid commitments came out of that English scene. So when I talked to Neil, I said, 'Come on, let's press the bet.' And once we talked it over with management and Bill Graham it was decided, if we're gonna do it, let's do it to the max, the nth degree, you know?"

With his tongue firmly in his cheek, Stephen's motivation for the gigantic tour was less ambiguous in this soundbite: "We did one for the art and the music, one for the chicks. This one's for the cash!"

Up to this point, no band had undertaken a tour of outdoor football stadiums. Stephen clearly relished the prospect of doing something not even The Rolling Stones had attempted. The whole thing would begin at the Coliseum, Seattle, in early July and rumble on to its September 14 conclusion, 35 shows later in London. While a huge team of organizers took care of the infrastructure required behind the ground-breaking tour, Crosby, Stills, Nash, and Young rehearsed at Neil's ranch.

Stephen was in particularly good shape for the work ahead, having just returned from a coral-diving vacation in Hawaii. The tour, he felt, would require rather different rehearsals and he outlined his plan of action. "Rehearsing outdoors at Neil's ranch was my idea," Stephen told *Rolling Stone*. "I said, 'Neil, we're coming to your ranch and we're going to build a stage across the road from your studio because we've got to learn how to play outdoors.' He didn't want all those people in his house, but it actually worked."

Some of the "potheads" and "sycophants," as Stephen called them, that surrounded each member of the band at the time might have felt the band should just naturally have done what they do on the tour, but Stephen wanted song arrangements for each song sorted in advance. So they grafted away outdoors among the pines, alongside the musicians hand-picked for the tour.

The rhythm section, this time, was hired without much argument. Initially Stephen had wanted Kenny Passarelli to play bass, but, outnumbered by Crosby and Nash, he conceded that Tim Drummond should get the gig. Joe Lala (percussion), inevitably, and Russ Kunkel (drums) completed the seven-piece band.

In glorious sunshine, the rehearsals went mostly without a hitch. The focus on what they needed to do was so fruitful that they even taped a few tracks by night in Neil's studio. One of these included the only known song in the Crosby, Stills, Nash & Young canon that had been written by all four of them. 'Little Blind Fish' remains unreleased to this day.

Could the fantastically positive vibes from the rehearsals at Neil's ranch extend through the months of touring together? Many fans and commentators doubted the project would ever make it to the end date in London, and at times you could see why. Arguments, tantrums, and seething discontent still surfaced occasionally. On one occasion, Stephen managed to destroy a huge CSN&Y ice sculpture logo backstage when he felt his bandmates had unfairly leveled criticism at him for hogging the limelight. But the four seemed determined to keep a cap on their spikier emotions this time, as Stephen explained: "There was a lot of manic energy around. The same kind of stuff that used to have The Who beating the shit out of each other. The same kind of stuff that broke up a lot of other bands. We kind of steeled ourselves to it."

That the tour, involving an entourage of 86 people, was excessive in every way imaginable was no surprise. The cocaine and caviar consumption, the egos and the cash involved, would all be documented almost as much as the music. Were there really monogrammed CSN&Y pillow logos designed by Joni Mitchell in hotel rooms along the way? Apparently so: "Excessive excess–guilty as charged," Stephen admitted to *Mojo*'s Sylvie Simmons.

Stephen also did some excessive reading before resting his head on one of those CSN&Y pillows every night, it would seem. He took Solzhenitsyn's *The Gulag Archipelago* on the road with him for the quieter moments.

With no experience of any tour on this scale before, Ken Weiss was still building up a business and personal relationship with Stephen that summer: "At this time, we were just together for barely two years and suddenly this monster tour was upon us. I learned a great deal on the tour, spent time with the other principals–well, at least David and Graham, and Bill Graham. Neil was always off on his own, wisely avoiding the madness–and especially so at its end, reviewing the financial documents and learning a great deal about the business of touring. But learning about touring from this tour was a bit like learning about sailing by piloting the Queen Mary. For many reasons, there really was nothing quite like it–before or since."

Stephen was certainly having the most fun, as he explained in a 1979 *BAM* interview when asked whether the spark from their first gigs together was still evident. "It was there, and we had some thundering good shows. Neil and I were into playing outdoors and really into the whole scene. I remember driving into the Kansas City ballpark. Neil and I were together, and he said, 'Hey, remember a few years ago when we talked about playing baseball stadiums and everybody laughed at us?'"

Graham Nash felt he had never seen Stills the guitarist in better form: "Stephen had moments when no one could touch him, not Clapton or Bloomfield or Beck or Santana, or anyone in that league."

The shows, with support acts like The Beach Boys, would typically last for more than three hours, with an intermission of 15 minutes at the midpoint. The first half would always kick off with a heavy-on-the-percussion-based 'Love The One You're With,' with more electric songs before a number of band and solo acoustic songs ahead of the break. The second half would be all electric, with space for Stephen and Neil to engage in their crowd-pleasing guitar duel. Stephen, Neil and Graham would take turns on keyboards on their own numbers, and the stage spokesperson was generally David Crosby.

After each energy-sapping performance, Neil Young would leave Crosby, Stills, and Nash to party back in their hotel. "Each night he packs up his guitar, wife, baby son, and dog and hits the road," David Crosby told Chris Charlesworth. It would be interesting to learn if Stephen ever found the time to finish *The Gulag Archipelago.*

When they weren't partying, Crosby and Nash in particular spent a lot of downtime in front of the TV watching the Watergate hearings. Stephen had his own take on what was going down at the time, as he revealed to *Rolling Stone*: "I saw the cards all lining up for Nixon to resign before they could impeach him. I had friends in Washington. They told me that Barry Goldwater and Alexander Haig went up to Nixon and said, 'Sorry dude, you've got to go.' Who knows how close Oliver Stone's movie was, but emotionally Nixon was pretty far out there. But his ego was such that he was going to fight until the end and then leave on certain terms so that you won't have Nixon to kick around anymore."

The music drew plenty of VIPs. When a curious Bob Dylan attended the Minneapolis leg of the tour at the Civic Center, Stephen dedicated 'Word Game' to him. After the gig, Dylan, Stills, and Tim Drummond adjourned to a hotel room until 5am, partying and playing each other new songs. "He played us all the songs from *Blood On The Tracks* on acoustic guitar," Drummond told *Rolling Stone*. "We were on twin beds, across from each other. Oh God, I can't tell you how great it was. At one point Stephen said something to him about the songs not being good. I was so goddamn embarrassed. He was probably coked out. Dylan, being the arrogant man that he was, said, 'Well, Stephen, play me one of your songs.' That was the end of it. Stephen couldn't even find one string from another at that point."

During the tour, there was more heartbreaking news of another friend's death, the kind of news that seemed to always haunt Crosby, Stills, Nash, and Young at the time. "My sister-in-law, Mama Cass, died in August during the tour," Russ Kunkel told *Rolling Stone*. "I was married to her sister Leah. I think we were in Houston at the Whitehall Hotel. I remember Graham sitting me down and telling me she passed away. She had a big role in their lives. She introduced Graham to Stephen. It was a very difficult day for us when she died."

When the tour finally, triumphantly, and perhaps miraculously, arrived at London's Wembley Stadium on September 14, England's national soccer stadium was filled with 72,000 fans. The weather was unseasonably warm, the support acts were rock legends in their own right (The Band, Joni Mitchell), and the crowd were so up for the four-hour CSN&Y set that they could have sung three blind mice and received a roaring encore. During one of the quieter, acoustic numbers, Stephen squatted on a chair, as Crosby, Stills, Nash & Young performed 'Blackbird,' with his five-month old son Christopher on his lap. Stephen had the lion's share of the 33 songs performed that day, with 'Love The One You're With,' 'Johnny's Garden,' 'Change Partners,' 'Myth Of Sisyphus,' 'You Can't Catch Me' / 'Word Game,' 'Suite: Judy Blue Eyes,' 'First Things First,' 'Black Queen,' and 'Carry On' all included.

'Black Queen,' almost always an electric show-stopper, was the opportunity for Stephen to plug in his Gibson Firebird and take center stage with the evening's heaviest riff. His stately solo performance of 'Myth of Sisyphus' at the piano gave the concert a welcome clean and refreshing break from the conveyor belt of greatest hits. But it was the rumbling rhythms of the familiar opening to 'Love The One You're With' (greeted by a huge roar) that kicked off the show, that lived longest in the memory.

The Wembley show brought a few criticisms. 'How could some overblown rock 'n' roll tour this big possibly be any good?' was the general angle. But the crowd that day–perhaps intoxicated as much by the sweet-smelling cloud of marijuana that hung over them on that breezeless day–lapped up every song and every bit of banter coming from the stage.

The British press, on the whole, were positive in their summing-up. "Powerful, unified, and genuinely impressive" was how the *New Musical Express* saw it, and *Sounds* decided "It was rock 'n' roll at its most potent."

Specific negative press was directed at the over-seriousness the band were guilty of at times. Stephen thought so too: "Before we came over we sat around for hours trying to think of a title for the whole show. In the end, I think, we came up with something very heavy ... very portentous, like 'The California Jam.'

"Now, I really wanted to call it 'Crosby, Stills, Bangers, and

Mash', and I mean, the other guys just did not want to know. But we should have done it because it would have put the thing in the right perspective."

Whatever any of the four of them said after the event, on the day Crosby, Stills Nash & Young appeared to enjoy themselves just as much as the fans who'd come to witness the end of one of the greatest rock 'n' roll tours.

Before going their separate ways, at least half of Crosby, Stills, Nash & Young appeared to jam the night away at an after-tour party at Quaglino's, in London's St. James.

Stephen and Neil joined members of Led Zeppelin and The Band to perform Neil's 'Vampire Blues' and 'On The Beach,' among other songs. The mouth-watering line-up consisted of Robbie Robertson, Rick Danko, Levon Helm, John Bonham, and Tim Drummond.

The tour made close to $12 million according to Graham Nash, but Crosby, Stills, Nash, andYoung, it seems, only pocketed $300,000 each.

Sensibly, Atlantic released a catch-all greatest hits album, *So Far*, with a Joni Mitchell painting of Crosby, Stills Nash, and Young on the cover, to coincide with the tour. It provided them with their third consecutive chart-topper in the US and managed Number 25 in the UK.

The day after the Wembley finale, Stephen headed across the channel to be reunited with Véronique in Paris and appear on stage at her concert at the Olympic, playing bass. In this same month, Véronique's album *Le Maudit* was released, with session musicians brought in from various current and previous Stills projects. Joe Lala, Conrad Isadore, Russ Kunkel, Donnie Dacus, Lee Sklar, and Kenny Passarelli all joined Stephen in supporting his wife's first album recorded in the US, in Hollywood and Sausalito. Since their marriage, concert appearances for Sanson in North America were restricted to the French-speaking Canadian city of Quebec, with regular return trips to tour in France.

Stephen couldn't help get drawn into some lively opinionated comments on how the music scene was shifting toward more visual performances when he was questioned by Cameron Crowe for *Creem* magazine. Hitting 30 soon, he acknowledged, was a chastening thought, and he wasn't much impressed by the new wave of glam rockers. But there were some exceptions: "For instance, you know whose band really impresses me? Rod Stewart's. They're hot. They play right. There's a few bands around who really play, but I think all of this mascara-rock, creep-rock, whatever you want to call it … it just turns my stomach."

When quizzed by Crowe, he predicted that the fickle audience for glam rock might vanish as soon as it had sprung up and added, "The only ones who ever pulled it off were The Rolling Stones. When they started, though, that's not what made them popular. What made them popular is that they played hot rock 'n' roll.

"That's why Alice Cooper is so hip, man," he continued. "He did his number. He's just a fine old Italian boy who's fun to get drunk with. He knew exactly what to do and how long to do it. And he'll never do it again."

Stephen evidently didn't feel threatened by this new wave: "And then there's good musicians who put on the high-heeled shoes that they can't stand in. To me, that's really sad. But then I'm an opinionated motherfucker, so …" he concluded.

After a break, Crosby, Stills, Nash & Young all reconvened in Nash's living room in San Francisco to try to kick-start the

Human Highway album idea again. They recorded in Graham's tiny basement studio and at the Record Plant in nearby Sausalito, but it wasn't long before Neil departed and Stephen did something that would create an even bigger rift in the Stills/Nash relationship than the episode with Rita Coolidge. First there was a major falling-out over a minor harmony part for Stephen's new song 'Guardian Angel.' If Nash dug his heels in and refused to budge over what he thought was a bad idea, what followed was an over-the-top response from Stephen. He took a razor blade and cut the master tape of the quartet's version of the Crosby and Nash song 'Wind On The Water' clean in two.

Somewhat unconvincingly, he later tried to brush off the incident. "The razor blade business was a joke," he said. But he admitted being drunk and was later suitably contrite. "Nash threw me out of his house. And I was ill-mannered enough to deserve it."

Back in Colorado for the winter, there was another less damaging but nonetheless intoxicated incident that halted another musical reunion. Stephen was invited over to guest on the Souther-Hillman-Furay Band's second album, *Trouble In Paradise*, at Caribou Ranch. Reuniting with old friends, Richie Furay, Chris Hillman, Al Perkins, Paul Harris and Joe LaLa, might have been fun, but the recording session didn't begin until 9pm. Sadly, having arrived four hours too early, Stephen was in no fit state to contribute much and left the studio, allegedly having consumed the ranch's entire stash of intoxicants.

However, his habit of frequently guesting on other people's recordings showed little sign of letting up. Stephen played acoustic guitar on Elvin Bishop's 'Rollin' Home,' on the former Paul Butterfield Blues Band member's *Juke Joint Jump* album.

The solo album Stephen had been holding back for release until now finally hit the record stores in June. *As I Come Of Age* was to have been the title of the album, but Stephen went for the less fancy approach again, naming it *Stills.* One of the reasons for the delay was that it was his first solo release after switching from Atlantic to Columbia Records. He'd never been convinced that Atlantic were putting enough effort into promoting his solo releases compared to the energy expended on CSN&Y. Leaving Atlantic and finding a better deal took some cunning on his part. "I had to convince one I was totally together and the other side I was totally crazed, right? And it worked like a charm," he joked to *Crawdaddy*.

"When we first heard he was on the label, I thought he would be nothing but trouble," a CBS executive was quoted as saying. "Surprisingly he's been really co-operative," he added.

It's fair to say that Columbia got a much better album than his previous Manassas offering *Down The Road*, but it came at a price, as bandmate Rick Roberts pointed out. "Stephen spends lots a cash. What it cost him to make *Stills* I could have made five albums. But they wouldn't have been as good. He is a genius. He's got better command of the studio than anyone I've ever met."

There were parts of *Stills* that dated back to recordings in London in 1971, which is why Ringo Starr is once again credited on drums for his contribution to the LP's stand-out track, 'As I Come Of Age.' It was a track that had been a long time in the making and had some late improvements added courtesy of new boy Donnie Dacus.

It was producer Bill Halverson who encouraged the 23-year-old to attempt to overdub a guitar part on 'As I Come Of Age.' Dacus proved just what an asset he could be by filling in the gaps brilliantly.

'Turn Back The Pages' and 'First Things First' were a couple of wonderfully optimistic high-tempo tracks recorded again with the Albert brothers at Criteria, Miami, and the remainder of the album is sprinkled with an old and new assortment, pulled in from other locations such as Caribou and Wally Heider's in L.A. Another high point was 'My Favorite Changes,' which Stephen once cited as one of his most tellingly autobiographical songs. Musically, it showed attention to detail you would so often associate with Stephen that had been so badly absent at times on *Down The Road*. Also one of his best arrangements, 'My Favorite Changes' drifted along delicately, interrupted by some beautifully fluid Stills electric guitar.

The cover photo for *Stills*, shot a year back during the CSN&Y tour rehearsals at Neil Young's Broken Arrow Ranch, showed a relaxed and healthy looking rock star, guitar in hand, wearing a Cleveland Browns football jersey. "I look at it now and go, 'I want that body back!'" he joked to *Rolling Stone*. "I wore football jerseys before it was cool. People like Jann Wenner [*Rolling Stone* co-founder] would always ask me, 'What's with the football uniform?' I'd say, 'We're in a football stadium and they're loud and colorful. And I like football.' The next year Mick Jagger shows up with a Philadelphia Eagles uniform at a show."

The album featured his recently appointed guitar partner, Donnie Dacus, who had writing credits on a couple of tracks. When Steve Lake interviewed the pair in New York for *Melody Maker*, there was great empathy.

"That's the reason I'm optimistic," Stephen began. "Donnie played a very large part in the direction of the album. There's none of that ..."

"There's none of that competition," interjected Donnie, "Like, I'm in music to have a good time and to be creative and Stephen's the first person that I've met to be creative with. He's the only person I've ever written a song with."

Stills eventually hit Number 19 (US) and Number 31 (UK) and got the thumbs-up from most critics. A tour to promote the album in early July was quickly undertaken, with Dacus and Joe Lala retained and joined by Rick Roberts (guitar), George 'Chocolate' Perry (bass), and Tubby Zeigler (drums). Not one for sitting on the fence, Stephen pronounced this new outfit to be "The best band I've ever played in."

Repaying the compliment, his band members were eager to set the record straight about their 'boss' in an interview with Barbara Charone in *Sounds* during that summer tour. They were surprised by the vitriol directed at what many considered, by reputation, a difficult, arrogant rock star.

"I don't know where he's gotten the reputation," Joe Lala pondered. "I've seen him get drunk and obnoxious, but then again I get drunk and obnoxious. But because he's Stephen Stills people like to say 'last night at so and so's ...'"

Donnie Dacus felt that the pressure of the past was a factor: "I'm sure that CSN&Y tag haunts him. It must be like a ghost shadow following you around."

Lala echoed Stephen's own assertions that the only thing that mattered was the music. "People resent him, 'cause they're jealous. If Stephen donated a million dollars to cancer research, certain sections of the rock press wouldn't have a nice thing to say about it. If you listen to the man's songs you'll see the kind of person he is."

Rick Roberts' conclusion that "When you live in a fish bowl as long as Stephen has you can't help being defensive" summed up the problem best.

"The sad thing," Stephen himself admitted, "is that out of

necessity I've become more tough-skinned with my art and a trifle less apt to react to sensitive situations. I've got to get rid of this image 'cause I'm bored with it. I ain't the asshole everybody wants to make me out as."

Out on the road with his loudest rock 'n' roll band to date, Stephen took a leaf out of Neil Young's book and traveled in style in a mobile home, complete with a well-stocked bar nicknamed 'The Pleasure Dome.' His old guitar sparring partner made the occasional guest appearance at some dates, notably L.A.'s Greek Theater, UCLA Westwood, and Stanford University. Both Stills and Young seemed to enjoy the experiences greatly, and at the Greek Theater Stephen announced from the stage that he had a new policy that would see him include one Neil Young tune per album in future.

Although the gigs were loud affairs–even 'Suite: Judy Blue Eyes' got a new electric treatment–his acoustic solo spots went to a new level. At the Greek he showed off his new Martin 12-string, developed by guitar technician Steve King. The new fatter sound was described as "sensational" by one reviewer as Stephen rolled out new additions to the set on this tour, such as 'Treetop Flyer' and his cover of his buddy Fred Neil's 'Everybody's Talkin' At Me.'

The occasional coming together of Stephen and Neil saw them both play an unannounced free set at Alex's, a tiny bar in the Santa Cruz Mountains near Neil's La Honda ranch, on New Year's Eve. Neil had said to *Rolling Stone*'s Cameron Crowe in the summer of 1975: "I think people have that friction business out of hand. Stephen and I just play really good together. People can't comprehend that we both can play lead guitar in the band and not fight over it."

Early 1976 would see them both in the studio together.

CHAPTER 24
"Eat a Peach"

"Neil Young backs me up better than anyone in the world. He understands what I'm going for. Neil allows me to explore my chops. What I want to do is make an album with Neil. We'd terrorize the industry."

Stephen's wish, as he explained it to *Sounds*' Barbara Charone, was about to come true. Equally enthusiastic was Neil, who suggested they secretly book time in Criteria Studios to see what a Stills and Young (without Crosby and Nash) album would sound like.

Toward the end of 1975, there had been a hint at what the aborted CSN&Y album *Human Highway* might have sounded like. Neil Young's closing track to his *Zuma* solo LP, 'Through My Sails,' was as perfect and laid-back a CSN&Y recording as anything they had combined on before. It was an odd inclusion on an album of some of Neil's most epic guitar sagas.

But before Stephen could hitch up with Neil, he would

complete work on a new solo album and watch as the Atlantic Records *Stephen Stills Live* album did some reasonable business for his former solo label and hit Number 42 on the *Billboard* 200. The album was an unpolished but at times stirring snapshot of where he was at back in 1974. Included among his own guitar pyrotechnics was his heavy-duty version of 'Rocky Mountain Way,' which was by now a crowd-pleaser when segued into 'Jet Set (Sigh).'

With Stephen already booked into Criteria in January and February, another band was working on a new album up the corridor. The Bee Gees were in Miami recording their forthcoming *Children Of The World* album. Stephen was on hand to add some guitar and percussion to those sessions, but the only thing that he helped out on that wound up on the album was the percussion on 'You Should Be Dancing.' Uncredited to avoid complications, his contribution met with the Gibb brothers' approval but not the record company, who reportedly wanted the end result, which they feared wouldn't sound commercial enough, cut from the record. Thankfully, the part wasn't removed and was a key feature of the single that would showcase the Bee Gees' new disco sound and give them their third *Billboard* number one single. Stephen's band members Joe Lala and George 'Chocolate' Perry ended up playing on other tracks on *Children Of The World*. Enjoying the opportunity so much, Stephen then lent a hand by playing bass on the demo of the countrified 'Rest Your Love On Me,' which eventually became the B-side to 'Too Much Heaven.' A song called 'Walk Before You Run,' written at Criteria by Barry Gibb and Stephen, was said to have resulted from a jam session with keyboards player Blue Weaver, drummer Dennis Bryon, and guitarist Alan Kendall. But it didn't find its way on to *Children Of*

The World or any future Bee Gees or Stills release. Barry, Robin, and Maurice Gibb had fun with it, though, as Stephen recalled: "We sang the chorus in four-part harmony and everyone went, 'Oh, oh, we better not, this would be too much to deal with! Gorgeous sound, though."

During this lengthy period at Criteria, Stephen offered Judy Collins some much-needed help. Although their love affair had ended abruptly in 1969, both had kept in contact. Despite her continued public success–with 'Send In The Clowns'–at this time, Collins was, in private, an alcoholic. The post-love-affair pain and suffering had subsided now, and Stephen offered Judy a place to stay when she most needed a break. He was at the time, with the help of his mother and sister Hannah, looking after son Chris in his canal-side home in Miami, after Véronique Sanson had returned to her native France. Swapping the cold of New York for the Florida beaches and Stephen's swimming pool had little effect on Judy's long-term health issues, but it would be comforting to know that a lifelong friendship would result after the misery endured during their break-up six years earlier.

Stephen's sessions down in Miami with Neil Young were productive. In a 15-day period the duo managed to cut 12 tracks under the guidance of the project's key presence, producer Tom Dowd, who had mixed the *Stephen Stills Live* album successfully back in November at Caribou. Some of Stephen's moody contributions– 'Make Love To You,' 'Black Coral,' and 'Guardian Angel'–were as far away from Manassas and his recent rock tour as it was possible to be. They provided a stark contrast with Neil's more predictable offerings, such as 'Long May You Run,' 'Fontainebleau,' and 'Midnight On The Bay.'

In March, without Stephen's agreement, Neil contacted

Crosby and Nash, who were enjoying increasing success as a duo, and invited them down to change the Stills/Young project into a Crosby, Stills, Nash & Young album. "Neil suggested all four of us make an album together," Stephen told Young biographer Johnny Rogan, "but that wasn't right because by that time we'd got all the tracks and half the singing done already."

The original tracks, and some newly arranged songs, were then enhanced by the addition of the Crosby and Nash vocals, and for a short period the album did indeed look like the follow up to *Déjà Vu*.

Halfway through the new sessions in Florida, however, Crosby and Nash were obliged to head back to California to meet deadlines set for finishing their *Whistling Down The Wire* album. What happened next was a scheduling nightmare, especially as Neil Young had returned west too.

The frustration Stephen felt about having to halt proceedings manifested itself in him closing all the doors in the studio while yelling at the top of his voice as he reportedly kicked in the console. Fifteen minutes later he reasoned that the best way to uncork the pent-up creativity that had been halted by the departure of his bandmates was to summon Joe Lala and George Perry, plug in, turn his amp up to the max, and play some noisy rock 'n' roll. With adrenalin pumping and wearing a T-shirt bearing the slogan 'I'm An Exhibitionist,' Stephen played so loud that bass guitarist Perry had to set up in the control room to be able to hear what he was playing.

Amid all the chaotic activity that spring, there were some lighter moments. With both the Eagles and Black Sabbath also sharing Criteria Studios at the same time Stills and Young were working away, there were bound to be tales of rock 'n' roll high jinks and pranks. Sabbath were recording tracks for their *Technical*

Ecstasy album and the band's British roadies David Tangye and Graham Wright recall Stills being less than friendly. "I remember him being drunk and writing all over Bill Ward's drumheads, about 'you stole the American blues' and 'ride back to England on your horse,' says Wright. "He was drinking a bottle of brandy and we kicked him out of the studio. I wish I had kept that snare head," Wright adds.

"I would follow Stephen Stills after he had been to the bathroom to clean up the Bolivian marching powder he had left on top of the toilet cistern!" David Tangye jokes. "I just remember that he left a carpet of snow in there!"

When it became clear that the wait to conclude CSN&Y recording sessions would be two weeks, the dynamics of the project changed again, with more frustration and deep resentment surfacing on both sides.

Clearly, Stephen and Neil needed more contributions from the departing duo, but with their own deadline looming–the beginning of a Stills/Young tour in a month– they decided to revert back to plan A. That meant erasing the Crosby and Nash vocals from the tracks they'd already banked.

When word got back to the duo in California, Graham, in particular, was more angry than he had ever been before with either of his two bandmates. It didn't matter that Stephen had a point when he'd reasoned that both parties should complete their duo projects then start again properly with CSN&Y when time allowed. Graham was incandescent with rage at the wiping of his and Crosby's vocals. While absolving Neil Young–who had put the whole thing together in the first place–of most of the blame, he let rip at Stephen with his emotions in an interview with *Sounds*. The reports that the sessions hadn't been fruitful met with incredulity from Nash. "For them [Stills and Young] to say the magic wasn't there or that we weren't hungry enough. I say bullshit."

The usually mild-mannered Nash's angry reaction to what Stephen had reportedly said about the reasons for dropping Crosby and Nash from the project? "I'll thump that fucker right in the nose when I see him again."

That last comment at least suggested they would be in contact at some point, but in his autobiography *Wild Tales*, he described the situation in even stronger terms: "I swore I would never work with them again."

Now CSN&Y wasn't just on hold. This time it looked like a dead end.

During all the on-off recordings in Miami, there was Stephen's latest solo album being readied for release. On *Illegal Stills*, interestingly, Stephen experimented by adding Crosby and Nash-like harmonies on the album, courtesy of his old friends Howard Kaylan and Mark Volman.

This second solo album for Columbia featured, rather like his new Stills/Young tracks, a lack of the one element most fans expected at the very least from him–his guitar playing. Moving further from his roots, some of the songs were barely identifiable as Stills songs. 'Midnight In Paris' was a good example. A really rather good potential hit single with some great hooks, it was more Donnie Dacus than Stephen Stills. He cut loose a little on Neil's 'The Loner' and 'Buyin' Time,' but the band he'd assembled for the loud and heavy live shows seemed a tad restrained on *Illegal Stills*. While *Rolling Stone* didn't bother to review the album at all, the British *New Musical Express* did highlight one real positive. The "exceptional" production work on the album by Stephen and Don

Gehman got the thumbs-up, with a very favorable comparison. "There is such a thing as the Stephen Stills sound," wrote Steve Clarke, "and like [Phil] Spector or [Brian] Wilson's sound it's a BIG aural landscape."

The reviewer concluded that "*Illegal Stills* is a well-paced album with a flowing sense of continuity totally absent from *Stills* and bears the mark of simply first-grade rock talent."

The finer points of the release were not enough to return Stephen to the upper echelons of the charts and *Illegal Stills* stalled at Number 30 (US) and Number 54 (UK).

With so many unforeseen diversions that spring, it was hardly surprising that a projected Stephen Stills tour of Europe was canceled at short notice. Stephen was at one point named in a letter by British chartered accountants Clifton & Co. as being the recipient of possible legal action due to the no-show at Cardiff City's soccer ground, in Wales. He was to have headlined at the outdoor festival in front of 40,000, with support from Eric Burdon, The Cate Brothers, The Kinks, The Pretty Things, and Bachman-Turner Overdrive.

"That's news to me," Stephen said later of the change of plan. "I know I have to go over there because that time, when I canceled, it was really a little close to the recording date to cancel, but it wasn't right at the last minute."

It must have come as something of a relief to all concerned when, on June 25, the Stills-Young Band tour opened at the Pine Knob Music Theater in Clarkston, Michigan. A relief to all concerned apart from Crosby and Nash obviously, who were still seething at the month's past events down in Miami.

The early Stills-Young Band shows weren't a shambles by any

means, but it did take the two chief protagonists and the band a number of dates to get to a tight enough level. Clearly the rehearsals hadn't been numerous or long enough, and Stephen's attempt to keep a rigid set list while they honed their performances clashed with Neil's common practice of changing material around from show to show to avoid boredom. At the Nassau Coliseum, Long Island, with support from Poco, the set list oddly didn't give the necessary scope for enough of the hoped-for guitar jams a lot of the crowd had come to see. Stephen and Neil mostly took turns doing their greatest hits and closed with an electric encore of 'Suite: Judy Blue Eyes.' Stephen, with–like Neil–hair cropped short, sported a black knee-length kimono. He sprinkled in some new songs, 'Buyin' Time' and 'Black Coral,' but the reviews were largely underwhelming.

As the tour rumbled on, they weren't able to get back to the studio to finish off the imminent Stills-Young Band album. One night, after a 20,000 sell-out show at Largo's Capital Centre in Maryland, Neil jumped in a Learjet and flew down to Miami to finish mixing the duo's now-titled *Long May You Run* LP. "If we both go, neither of us will want to come back," he told Stephen, according to *Rolling Stone*'s Cameron Crowe. The irony of that statement wouldn't be lost on anyone remembering it a week or so later.

Despite the hectic toing and froing by Neil to Miami, the quality of the tour's live performances began to improve. Now, it seemed, they were well-enough practiced to begin to enjoy themselves. "I got to the point where we were tight enough to cut loose," said Stephen.

The Richfield Coliseum date, in Cleveland, Ohio, on July 15, was by all accounts the breakthrough gig of the tour. If, as some commentators had suggested, Young had tried to help boost his friend's flagging career by inviting him out on the road, this explosion of scorching guitar solos and after-show euphoria proved that the duo were a top rock draw. That night, and after several following performances, Young heaped praise on his partner and, in a bid to reverse recent negative press, told Cameron Crowe: "Now you have something to write about." Young's enthusiasm for the tour at this point made what happened next all the more puzzling.

After another decent Stills-Young Band show at the University of Columbia, South Carolina, the tour came to an unscheduled and abrupt end.

Although it was common for Stephen and Neil to travel to each new tour destination independently, when Stephen arrived in Atlanta, Georgia, he soon discovered that his partner wouldn't be joining him.

Neil delivered the news that he was departing his own tour in memorably brief fashion. The telegram to Stephen informing him read, "Dear Stephen, funny how things that start spontaneously end that way. Eat a peach. Neil."

Surprisingly, there was no fall-out, no anger, no cataclysmic meltdown from Stephen. Perhaps he had half seen the premature end coming. However, if Neil had partly organized the tour to help Stephen's career, then this turn of events certainly left Stephen in a very much worse position. Whatever the reasons for Neil's casual exit two months early, Stephen was now lumbered with tour dates that would either need to be canceled or fulfilled without Neil.

Bravely, Stephen decided to do as much to continue the tour as he could, including at least one daunting date following support act Lynyrd Skynyrd in their home state of Florida. If the business of filling in tour dates to honor agreements was a struggle, it was nothing to the struggle he was having with his failing marriage to Véronique that summer. On a return visit home to Colorado, he discovered that his wife of three years had filed for divorce.

"Colorado was a little remote for her," Stephen later reflected to Dave Zimmer. "Also my French never quite got over the hump, you know? And she just couldn't get used to America. She just couldn't. So the situation got more and more frustrating and the marriage died of natural causes, I suppose."

There would be no reconciliation in his marriage, but, happily, his publisher and personal manager Ken Weiss was about to help in the reconciliation of Crosby, Stills & Nash, with the emphasis on the Stills and Nash part.

CHAPTER 25
Reconciliation

Stephen left his marital home in Colorado in the summer of 1976 and moved back to California. Here he began to tackle his problems head on by seeing a doctor in Santa Barbara. "We see each other about once a month," he later revealed to *Crawdaddy*'s Peter Knobler. "There's a certain amount of neurosis that goes with going out there and doing a psychological striptease in front of 10,000 people, and you've got to learn how to deal with it.

"Sometimes you've just got to close your eyes and charge," he said of his recent lack of confidence and fear of the stage. But the monthly sessions in Santa Barbara were mostly to help him deal with the collapse of his marriage.

Curiously, he began spending most of his time in the penthouse of the Beverly Rodeo Hotel in Beverly Hills, only 10 minutes from his house.

Taking care of business and offering some friendly advice was

Ken Weiss: "This was not an easy time to say the least–certainly the worst period of his life to that point, something of which I am sure he would agree. Lots of room-service food was flowing in, rather tasty as I recall, and we were not going out at all. He was obviously depressed and distressed–and not much creativity was taking place. And to make matters more uncomfortable–or it seemed–David [Crosby] and Willy [Nash] were playing a date at the Greek Theater the next night, just a few miles away in Hollywood. I tried reaching them but was unable to–perhaps by intent on their part. So I made some calls to my various contacts, I'm not sure which or whom, perhaps John Hartman, who was their manager at this time. Anyway, I made arrangements for Stephen to go, quietly. I was clearly not sure that he would go, especially given that I had to convince him it was a smart thing for him to do, at least for his emotional well-being. Of course I considered the implications in doing so."

At this time the implications Ken Weiss referred to were the compounding of the rift that had developed in the spring surrounding the Miami sessions for the aborted CSN&Y album.

"So it is with that backdrop Stephen quietly arrived backstage at the Greek Theater," continued Ken. "I do not believe either one of the two guys imagined Stephen would be there. But there he was, and by Stephen's account, a few hugs later all was forgiven–though likely not forgotten. At the end of the show, Stephen walked out on stage to perform 'Teach Your Children' with them for the encore. An audience going wild and showing such affection was even more than I had hoped would take place. It's also worth noting I did not go to the Greek that night. But I really believed it would be better if I were not there. It was far more pure and natural this way. I was more confident than not that they would work it out, but more importantly, it would help

Stephen get back to what he does best. Divorce was not one of those things."

That night after the gig, Graham Nash, encouraged by his girlfriend Susan Sennett, invited "the Stephen I'd always hoped I'd see back again" home with him.

Tellingly, Susan had this to say: "... all I'd heard was what a monster Stephen Stills was. I'd figured anybody Graham could hate this much, he must really love. And when I met Stephen, here was this shy man who didn't seem so terrible. I liked Stephen."

The clear-the-air drinking session that followed ended when Graham revealed: "I piled him back into his room at 4am."

According to Ken Weiss, the campout at the Beverly Rodeo soon ended. Stephen returned home with an outlook brightened by his reconciliation with Crosby and Nash again.

A few days after the Greek Theater reunion, Stephen was back in circulation helping Jimmy Webb to celebrate his 30th birthday. Among other invited guests was Stephen's old friend Ringo Starr and 400 others, reportedly invited to the songwriter's Encino home for a steak dinner.

The release of the long-awaited Stills-Young Band album *Long May You Run* in October did at least return Stephen to the upper reaches of the albums charts. Despite the earlier fall-out from the tour, the record (released on the Reprise label) crawled to Number 26 (US) and Number 12 (UK). The mellow groove throughout didn't reflect any of the hoped-for Stills/Young guitar jams that the large attendances at the live dates grew to love. The title track was the one classic that will bear repeating down the decades, but most of the remaining new songs would fail that test of time. Reviewers were often positive about Stephen's 'Black Coral,' which was his best contribution according to some.

Maybe it was, but Stephen appeared to be drifting far away from his musical roots with the song, which came from a personal experience, as he told Chris Charlesworth: "My songs on that album were written somewhat before Neil's were mostly done [in the studio]. My 'water' song, the one about diving ['Black Coral'], was actually written after I'd gotten into some very deep diving. I have been down 288 feet."

As you would expect from any recording involving Neil Young, the album was mostly cut live with very little overdubbing, but the general conclusion was that it lacked the heart and soul most had expected from the duo. Few reviews let them off the hook entirely, but it didn't receive the mauling some had feared, although almost all the critics pondered on the notion that it might have been so much better had the transformation to a CSN&Y album taken place.

Perhaps the best thing about the album was Tom Wilkes' evocative cover design, which featured a sketch of two feisty buffalo. It didn't prove to be a metaphor for the attitude displayed by Stephen and Neil on this record.

Surprisingly, when Stephen took to the road for a solo tour of smaller theaters and colleges in October and November, it was the first time he had undertaken dates without support. "Between bands," as he put it, he would only 'plug in' at the end of the show for an electric 'For What It's Worth,' as he explained to Chris Charlesworth: "I just get out there with six guitars, a banjo, and a dobro, plus a 12-string and maybe one little electric guitar for the last number. I even have my music book with me at the piano in case I forget the words or something. Hell ... I'm not proud."

His profile improved a little when *The Best Of Stephen Stills* was released in early December, again courtesy of his old solo label

Atlantic. It was a decent introduction to anyone not familiar with his best songs, but fans didn't find anything new on the release and avoided it.

In the run-up to Christmas 1976, a year he admitted had been his worst ever, Stephen booked time at the Record Plant in L.A. and began recording 'Run From Tears,' 'See The Changes,' and 'Dark Star'–three songs immeasurably better than anything of his included on *Long May You Run*. Further healing old wounds, Crosby and Nash (whose *Whistling Down The Wire* had easily outshone the Stills-Young Band release) decided to reunite again following first a get-together at Graham's house in San Francisco and then a visit to the Record Plant.

Pooling resources–Graham had recently written 'Just A Song Before I Go'–the three took a short break in early 1977 and then headed east to rent a Spanish-style villa on Pine Tree Drive near Criteria Studios in Miami, Florida. It would prove to be a happy, domesticated scene, and just the environment Stephen needed at the time.

Back on form and working hard in the studio, Stephen was suffering a bout of sickness and a back problem. "Right now, I'm a cripple," he told *Rolling Stone's* Cameron Crowe.

His hearing was shot and he'd started wearing glasses, but despite all that the fact that he'd stopped drinking had most to do with the close bond developing again with Crosby and Nash.

Of the on-stage drinking he told Crowe: "It made me braver but I just wasn't pulling it off. I sat in with the Average White Band, man, the other night and I had three gulps of Scotch and I was completely *blind*. Just … completely … on … the roof. I have definitely quit."

Emphasizing this turn-around, Stills brought five songs to record that would end up on the eventual album to be titled simply

CSN. 'See The Changes' showcased the clear-as-a-bell three-part harmony that the trio had developed on their debut album, and 'Dark Star' was a chugging rocker with some powerful guitar riff embellishments.

Maybe the biggest shock in Graham Nash's autobiography was the fact that he stated with no ambiguity that the "achingly self-revealing" lyrics in Stills' 'Dark Star' were about his bandmate's relationship with Joan Baez. As Stills has never introduced the song in the past or will most likely never introduce it in the future with a "this one's for Joan," we'll have to respect their privacy and leave that revelation hanging.

In February, the three took a break from recording when Graham traveled back to England to visit his sick mother. On a dreary day in Manchester he wrote 'Cold Rain,' which was immediately added to the album on his return to the Miami recording sessions. The whole project, which had started so well, gradually ended with the old arguments and even a visit from a curious Neil Young, who turned up unannounced while in the area. But this time there was to be no argument big enough to halt the completion of work and no place for Young to join in.

Even the album cover shoot got done without a hitch, the three snapped–in the correct CSN order this time–aboard a beautiful sailboat, miles out at sea. The schooner, the William H. Albury, was hired by Crosby and they sailed to The Bahamas for a week-long break accompanied by Joel Bernstein, who photographed all three looking happy, tanned, and relaxed.

In early summer, Stephen was once more drawn into the orbit of The Rolling Stones when they arrived in New York to overdub and mix their *Love You Live* album. One night, work ground to a frustrating halt when Mick Jagger's search for an important piece of recording equipment came up against a locked door with no available key. Hanging out at the Atlantic studios that night was Stephen, who had the gumption to telephone Ahmet Ertegun to locate the problem key. According to *Rolling Stone*, the call went something like this … "Listen, I hate to bother you so late … Well, Mick Jagger and I are down here at your studio. Now, we both sell an awful lot of records for you and Mick is trying to mix the Stones LP, and he needs a part which these people can't seem to get for him … I don't know, they don't have a key or something … Sure man, I'll put him on."

After handing the phone to the night manager, the problem was quickly solved and work continued.

Although Mick and Stephen appeared to get along well, as Ronnie Wood recalled, Keith Richards didn't. "Every time I think about Stephen Stills, I can't forget that Keith couldn't stand him and there was nothing Stephen could do to change that.

"We were sharing a studio once at Atlantic Records in New York and Stephen wanted to play one of Keith's guitars. But Keith said no and actually locked all his guitars away to keep Stephen from playing them. Then Keith put a sign up on the door that read 'No Stephen Stills Allowed.' I'm not sure Keith knows why he didn't like Stephen, but he used to say, 'Stills doesn't know how to do drugs properly.' An odd reason, especially as I don't think any of us knew whether Stills did drugs at all!"

Despite Ronnie Wood's assertion, it appears that Keith and Stephen might have buried the hatchet by July 13, when reports suggest they jammed together.

Stephen's admiration for Keith was evident in a later interview he did for *Guitar World*'s Gary Graff. "To become a decent lead guitar player you've got to play rhythm first. That's why Keith

Richards is also one of my favorite guitar players. He just lays down a pocket that will not quit. It's always cool, and you can put a whole stadium on that rhythm guitar and the place jumps."

In June, *CSN* was released and Crosby, Stills & Nash began a summer/fall US tour. Surprisingly, it was their first as a trio. A few days into the tour, Stephen arranged an extraordinary visit to the White House, where the three were presented to President Jimmy Carter in the Oval Office. The cordial five-minute meeting on June 9 1977 was sandwiched between the President's Middle Eastern policy lunch discussion with Senator Hubert Humphrey and early afternoon NASA budget meeting. Inevitably, the trio were asked if they would consider a concert for Carter and, according to Graham Nash, one of their party smoked a joint inside the Oval Office. Otherwise the meeting of minds was uneventful and short, but at least it was captured on camera for posterity.

Indications were that, yet again, the longer the three were together the more they began to get on each other's nerves. But the rekindled success they were enjoying far outweighed any minor difficulties as the new album peaked at Number 2 (US) and Number 23 (UK). *CSN* also provided the band with their highest-placed *Billboard* hit single, with 'Just A Song Before I Go' hitting Number 7. Stephen's 'Fair Game' was the follow-up single, which fell just short of the Top 40.

The album reviews were positively gushing. British journalist Phil Sutcliffe, who described CS&N as "soft and tough," summed the mood up perfectly: "It strikes me they've completely outflanked their critics."

Peter Herbst's *Rolling Stone* review was headlined "CS&N

all grown up" and analyzed the reasons they work so well as a team. "Stills prevents Crosby and Nash from being cloying, and they restrain his usual stridency." And, while harking back to the "amelodic ramblings he's churned out over the last four years," Herbst declared, "Stills' tunes are superbly focused" on *CSN*.

Reviews on the road were equally good. A sold-out show at Madison Square Garden in New York was witnessed by a doubting Barbara Charone. She wrote: "Diehard cynics would be hard put not to be positively affected by the excellent sounds." Stephen was mentioned in dispatches for "the highlight of perhaps the whole show" for his 'Turn Back The Pages,' which gained him a standing ovation. "Fag in mouth, eyes closed," Charone reported during 'Military Madness,' "Stills finally lived up to his guitar star reputation, now more truth than fiction."

Later in the year, Stephen gave an insight into why he was in such great form during the tour. "I did my share of being crazy," he told *Crawdaddy*'s Peter Knobler. "I don't like to party too much anymore. I don't drink hard booze, except for Cognac. Booze is nice but I don't like to get falling-down, knee-walking drunk anymore. I used to hit the stage in that condition and pull it off, but God knows how."

With a successful 1977 tour and album behind them, Crosby, Stills & Nash reconvened once again at Criteria to begin the process all over again in January 1978. But these sessions were lacklustre, and the new songs less plentiful. Super-session guitarist Danny Kortchmar was called in to liven up proceedings and ended up co-writing scorching guitar boogie 'Can't Get No Booty' with Stephen.

"We just made it up at the end of a very long and frustrating CS&N session, Stephen told Dave Zimmer. "We cut it in about 45 minutes. Then I wrote the verses, dubbed them in the next day, and it was a record."

As Stephen agreed, 'Can't Get No Booty' wasn't a CS&N kind of number, or even a Stephen Stills number. "It's kind of silly. 'Can't Get No Booty' is really a put-on, if you listen to the words. The subtitle of it is 'White Dopes On Punk.' What I wanted to do when I cut that thing was to make up the name of a group, like The Nerds or something. Then I was going to just put it out and see what happened. And I bet it would have been a smash, but coming from Stephen Stills I guess it took everybody aback a little."

The track would find its place on a new Stills solo album, *Thoroughfare Gap*, that came out of the disintegrated CS&N sessions.

This time there were no hard feelings or anger when the CS&N recording sessions in Miami broke down. Happily there was still a good sense of what they might achieve going forward, but it wouldn't be happening that spring. The band dynamic had now switched to a less volatile, easy-going vibe that, significantly, had seen Graham Nash adopt the role of head boy. Their recent return to form was recognized by the award of a star on Hollywood's legendary Walk of Fame in June, and Stephen and Graham (but no David Crosby) were present to receive the honor. Soon after, they began another long Crosby, Stills & Nash tour, this time without a new album or much new material to promote. When that wound down, they celebrated Graham Nash receiving his American citizenship on August 14. Stephen was there to support him at L.A.'s Dorothy Chandler Pavilion. To mark the occasion appropriately, he took Graham for a slap-up meal of hotdogs and Cokes at Pink's hotdog stand.

The recording sessions for *Thoroughfare Gap* over, Stephen

filled in the time before the record's release with a visit 'back home' to New Orleans for the Muhammad Ali versus Leon Spinks heavyweight title fight. And there were yet more high-profile guest appearances. Mimi Fariña's Bread & Roses Folk Festival in San Francisco saw him added as a last-minute addition to the bill that included Hoyt Axton. A month later and he was back at the Troubadour, where it all started for Buffalo Springfield, on stage jamming with new L.A. outfit The Knack.

Thoroughfare Gap was released in October and the material provided a big stick with which Stephen's critics seemed happy to beat him. Stephen described it as "disco and swamp rock." Had his earlier association with the Bee Gees gone to his head? Some reviews suggested Stephen had turned in a disco record. In truth, the songs were a typical variety of styles. The title track was a beautiful, tumbling, guitar-led rootsy number where, once again, Stephen was drawing on his southern history. "That's what it is about," he told Dave Zimmer, "and the title of the album was named after an escape route used during the Civil War. Mosby's guerillas used to run through 'Thoroughfare Gap' when they felt harassed. They'd just disappear into the Blue Ridge Mountains. For me, the record represents a little gap between one part of my career and the other: a cut in the pass."

Clearly an enduring fan favorite, 'Thoroughfare Gap' was one of the first songs guitarist George Terry remembered cutting with Stephen. "What always stood out to me about Stephen is his great acoustic guitar-playing, an instantly recognizable voice, and of course his melodic story-telling song-writing. A song I did with him that is a great example of his lyric story-telling is 'Thoroughfare Gap,' which I believe is about Neil Young's Lionel trains. On guitar, Stephen has a style of his own and the claws of an eagle. His fingerstyle picking is aggressive and clear. His use of alternate tunings is masterful and sets the tone of many of his songs."

As to criticisms of his perceived attempt to record dance music, Stephen had this to say: "There are elements of disco I really like–the percussion and guitar. I have played on so many Bee Gees songs I don't know which ones I played on and which ones I didn't. 'Cause Barry [Gibb] is an old friend of mine, and I just sat in and played chickum-chit, chickum-chit, a little wacka-wacka guitar, then said, 'Use 'em or don't use 'em, I had a great time. You don't even have to use my name.'"

Of *Thoroughfare Gap*, he continued: "Maybe some of the tunes weren't as good as the others I've written, but I am just messing around trying to find something new. I can't do the same thing for eight years. That's called artistic suicide."

But adding cover version 'Not Fade Away' didn't seem to suggest he was trying much that was new. "I went to see *The Buddy Holly Story* [movie] and the next night I went to the studio and cut 'Not Fade Away.' Kind of a combination of the Stones version and the original version," he explained at the time.

The powerful 'Can't Get No Booty,' mentioned earlier, was addictively catchy, but the remainder of *Thoroughfare Gap* didn't offer nearly enough to suggest the form he had shown when donating some truly great songs for *CSN* was continuing. A *Billboard* chart placing of Number 83 was a damning indictment of Stephen's musical direction that fall.

One area where his career was moving forward lucratively was in the publishing business he had set up with Ken Weiss, who remembered his favorite 'cover story' when pitching to The Pointer Sisters' producer Richard Perry. "I thought a version of

'Turn Back The Pages' would work for the record, but I had to get it to their studio fast. Remember, there were no mp3's or email then. So I marked the song and sent the CBS *Stills* album over there. Ordinarily I would make a separate cassette of the song, but time was of the essence so I sent the album instead. Just as well as it turned out. Nothing more was heard until I got a call from Elektra asking for a license. Only it was for 'As I Come Of Age,' a song also on *Stills* but not one I ever would have pitched to the Pointers. Maybe they listened to the record and liked a different song or they just knew the song. In any event, the album *Energy* was a great success, driven by their version of Bruce Springsteen's 'Fire' and Allen Toussaint's 'Happiness.' I liked their recording of 'As I Come Of Age,' even if in most places it sounded more like a quartet of Graham Nash's than The Pointer Sisters. No matter– royalty statements were very healthy and we were very pleased."

CHAPTER 26
'Southern Cross'

In January 1979, Stephen unveiled the new band he had successfully auditioned back in November. Trusted sidekick, Dallas Taylor, returned, joined by Gerry Tolman, George 'Chocolate' Perry, Carl Pickard, Mike Finnigan, and Delaney & Bonnie vocalist Bonnie Bramlett. So confident was he that rehearsals had delivered what he wanted, Stephen's band played four sets at the Roxy, with a recording truck parked outside the Sunset Strip venue.

The newly formed band then experienced a typical Stills 15-hour recording session at the Record Plant, partly to test out the studio's brand-new 32-track facility. Then it was off to Cuba for an historic appearance at the first American/Cuban music event on the Communist island. As Stephen pointed out, he was, perhaps, the natural choice as the first rock star the Cubans approached, "… because of my language, because I'd lived in Latin America and they knew I was politically astute."

The Havana Jam performance saw Stephen sing a new Spanish composition, 'Cuba Al Fin,' for the 4,000-strong crowd, written in President Fidel Castro's honor. Rita Coolidge, Kris Kristofferson, and Billy Joel were among the other CBS acts on this ground-breaking bill at the Karl Marx Theatre.

Perhaps surprisingly, there's little controversy back in the US about the US artists participating in the Havana Jam, but an unsavory news story did blow up when the Stills band tour rolled into Columbus, Ohio. Also drinking in the Holiday Inn bar that night alongside some of the Stills band members was British new wave artist Elvis Costello. "He had the nerve," Mike Finnigan said of Costello, "to call Ray Charles a blind n****r."

The angry Finnigan, who happened to have his mother with him that night, was dissuaded from thumping Costello, but Bonnie Bramlett had no compunction and decked the Englishman with one punch. The news headlines spread quickly across the US but failed to overshadow the excellent performances the band were accomplishing.

That band, apart from Tolman, Finnigan, and Stills, was no more by June. A major change round in personnel saw Lala, Vitale, and Perry all leave to fulfill other commitments, with Pete Escovedo, Bill Meeker, and Gerald Johnson replacing them on percussion, drums, and bass respectively. Also gone (to The Allman Brothers) was Bonnie Bramlett, with singer Brooks Hunnicutt coming in to great effect on lead vocals on 'Love The One You're With' and other important vocal parts. When Stephen's new California Blues Band played New York's Central Park on July 2, the set list, infused with a number of old blues standards, was worth noting: 'Precious Love,' 'Red House,' 'Go Back Home,' 'Got To Find Love,' 'Love The One You're With,' 'Cuba Al Fin,' 'Part Time Love,' 'For What It's Worth,' 'Cherokee,' 'Turn Back The Pages,'

'Thoroughfare Gap,' 'Come On In My Kitchen,' and 'Woodstock.' The final number was selected to capture the spirit of the day during what was a Woodstock reunion concert, almost 10 years on from Crosby, Stills, Nash & Young's legendary appearance at the original festival. The rest of the set list was anything but a nostalgic look back at past glories. Stephen was pleasing himself with a repertoire leaning heavily on the blues. "The most relaxing, fun tour I've been on in many years," he told the large Central Park crowd.

Now divorced from Véronique Sanson, Stephen had been dating actress Susan Saint James. But in July that relationship had ended. Reportedly introduced to Stephen by *The Life and Times of Grizzly Adams* star Dan Haggerty, Saint James had been sharing Stephen's Bel Air home for months. A month after their engagement was broken off, she told the *Rockford Morning Star*'s Alan Markfield that "our different lifestyles pulled us apart," adding: "I don't figure I'll get over Stephen Stills for a year. I still adore him and can't bring myself to date anyone else at all."

Rarely at home, Stephen continued his seemingly impossible mission to play with every artist he thought he could learn from and joined a bunch of accomplished musicians contributing to Hoyt Axton's hit country album *A Rusty Old Halo*. Jeff 'Skunk' Baxter, Garth Hudson, James Burton, and Dr. John all featured. And 1979 also saw him enter the studio to play with Donnie Dacus again, during sessions for *Chicago 13*. The band recorded–with Stephen on guitar–a version of his 'Closer To You,' which eventually got released on the album's re-issue years later.

Before the year's end, Crosby, Stills & Nash were hurriedly reformed for a final night's performance during a series of high-profile benefit concerts in aid of Musicians United for Safe Energy.

The MUSE gigs, organized by Graham Nash, Jackson Browne, Bonnie Raitt, and John Hall, persuaded Bruce Springsteen, The Doobie Brothers, and Carly Simon and James Taylor to join them for the Madison Square Garden gigs–later released as the *No Nukes* triple album and *No Nukes* movie. A week before the five-night extravaganza, organizers still didn't have a headline act for the final night. Jackson Browne it was who persuaded a reluctant Graham Nash to call Stephen and David Crosby. Nash had reservations CSN were apart for good reasons and would in any case be totally unrehearsed for such a reunion. But the call went out and Crosby and Stills flew to New York and performed shaky but inspired renditions of their greatest hits for the show, album, and movie. In an effort to get the album into record stores in time for Christmas, Graham Nash reportedly worked seven consecutive days in November with just two short naps. With Jackson Browne and a team of engineers also working around the clock, Stephen dropped by to help finish the mixing and the deadline was met.

In 1980, Stephen cut an album in Muscle Shoals that no one will hear. Impounded in the vaults was a stack of material that Columbia didn't approve of. The record company had decided to send him down to Alabama to work with producer Barry Beckett, concerned that the somewhat experimental recordings he had been readying from his home basement sessions, with among others Herbie Hancock, weren't to their liking.

"I was getting tired of wearing so many hats–singer, guitarist, band leader, producer, engineer–and I think I was losing a little perspective on my own music," Stephen told Dave Zimmer. "Barry and I got along great. He was real efficient and allowed me the freedom to explore my musical chops more."

Stephen's assertion that "we had a nice combination of songs" may have been true, but the album never saw the light of day amid little co-operation between Stephen and his record company. However, one gem of a song recorded during the Muscle Shoals sessions would have to wait two years to get released, but it would become a staple in most Stills and CS&N sets in future.

The background story to that gem of a song, 'Southern Cross,' was unusual, as Ken Weiss revealed. "In 1980, I was working with a couple of very good songwriters and performing artists called The Curtis Brothers. The principal songwriters were Michael and Richard Curtis, who were under a previous publishing contract to my company, under which I controlled the rights to a song of theirs called 'Seven League Boots.' I always believed it was a terrific piece, though I was not enamored of the lyrics. So Stephen and I were hanging out one night, playing some music, and I pulled out 'Seven League Boots'–and he loved it–and felt as I did about the lyrics. We sat up for a few hours and then again the next day while he played around with some ideas for it. Finally, he had something that was shaping up quite nicely–a song for which he changed most of the lyrics, and very much the overall attitude of the song– and retitled it 'Southern Cross.' Shortly after, Stephen recorded the song for what would have been his next solo album for CBS."

Years later, 'Southern Cross' would get the singular honor of being selected by a guest on the world's longest-running BBC radio show, *Desert Island Discs*. In 1998, land-speed record-breaker Richard Noble chose the song. A similar accolade would be given at various times to 'Carry On' (chosen by photo journalist Nick Danziger) and 'Season Of The Witch' (selected by writer and naturalist Richard Mabey).

CHAPTER 27
Stephen Stills 'Rock Segovia'

"Nobody talks about a friend of mine like that. It's bullshit journalism. If that writer walked in here right now, I'd deck him." So said Stephen following a particularly critical review by *Rolling Stone* of Graham Nash's March 1980 album *Earth & Sky*.

In a sign that the pair appeared to have fully repaired their previously fractured relationship, a new recording and performing permutation seemed to be forming. Stills and Nash on a bill without Crosby came about by accident when both found themselves on vacation in Hawaii and sharing a stage during a political benefit for JoAnn Yukimura.

Crosby had been isolating himself from his partners. Crosby, Stills & Nash tour manager Mac Holbert later summed up the state of their union at the time: "All three of them had always felt a tremendous responsibility to their audience. David now felt a greater responsibility to his addiction."

Saddened and hamstrung by Crosby's inactivity, Stephen and Graham, with the help of keyboards man Mike Finnigan substituting for Crosby's third vocal part, began recording a new album. Stephen and Graham's optimism that they had good songs didn't cut it with Atlantic, who insisted they wanted a CS&N record, and by Christmas. In the end, the public got a CS&N record. *Replay,* a greatest hits album, was Atlantic's attempt to fill the void. Ironically, *Replay* contained just one Crosby composition, 'Shadow Captain' from the *CSN* album just three years earlier.

Away from the unproductive sessions in the studio, Stephen's California Blues Band completed some dates in Europe and Graham Nash joined the party in Germany.

In August, Stephen got the call to help out Ringo Starr when his old friend was a month into recordings for his eighth solo album, *Stop And Smell The Roses*. Along with Harry Nilsson, Paul McCartney, George Harrison, and Ronnie Wood, he was asked to contribute a song and produce it. "No pressure at all. You're a producer: produce. Aaaargh!" was Stephen's reaction to the request. The result was 'You've Got A Nice Way,' which Stephen, who played guitar and sang backing vocals, had written with Michael Stergis.

Stergis would become Stephen's go-to guy for finishing off songs during this period. Perhaps, more accurately, it was Stergis who would go to Stills–sometimes in the dead of night. "He'd say, 'I have this idea for a song, but it needs a little something else. Wanna come up?' Stergis told Dave Zimmer. "I'd never not go up to Stephen's house, even if it was two or three in the morning. We'd always end up with something ..."

Back in the studio, Stephen and Graham chose Sea West in Hawaii, a small recording facility on the north shore of Oahu, where they rented a seaside home once owned by Elvis Presley.

Stephen was enjoying the escape from pressure and becoming 'Mr Healthy,' as Graham Nash observed. "What I enjoyed about Hawaii was seeing Stephen get up at 10 in the morning, go into the kitchen, drink orange juice, then go play tennis for a couple of hours, swim, then go into the studio–fresh and clear."

The songs were flowing, the mood was good between the two of them, but when they returned for more work at L.A.'s Rudy Records, there was still the nagging problem that Atlantic wouldn't want a Stills & Nash record, however good it sounded.

So with the enduring belief that what they were doing was right, despite the failure of the record company to back them, Stephen and Graham decided to finance the work themselves and keep going.

At Rudy Records, Stephen cut a wonderful version of Traffic's 'Dear Mr Fantasy' on November 17 and enlisted the help of the best vocalists they could get to cover for the absent Crosby on tracks they had stored up. Art Garfunkel produced a terrific third vocal part on Stephen's 'Daylight Again' and Timothy B. Schmit did such a good job on Graham's 'Wasted On The Way' that it fooled Ahmet Ertegun into thinking Crosby was on the recording when the Atlantic boss visited the studio.

Almost at the eleventh hour, Nash made countless calls to the seemingly unavailable Crosby before finally persuading him to come down to Rudy Records and add something to the mix. What happened next was a perfect compromise in some ways. Still physically and mentally out of it, Crosby added little to what Stephen and Graham had been working on for the past year, but he did have two songs he could add to their album. 'Might As Well Have A Good Time' duly got the 'real' Crosby, Stills & Nash vocal treatment, and the excellent, slow-burning 'Delta' was a strong addition to the now 11 tracks.

Daylight Again would now get the Atlantic thumbs-up and was readied for release in early summer 1982.

The year closed on a personal high for Stephen, when his father William Stills turned up at his California Blues Band gig in Baton Rouge, Louisiana, in December 1981. Stephen recalled with some pride the words his father said backstage that night. "Son, you've done all right. You've got my respect."

The year ahead would involve Stephen in a great deal of Crosby, Stills & Nash activity surrounding the release of their new album and an extensive tour. But before either happened, they had to know that David Crosby was in good enough shape to withstand the rigors of touring. One opportunity to gauge how that would work ended badly. On his way to join Stephen and Graham at an anti-nuclear rally, David crashed his car into a fence on the San Diego Freeway, with the consequence that police then discovered drug paraphernalia and a pistol. The resulting fine, probation, and drug rehab order was compounded by a further incident a month later when he was found in possession of another gun and cocaine.

Unbelievably, somehow Crosby added his name to the bill of a very high-profile Stills and Nash booking on June 6 at the Rose Bowl in Pasadena. The Peace Sunday Benefit attracted an astonishing 85,000 people. With Nash on the organizing committee, Stevie Wonder, Tom Petty, Stevie Nicks, Joan Baez, and Bob Dylan were all scheduled to appear, but there was sizeable interest that a rare appearance by Crosby, Stills & Nash would give the event a new angle.

If half those in attendance expected Crosby to make a mess of this reunion they were surprised by the clarity of his vocals, most notably on 'Long Time Gone,' which got an airing exactly 14 years after the assassination of Bobby Kennedy, for whom the song had been written. Guesting on stage with the trio toward the end of the set, at Stephen's invitation, was Dave Mason, who joined the band for 'Hoochie Coochie Man' and 'Rocky Mountain Way.'

The event was not just a huge success for Graham Nash and the message delivered that day, but a vindication of his decision to do whatever he could to get the trio back together.

And so, after some testing rehearsals on a soundstage at Hollywood's Zoetrope Studios, Crosby, Stills & Nash hit the road once again.

"There aren't many bands that can build a catalog of songs over a 14-year period and still have the chops to do 'em all justice. The Stones and The Who have done it. Now we're doing it again. You see, we ain't about to let our rock 'n' roll die yet." Stephen was in combative mood ahead of the tour.

Was he perhaps a little defensive? After all, this was the summer of a second 'British Invasion,' this time fronted by synthesizer-driven hits. Rock 'n' roll had survived the punk revolution, but how relevant could the Woodstock generation be now?

Had Crosby, Stills & Nash now realized that the fans, old and young, that were buying their tickets wanted to hear their unique brand of music and not see them adapt and change to the styles around them?

Stephen had been guilty of adopting some elements of the disco movement years and got badly burned.

In the event, their touring set list this time was chock full of their radio-friendly hits as opposed to numbers where Stephen might have previously cut free on guitar. 'Love The One You're With,' 'Southern Cross,' 'Just A Song Before I Go,' and 'Wasted

On The Way' were all in evidence: 'Black Queen' and some of his heftier material were absent.

But, ahead of the album release, there was a hitch involving Stephen that needed to be addressed urgently. "A problem arose with CBS involving Stephen's previous recording contract," remembered Ken Weiss. "As all parties, especially Atlantic, desperately wanted a new [CS&N] version of 'Southern Cross' on the record, we made a deal with CBS that allowed us to avoid delays with the album's release, and schedule the supporting tour, and a television special. While the easiest–and cheapest–way was to discard the song and release the album, there was no appetite for that–not by Stephen, by CS&N, by Atlantic, and certainly not by me. We knew the track was hot and had to have it on there."

Once that difficulty had been overcome, there was just the little matter of a suitable image for the *Daylight Again* album cover to be agreed.

The severity of Crosby's condition at the time was underlined by the stark fact that those around him were living with the fear he might drop dead at any moment. He was in terrible shape. Little wonder then that *Daylight Again* was the first Crosby, Stills & Nash album not to picture the three of them on the cover. A landscape by artist Gilbert Williams, more in keeping with the other worldly fantasy covers by Roger Dean for his series of Yes albums, seemed incongruous.

With six out of the 11 tracks written or co-written by him–'Turn Your Back On Love,' 'Southern Cross,' 'Since I Met You,' 'Too Much Love To Hide,' 'You Are Alive,' and 'Daylight Again'–the release was something of a triumph for Stephen and no doubt a relief. The process working with Graham had been a happy one, but the outside forces and pressure from Atlantic and Crosby's unavailability had led to lengthy delays and problems. Aside from the revitalization in his career that 'Southern Cross' would give him, the title track would be another timeless Stills classic. Here's how Stephen described the genesis of 'Daylight Again' (and precursor to 'Find The Cost Of Freedom') in his notes for the *CSN* box set.

"I was on tour and we'd done four nights running. I was in Williamsburg, Virginia, drunk and burnt out, and dead tired. At the end of the concert I began to play the song. I didn't have any words, but I continued to play. I closed my eyes and went into a trance and saw a movie. It was a talking dream where I went back 112 years, to the Civil War. The lyrics just flowed through me like an automatic poem. I sang them as they came into my head and a whole story unfolded. When the concert was over I rushed backstage and madly tried to reconstruct the lyrics."

Five years since their last studio album, and 17 months in the making, *Daylight Again* proved to be a success and peaked at US Number 8, with three singles, 'Wasted On The Way,' 'Southern Cross,' and 'Too Much Love To Hide,' hitting Number 9, 18, and 69 respectively. Reviews were not generally as positive as they had been for *CSN*, but as the year unfolded Crosby, Stills, and Nash were happy in the knowledge that their unique brand of music was still making its mark, boosted by two big radio hits and a specially made TV video for 'Southern Cross.'

The tour promoting *Daylight Again,* from Connecticut to Iowa, ran with a short break from July to November, and despite another arrest for Crosby during the break–this time charges were dropped–he came through the tour relatively unscathed. Stephen, meanwhile, lent his support in the re-election campaign for Ted Kennedy in Worcester, Massachusetts. In front of a crowd of 2,000 assembled at a Kennedy family lakeside picnic, he performed 'Teach Your Children.'

With touring done and no possibility of all three getting in the studio anytime soon, there was an opportunity to get a new live album compiled and the band's first video was aired, a year after the MTV era began.

The band's cable TV network video debut on Showtime comprised 80 minutes of footage of Crosby, Stills, and Nash live at the Universal Amphitheatre in L.A. *Daylight Again*, as it was titled, was first broadcast in May and would be repeated down the decades and go to worldwide release on DVD.

Ahead of those releases in 1983, Stephen spent time guesting on Firefall's *Break Of Dawn* album down at Criteria in Miami, and grabbed the chance to cut loose by joining the Grateful Dead for two nights at the Brendan Byrne Arena, East Rutherford, New Jersey. He covered songs by Buddy Holly, Chuck Berry, and The Dixie Cups, along with Stills/Dead versions of 'Black Queen' and 'Love The One You're With.'

A proposed Crosby, Stills & Nash summer tour of Europe was nearly compromised by David Crosby's appearance in a Dallas court, but although found guilty of drug possession and firearms charges, the judge postponed sentencing. So the trio set off for France, but uncertainty was never far away as dates in France, Spain, and Italy were abruptly canceled due to various problems, not least atrocious weather. Finally, they completed their tour in London. It was a show which many speculated at the time might be their final appearance together.

A good number of the Wembley Arena reviews seemed preoccupied with the trio's weight gain, lack of any hair left to cut, or out-of-date Californian idealism. The positives seemed to be grudgingly handed out, but at least most acknowledged the response to one of Stephen's contributions and *The Sunday Times'* Derek Jewell gave this flattering comparison: "The exquisite 'Suite: Judy Blue Eyes' was, predictably, the most rapturously received as Stephen Stills expanded majestically on his recorded guitar interlude like some demonic rock Segovia."

Ignoring the cheap jibes about Crosby's waistline, Stills' balding pate, and Nash's outdated rhetoric from other broadsheet papers, Jewell prefaced his piece by stating: "CS&N sang their keening, exotic harmonies with the diamond-hard dazzle of old and a grip of iron."

Midway through the European tour, Atlantic released *Allies*, a live album from recordings made in Houston, Texas, in 1977, the New Universal Amphitheatre, Universal City, in 1982, and two new numbers: 'Raise A Voice,' penned by Nash and Stills, and 'War Games' by Stills, cut earlier in the year in L.A.

With the *Allies* album doing reasonable business, the tour over, and very little, musically, to occupy him, Stephen did what all keen golfing tourists do while in the UK and headed for a vacation in Scotland. Meanwhile, Graham was occupied with a short reunion with his former British band The Hollies and David Crosby was contemplating a stretch in prison.

CHAPTER 28
Stephen Gets Mad . . .

Stephen began 1984 with a new solo recording deal. Surprisingly, he was back with Atlantic and his mentor and friend Ahmet Ertegun. Atlantic's obsession with CS&N product over lesser financial rewards from Stephen's solo records hadn't changed. "CS&N should not be allowed to peter out," was Ertegun's mantra once again.

Amazingly, CS&N weren't done yet as they reconvened somehow, with the ailing Crosby, for a summer and fall tour. But if Atlantic were hoping for new material to market that Christmas they were disappointed.

What Atlantic did release, though, was a brand-new album from Stephen. *Right By You* hit stores just before the CS&N summer tour in August. Few would argue that it was Stephen's weakest solo offering to date, but there were at least some noteworthy moments courtesy of friends and family. Son Christopher co-wrote 'Stranger,' Graham Nash added vocals to the majority of tracks, Joe Lala was back, and there was some interesting assistance from Jimmy Page. The Led Zeppelin guitarist added some nice touches to three of the album's tracks, and whereas most of the album was recorded in familiar territory in L.A. and Miami, the Page contributions were made in England. "Stephen had visited my aptly-named recording studio, The Sol, on the River Thames in Cookham, Berkshire, so that I might supply some overdubs to his tracks '50/50,' 'Right By You,' and 'Flaming Heart,' which were recorded on the 4th and 5th of May of [1984]," remembered Page. "I greatly respected Stephen's work and would have preferred to have worked with him from source, but as it was, it was just overdubbing the session in England that had originated in the States."

Stephen remembered his visit to Jimmy's place in Berkshire with fondness: "A very sweet guy. Scatterbrain, but he played on the record and was just lovely and we shot snooker all night and then got in a boat on the Thames and rowed up and down. I guess this is how they used to pick up girls, but we were middle-aged geezers by then so it just wasn't going to work," he joked.

Generally, the quality of the material on *Right By You* was stretched thinly. Included was the obligatory Neil Young track he'd spoken of on all future records at one point. This time Stephen chose 'Only Love Can Break Your Heart,' but the disappointing version here was probably what *Billboard* magazine were driving at when they heralded the album by saying it "should enhance its potential for softer rock and pop fans."

Better by far was the old country classic 'No Hiding Place,' which reunited Stephen with Chris Hillman on mandolin and vocals and Joe Lala whacking a cardboard box. With Herb Pedersen (banjo and vocals), Gerry Schett (bass), Bernie Leadon (guitar and vocals), and Mike Finnigan and Graham Nash (both vocals) also chipping in, it felt like a glorious return to Stephen's Manassas days.

In an interview, Chris Stills, who began his song-writing career on *Right By You,* revealed how he first became aware of his dad's rock 'n' roll history.

"I went on the road with my dad a lot as a kid but I didn't pay attention," Chris told *Mojo* in 1998. "I remember running around these big arenas with Graham and David's kids, with 'access all areas' passes, and it was a wild thing. Then I started listening properly and really got off on it. I was 12 when one of my dad's guitar techs taught me to play 'Rocky Raccoon.' After that I just watched his hands all the time. I remember someone playing me 'For What It's Worth' and I thought it was the most amazing thing I had ever heard. I asked what it was and I was told it was my dad. I'd never heard Buffalo Springfield and I said, 'No, my dad's in Crosby, Stills & Nash!' That song was an epiphany for me. I just played it over and over again."

More politically active than ever before, Stephen appeared at a rally in Philadelphia in support of Democrat Presidential candidate Walter Mondale. The October 22 event at JFK Plaza saw him play three or four songs on a bill featuring B.B. King and Peter, Paul & Mary, with whom he concluded proceedings on 'This Land Is Your Land.'

Somehow, Crosby, Stills & Nash were on the road again in the summer of 1985, with two tours stretching from June through to the end of September. The first half of the year saw a wretched Crosby hospitalized for rehab and sent to Dallas county jail, where he was thrown in solitary confinement for allegedly stealing and failing to work.

At times during the concerts that summer Crosby seemed in

a distant world of his own, but did enough to get fans to really root for him when called upon to take a leading role on vocals. At times his bandmates weren't so understanding.

CS&N tour manager Mac Holbert graphically recalled how Stephen handled one incident with Crosby in Norfolk, Virginia, in an interview with the *4WaySite* website: "The last straw for me was one night in Pittsburgh when David was experiencing withdrawals during a show and left the stage in the middle of the concert and came backstage to the dressing room, where I was sitting on the couch going through receipts. He stormed in and screamed, 'Get off the fucking couch.' I leaped up and he assumed a prone position. I sat down across the room from him feeling slightly stunned by this sudden intrusion. Then the door opens and Stephen storms in, walks over to the food table, picks up a five-gallon container of ice water and proceeds to walk across the room and dump the entire contents on Crosby's head. He then threw the empty container aside, yelled at Crosby 'Get your fuckin' shit together!' and exited. I'll never forget the pitiful looks on David's face as he sat trying to understand what had just happened. He looked like a drowned alley cat. He slowly dried himself off and eventually made his way back to the stage, where he finished the show. I knew at that point that he no longer had any control over his addiction."

On July 13, the CS&N touring schedule was interrupted for an appearance in Philadelphia for Live Aid. Neil Young joined them for the first reunion on stage by the quartet in 11 years. Crosby's condition wasn't the only problem the four had to overcome on the day. Sound difficulties spoiled their appearance, but Stephen's chiming guitar carried them through. Wearing what looked like a Rear Admiral's jacket, Stephen found time to catch up with numerous musicians backstage, including Jimmy Page and The Rolling Stones, and even Jack Nicholson.

The media's preoccupation with how much longer Crosby could survive clearly angered an irritated Stephen, who still felt his bandmate could pull through: "I'm sick of this *Perils of Pauline* attitude in the press," he told *Rolling Stone*. "It really makes me ill. It's not like this is some rare disorder or something. You got ball players with the same problem."

Crosby's problem, though, did not go away. The IRS were now on his trail and seized possession of both his home and his boat, leaving him homeless, penniless, and on the run, circumstances that would lead to almost half a year in jail until August 1986.

Maybe it had been the Stills/Young reunion at Live Aid that had started the ball rolling, but in January 1986 Stephen and Neil were back playing together. No Stills-Young Band this time. In Stephen's home basement, the two of them reunited with members of Buffalo Springfield.

A year earlier, after Dewey Martin had re-joined the line-up, which also featured Bruce Palmer, the band was, with Stephen and Neil's permission, renamed Buffalo Springfield Revisited. At The Palomino Hollywood, Buffalo Springfield Revisited featuring Martin and Palmer had Stephen join them on stage for a couple of numbers. Now all five original members, with the addition of Revisited keyboard man Harlan Spector, met at Stills' Encino home, where they jammed in his basement but made no plans to reform officially and commit to concert dates. This short-lived reunion was nevertheless filmed and apparently showed a genial and productive session.

Another reunion with Neil, Graham, and indeed the recently

released David Crosby, came about when all four reprised their Live Aid set, with a couple of additional songs, to play together once more at Neil and wife Pegi's Bridge School Benefit concert in October. The gig, in front of 17,000 at San Francisco's Mountain View Shoreline Amphitheatre, was the first of an annual event to raise money and awareness to provide facilities for children with severe physical and speech impairments. This first show had a bill featuring CSN&Y, Nils Lofgren, Don Henley, Tom Petty, Robin Williams, and Bruce Springsteen.

It was the era of the benefit gig, and a couple more were undertaken before the year was out: at Madison Square Garden, New York, by CS&N, appropriately enough in aid of fighting crack cocaine addiction, and a war veterans' benefit in Kansas City undertaken by Crosby and Stills, this time without Nash.

CHAPTER 29
The Life-Changing 'Treetop Flyer'

Although no stranger to solo acoustic touring, Stephen joined Graham and David for the trio's first unplugged tour in January 1987. The shows were well received and the wayward Crosby appeared to be back to something like his best. Yet another benefit, this time for Greenpeace, in Santa Barbara, found them joined by Neil Young and the reception they got, particularly when Crosby previewed new songs–such as the ode to rehabilitation 'Compass'–was encouraging.

The success of the gig prompted the four to consider entering the studio to cut what amazingly would be the long-awaited follow-up to *Déjà Vu*.

This time it would be a Neil Young initiative, with the idea that a Crosby, Stills, Nash & Young album was just the focus David Crosby needed to complete his transformation.

But it was domestic issues that were top of Stephen's agenda. His son Christopher left the U.S. to attend the American School of Paris and live with his mother Véronique, and Stephen married for the second time.

He and his partner, model Pamela Ann Jordan, had met at a party in Milan and were married at the Georgetown Presbyterian Church in Washington, D.C. in early December. Among those attending the ceremony, and the wedding reception at the International Club, were David Crosby, Graham Nash, Robert Kennedy, Jr., former Eagles guitarist Joe Walsh, former Arizona governor Bruce Babbitt, and former president Jimmy Carter's sons, Chip and Jeff.

The marriage brought with it a move to a new home in Beverly Hills and, soon, a daughter, Eleanor Mary Stills.

On May 14, 1988, there was another big rock event where Crosby, Stills & Nash played a significant part. The 40th anniversary of Atlantic Records was celebrated with a mammoth 13-hour concert featuring all the record company's major acts. Led Zeppelin, Genesis, and the Bee Gees were among the biggest bands that turned out for the concert party of a lifetime at Madison Square Garden, where Crosby, Stills & Nash, introduced by movie star Michael Douglas, performed 'Wooden Ships,' 'Our House,' and 'Suite: Judy Blue Eyes.' Stephen had earlier had the honor of introducing B.B. King. The proceedings were broadcast live on TV and a four-disc album was later released.

Soon after, the trio were off on their annual summer tour, despite the year-long distractions of a new CSN&Y album for Atlantic. With Neil Young in charge of proceedings, the new album had begun with a hazardous-looking re-enactment of the previous attempt. Again, work began with just Neil and Stephen, at first, up at Neil's ranch. Then Graham and David were invited after two weeks to see what they might add. Sessions were harmonious and relaxed as 14 new songs were cut and mixed locally at Redwood Digital, Woodside, A+M Recorders, and Record One. The idea this time was to create a 'real' CSN&Y album, as opposed to the fragmented solo contributions that dominated *Déjà Vu*. "Now I'm the driving force in the band," Neil stated, and having controlled their first studio album, it was Stephen's turn to take a back seat. None of the songs Stephen brought to the project were up to the standard of previous Stills offerings to a CS&N or CSN&Y album. 'Got It Made,' 'Drivin' Thunder,' and 'Night Song' were collaborations with Neil and 'That Girl' with Joe Vitale and Bob Glaub. If this album was to succeed, it would not be on the strength of Stephen's contributions this time. But there were few tracks, aside from David Crosby's heartfelt 'Compass,' from any of the other three that fans might point to as future CSN&Y classics.

The extraordinarily catchy 'American Dream' by Neil was perfect as a pop single and video for MTV, but it didn't sound much like anything Crosby, Stills, Nash & Young had done before. That might have been a good thing, but how would it sound live in concert? If this was an attempt at a new direction, it didn't look like it would lead anywhere. If Neil had at one point in his career metaphorically headed for the ditch, here he had the top down in the fast lane. 'American Dream' was positively jaunty and scathing at the same time.

There would be a couple of live appearances around the November release date of *American Dream*, but no tour by the quartet this time. A UNICEF benefit appearance and a short set at Neil and Pegi Young's second Bridge School Benefit would prove that relations between the four were good, but there seemed to be no enthusiasm for the commitment of a lengthy tour in support of the album. A peak chart position of Number

16 in the *Billboard* 200 reflected the cool reception the record had received in the press. Stephen and Neil's bouncy 'Got It Made' was the first single released, which flopped at Number 69. Belatedly, 'American Dream' was then chosen as the follow-up, but this sank without trace in the US while bizarrely becoming a minor hit (Number 55) in the UK. That territory's best-selling music magazine, *Q*, had conflicting comments when delivering its verdict on the album. "... just the hotchpotch we expected," wrote Tom Hibbert. "Oh, but those harmonies are thoroughly evocative; the codgers' bodies may have run to fat, their faces may have seen lovelier days, but the voices haven't packed in yet."

At this point it would probably be fair to say that Stephen's body was the one in least good shape. The early part of 1989 saw him playing very much smaller venues solo, seemingly waiting for the annual CS&N tour later in the year. As he later admitted, "The end of my enjoyment of success happened in the summer of 1980. And I believe I poured myself into a bottle of whiskey for about 10 years. Pretty much missed the '80s. The trauma of John Lennon being shot in such ridiculous fashion took a great deal of the pleasure out of it for me."

At least the decade finished on a positive note when Crosby, Stills, and Nash were in Europe to witness the celebrations surrounding East Germany's new-found freedom, with the opening of passage between East and West Germany through the Berlin Wall. Three- or four-hundred fans stood in the cold to hear their extraordinary performance in front of the Brandenburg Gate, arranged at short notice with the blessing of the West Berlin police.

"We just showed up yesterday and said, 'Hi, we're here, we want to sing,'" Stephen told the quickly gathering crowds.

Later, he admitted, "We blew 20 grand just to stand on the

wall. But we wanted to do as much as we could to show our support."

On the hastily erected stage, Crosby, Stills & Nash performed a brand-new song, encouraging the forthcoming initiative to dismantle the wall. 'Chippin' Away' was released as a one-off single in Germany, but didn't have much traction beyond the vibe of the day.

The Nineties began with Crosby, Stills & Nash in the studio recording their fourth album as a trio. For whatever reason, the recordings once again failed to see much of the group doing what everyone felt they did best–singing those pitch-perfect harmonies into one mic all together. The speedily recorded album seemed doomed from the outset. Where their previous CS&N album *Daylight Again* necessitated the need for guest vocalists to fill the void left by the often absent Crosby, here they had the opportunity to at least create the special three-part harmony for real. However, the vocal performances failed to match their own high standards. The strength of some of the songs on *Daylight Again* was not replicated here either.

There were some positives: *Live It Up,* as it would be called, did have some intriguing guest musicians to keep things interesting. The small contributions from Roger McGuinn, Peter Frampton, and Bruce Hornsby weren't enough to save the project from being a bland and perhaps even terminally damaging release. Perhaps the one saving grace was Stephen's 'Haven't We Lost Enough?'–a truly great acoustic song made for the three-part harmony that CS&N delivered perfectly on this one track. Another classic Stills lyrical melodrama, the song was the result of Stephen's collaboration with REO Speedwagon's Kevin Cronin years earlier.

"Kevin Cronin and I were living in Encino, and in similar conditions romantically, that is the end of relationships. And while commiserating with each other one night we decided to write a song. We finished it in the studio one night several years later, and recorded it the next day," Stephen wrote for the notes to the *CSN* box set. "One of my best efforts in years," he concluded.

The public and press response to *Live It Up* when released in June was poor. David Crosby told *Record Collector* soon after release that the band themselves were generally unhappy with the project. "Stephen likes to call it the *Live It Down* record," he revealed.

The *Billboard* chart peak of Number 54 for *Live It Up* said much about CS&N's current disappearing act in the music scene. It wasn't just the dearth of any really great new songs that they were suffering from. There seemed to be a distinct lack of any real musical direction in what they were trying to achieve at the time. Inexplicably, embracing the MTV era proved to be the direction they would benefit most from.

The *MTV Unplugged* format was a perfect fit for a band driven by three-part harmonies and Stephen's strong acoustic guitar-playing. So it proved on September 30 when they performed a nine-song repertoire for the show at New York City's Ed Sullivan Theater. The song selection was dominated by Stephen's 'Helplessly Hoping,' '4+20,' 'Daylight Again,' 'Find The Cost Of Freedom', 'Suite: Judy Blue Eyes,' and 'Southern Cross.'

In an interview for the Rock and Roll Hall of Fame, Stephen recalled: "I was so sick I couldn't talk. I couldn't get anybody to realize it was really stupid to do this when I was sick. So, we did not do that well, and it should have been one of our finer moments."

He may not have been up to par for this important

TV appearance, but Stephen's somewhat restrained vocal performance was refreshingly good considering his reluctance to perform at all.

There was a fascinating guest appearance by Stephen a few weeks later on a new TV show, *The Inside Track*, hosted by Graham Nash. Judy Collins was Graham's main guest, and during the section of the show when he reminisced about the Sag Harbor days back in 1969, on came Stephen and sat down without a word to play guitar on the song he had suggested Judy include, 'Someday Soon,' on her *Who Knows Where The Time Goes* album. There was a wonderfully happy vibe to the broadcast, which clearly showed two old friends and accomplished musicians at the top of their form, enjoying each other's company.

Stephen's vocal pipes were in demand in February 1991 when, as one of 100 choir members, he contributed to charity record 'Voices That Care' in Burbank, California. Recorded by a supergroup of musicians, entertainers, and athletes, the single and supporting documentary music video were intended to help boost the morale of U.S. troops involved in Operation Desert Storm and benefit the International Red Cross organization. The single hit Number 11 on the *Billboard* Hot 100. There was another call for Stephen's services this month when Tatum O'Neal organized husband John McEnroe's 32nd birthday party. A huge stage was erected on Malibu Beach while McEnroe was playing Pete Sampras in an important match in Philadelphia. Anxiously, Tatum rang to check the tennis player and rock fan wouldn't be late for his own party, but happily McEnroe arrived in time to jam with an all-star band featuring Stephen, Bruce Springsteen, and another fan of Stephen's, movie star Bruce Willis. Sadly, no recordings appear to exist of the reportedly fabulous job the band made of their rendition of 'C.C. Rider.'

More extensive touring by Crosby, Stills & Nash in 1991 meant a trip to Australia and Japan in the spring. It was Stephen's first visit to Australia since the Manassas flying visit, and this time the experience was a good deal more relaxed. Reports suggested that the concert appearances Down Under were some of their best yet.

On a more personal level, 1991 was a significant year of change for Stephen. His 20-year association with publisher and former personal manager Ken Weiss ended amicably, with both remaining good friends in the years ahead. It was also a period where he felt the need to cut another bunch of songs, which he decided to release on his own Gold Hill label. The resulting album, *Stills Alone*, although disjointed, had an interesting collection of songs. He chose three covers of favorites–Lennon & McCartney's 'In My Life,' Bob Dylan's 'Ballad Of Hollis Brown,' and Fred Neil's 'Everybody's Talkin''–and a mixture of mostly unreleased originals from a variety of periods throughout his career. Recorded mostly alone, hence the title, *Stills Alone* was cut at Audio Vision, Miami, and the Record Plant. In the great scheme of things, the project wasn't planned–it just happened, as he explained to *Record Collector*: "I was bored. I'd just finished a tour, and my voice was in good shape, my chops were up, and I just said, 'I've got to get something on tape here, or else I'm gonna go nuts.' So I went into the studio and sang for a week. I did a couple more out west, and then said, 'Let's put this out and see what happens.'"

The most interesting of the covers was a reduced version of a classic, due to circumstances beyond his control. "When I was cutting Dylan's 'Hollis Brown,' I was trying to figure out how to cut the song down, but I didn't want to leave any of the verses out. Then the wind from the air conditioning takes the middle sheet of paper and blows it away, and that was the edit! Edited by the wind!"

The high points on the album were undoubtedly new recordings of songs such as 'Treetop Flyer' and 'Isn't It So.' The former was certainly the case for one young fan. In fact the whole album was cited as a life-changing release for Ray LaMontagne. The chart-topping singer-songwriter was a shoe factory worker in Lewiston, Maine, back in 1991 when his radio alarm clock woke him as usual for work at 4am. On this particular morning, the music he awoke to was Stephen's 'Treetop Flyer.'

"It's like a light went off and everything became very clear to me," LaMontagne recalled later. "That period of my life was a dark, dark time, but I knew at that moment exactly what I wanted to do; I wanted to play music."

LaMontagne skipped work that day, headed for the nearest record store, bought *Stills Alone*, then sold his VW van to buy a Martin guitar. His alarm clock epiphany began a hugely successful career in the music business.

The August release of *Stills Alone* didn't encourage many others to buy the album, but the next project that he had a hand in was very much more considered in its development. The long-awaited and inevitable *CSN* box set hit stores a month later. Here was a release to excite all die-hard fans of the band. Of the 77 tracks selected and produced by Graham Nash and Gerry Tolman, 26 were rare or unreleased recordings. The non-musical content in the beautifully packaged accompanying book, containing song-writing notes by the writers of every track, brought new insight into old favorites.

There was obvious satisfaction and pride at what had been captured on the box set, and the upswing in positive reviews and opinions continued throughout stage appearances. Particularly gratifying was the reception the band received on their 1992 tours. The London leg of their European tour was the most uplifting. After a nine-year absence, British fans were clearly happy to see the trio in such great form during two sold-out nights at the Hammersmith Odeon, as *Q* magazine reported. "The audiences were ecstatic," wrote Robert Sandall, "the celebs were out in force (CS&N's guest list included Dustin Hoffman, Bob Hoskins, Terry Gilliam, Dave Gilmour, and Boy George), and today's broadsheets are uniformly appreciative."

Indeed they were, with *The Times*' Alan Jackson chiding Crosby and Nash a little but highlighting Stephen's role: "A handsome Stephen Stills eschewed such self-depreciating small talk, preferring to allow his guitar to speak for him on a spell-binding coda to 'Suite: Judy Blue Eyes.'"

Tellingly, there was a new, raw honesty about Stephen when he told Sandall: "I just want to please the folks, you know. In an acoustic show some of the new material, either by virtue of how it's written or how it's arranged, doesn't come off as good as the old stuff. Maybe it isn't as good."

There was a new dynamic in the band that had Graham Nash as leader and chief spokesperson now, but Stephen's relationship with the press was flourishing. There was a growing respect for his restraint in interviews and journalists began to warm to his self-depreciation. The ego had landed, even disappeared, and been replaced with a good deal of wit and humor that would increasingly endear him to the press. The European tour was such a success that the trio returned again before the end of the year, this time including a date at London's Royal Albert Hall, where they had first wowed a UK audience in 1970.

Shortly before the return to Europe, Stephen put Susan Nash in touch with one of the commanding officers of the Pacific Fleet to enable her to hire a helicopter full of emergency supplies and get permission to land it on the island of Kauai. The supplies were for the people devastated by Hurricane Iniki, and Crosby, Stills, and Nash followed this up by raising more than $1 million for the Hawaiian people affected by the storm, the proceeds coming from two acoustic concerts in Honolulu and one on Kauai.

Following work in the studio at various times throughout the first half of 1994, a new CS&N group album was readied for release in July. *After The Storm* was actually finished when Stephen came up with another track, 'Only Waiting For You,' which they recorded when a break in their tour schedule allowed. The album was still released on August 16, with the new track kicking off proceedings nicely. Significantly for Stephen, this album included contributions from son Christopher and daughter Jennifer. Jen added vocals to 'After The Storm' and Chris played acoustic guitar on a cover of The Beatles' 'In My Life,' Spanish guitar on 'Panama,' and piano on 'These Empty Pages.' The other innovation on the record was the recruitment of a producer from outside the band, Glyn Johns. His overall direction was for Crosby, Stills & Nash to play to their strengths. "Bands that have been around as long as they have naturally try to change with the times and adapt what they do," he told the *Los Angeles Times*. "But I felt now would be a great time to have a record that related a little more to what they used to be. That's what I set out to achieve, and they readily climbed on board."

It sounded like a sensible policy, but the *Billboard* chart stats did not make great reading when *After The Storm* hit the record stores. With a chart peak of Number 98, it looked like the public had turned their back on the new material CS&N were pushing.

If Glyn Johns' idea had been to point the band in the direction of "what they used to be," they pretty soon got the perfect opportunity to try to recapture the vibe surrounding CS&N during their first year together when the organizers of Woodstock II booked them for the massive 25th anniversary festival.

Staged this time at Winston Farm, Saugerties, New York, the event was blanked by Neil Young, who took against the whole principle of the August 13/14 weekend. Newer acts Nine Inch Nails, Metallica, and Red Hot Chili Peppers joined Woodstock veterans like CS&N and Santana in celebrating the world's most famous festival's big birthday. It was also CS&N's 25th anniversary, and with age came the need for a more comfortable experience than the band endured back in 1969. "We just want to arrive early and get a good parking space," joked Stephen to the *Los Angeles Times*. "We've got a much nicer tour bus this time around, and as long as I'm on the bus I know I'll be comfortable."

The band inevitably included songs in their set list that they had played at the first festival, but it was the closing number, 'Woodstock,' and a thrilling 'Déjà Vu'–with John Sebastian reprising his harmonica part on the recorded track–that received the best reaction from the huge crowd of 350,000.

By the end of 1994, Crosby, Stills & Nash were forced to take an indefinite break. David Crosby had been told that unless he underwent a liver transplant soon he would die. Preparations for the operation in late November were worryingly abandoned when the liver prepared for the transplant was discovered to be cancerous. A second liver and operation fortunately proved successful, but a long recovery and recuperation period for the 53-year-old meant that the trio would not be working together again any time soon.

Away from the music, in 1996 Stephen got married for the third time. "I finally got my best friend to marry me," he said of his partner, Kristen Hathaway. The 33-year-old recording studio manager and Stephen chose the Ritz-Carlton in Palm Beach, Florida, as their wedding venue, a popular hotel Crosby, Stills & Nash had previously visited. But it was a long way from home in L.A. "It was far enough away from everyone so that basically we could insult all our friends by not inviting anyone," joked Stephen to the *Indianapolis Star*.

Unhappy family news was sadly what followed next when Stephen's 26-year-old son Justin was critically injured. In a coma as a result of a snowboarding accident near Mount Charleston, west of Las Vegas, in February 1997, his subsequent treatment and recovery was featured in an episode of Discovery Health's TV documentary series *Trauma: Life In The ER*. Justin's mother was Harriet Tunis, with whom Stephen had settled a paternity suit back in 1972, shortly after Justin was born.

Lack of activity on the road or in the studio meant time for other new projects, and Stephen continued to sporadically work with different media. A year earlier he had busied himself converting a song written for the *Stills Alone* album, 'Isn't It So,' into the theme tune for hit TV series *Second Noah*. Now he was venturing into movie work. His recut of 'Love The One You're With' (more like the live shuffle R&B version, according to Stills) and 'Nacio Para Correr,' co-written and performed with Joe Vitale, plus some additional instrumental recordings, were included in the movie *Prefontaine*, the biopic of athlete Steve Prefontaine.

The plans for CS&N to record another studio album and tour in the summer seemed to have him in a settled phase, with the "screaming egos," as he put it, a very distant memory. "We're too old for that, all the prickly pears are in the Eagles."

CHAPTER 30

A Double Hall Of Fame Induction

"If I had to come in a rowboat and stand outside, I would have," said Stephen of the invitation to attend his double induction into the Rock and Roll Hall of Fame. It was a pointed comment reflecting the no-show of his Buffalo Springfield partner Neil Young, who rejected the opportunity to join the celebrations.

Two days before the 1997 Hall of Fame shindig in Cleveland, Ohio, Crosby, Stills & Nash were back on stage across the city remembering a horrific event 27 years earlier. With 'Ohio' as the key point in their set, they performed an outdoor free concert at Kent State University, in memory of the infamous killing of four students shot dead by the National Guard during anti-war and anti-government protests. The ticketless concert, held after the annual commemoration ceremony, attracted a crowd of 7,000.

The Rock and Roll Hall of Fame Buffalo Springfield and Crosby, Stills & Nash inductions on May 6, 1997 were overshadowed to an extent by Neil Young. Sending a fax to VH1, his bandmates, and the Rock and Roll Hall of Fame, in which he refused to accept his Buffalo Springfield award personally, his lengthy statement drew to a close with the words, "Although I accept the honor in the name of Rock 'n' Roll, I decline to take part in this presentation and be trotted out like some cheap awards show."

In other respects this was still no happy reunion for Buffalo Springfield.

With Neil absent and separate tables for the remaining band members who did attend, there was no celebratory live performance to mark the occasion. Bruce Palmer and Stephen weren't even talking to one another. Whether Stephen was consumed by the honor of being inducted twice in one evening, or whether he was preoccupied with the business of playing with CS&N on stage, his good humor surfaced in a quip to Richie Furay about Neil Young's no show that reminded the pair of their buddy's departure from the band back in the Sixties: "Hey, Rich, he quit on us again!"

Despite the rather strained and truncated celebration of the career of Buffalo Springfield, Stephen did manage to play the band's classic single 'For What It's Worth' (joined on stage by Tom Petty, who had inducted Buffalo Springfield) during the Crosby, Stills & Nash set, a song list which also included 'Wooden Ships,' '49 Bye-Byes,' and 'Teach Your Children.' The trio's old friend James Taylor inducted Crosby, Stills & Nash and Stephen became the first person to be inducted twice on the same night in the history of the prestigious awards.

If Stephen's joy in making rock 'n' roll history was tempered by the absence of Neil Young, he didn't show it. And Neil wasn't the only notable no-show that night. Joni Mitchell, also inducted, cited personal pressures associated with her reunion with a daughter she had given up for adoption 30 years ago, and Graham Nash accepted the award on her behalf.

The double induction into the Rock and Roll Hall of Fame was evidently a watershed moment that encouraged Stephen to reflect, with some experience, on the trials and tribulations of being an ageing rock star.

He opened up with some revealing honesty when interviewed by Greg Kot of the *Chicago Tribune*.

"Being middle-aged and on stage you're a target if you're not one of those obsessive people who runs all the time and stays in shape. I always felt as a reader of reviews that it's much more fun for the music critic to write the carve-up-the-turkey review. And you sound too much like a fan if you write a gushing review. So I understand why some reviews are the way they are. I just saw a writer the other day who hammered us a few years ago and I said, 'Hey, long time no talk to. And about that review you wrote a while back ... you were right.' All my entourage was whining about this review and I said, 'Hey, read it again. It says we were sloppy, we were out of tune, we wandered around between songs as if we didn't know where we were–and we didn't!' Some kid asked me whether I was disappointed when I see some acts go through the motions and I said, 'Son, everyone goes through the motions at some point. I've seen the touring schedules of some bands and I know after a day of travel and doing interviews and then trying to play, they're going to go through the motions.'"

Around the same time, he also defended an artist's right to do whatever he wanted to do with the music he or she had created. Agitated that he was being accused of 'selling out' when 'For What It's Worth' was used in a padlock commercial, he had this to say: "Either incredibly rich entertainers or incredibly poor ones argue about this," Stephen began, "and I'm stuck somewhere in the middle. A commercial is a commercial: big friggin' deal. The mechanicals [publishing fees he receives] are real nice and help out. God forbid if David Crosby gets sick again and I can't tour anymore, or something happens where I can't get around, what am I going to live on? I'm going to be living on mechanicals. So I don't want to hear it."

There was to be yet another induction ceremony in September. This time Bruce Willis did the honors, inducting Stephen into the RockWalk outside Hollywood's Guitar Center, at 7425 Sunset Boulevard.

"As a founding member of Buffalo Springfield and a cornerstone of Crosby, Stills & Nash, he left a mark on an entire generation. He continues to play today and he played over 60 countries last year. He continues to be a creative and innovative force, and I'm very proud to call him my friend," announced Bruce Willis to the hundreds of fans gathered on the street.

"I have pounded these pavements myself before I could afford a car," responded Stephen, "so I know what it feels like to look at the sidewalk, and this is really neat."

Perhaps an even bigger accolade shortly afterward was the call to work with hugely popular hip-hop outfit Public Enemy. The result would be a single release, 'He Got Game,' from the soundtrack to the Spike Lee movie of the same name. The track incorporated parts of Stephen's 'For What It's Worth' and ended up as a Public Enemy featuring Stephen Stills collaboration. The New York rappers invited Stephen to revisit his famous guitar part, add vocals, and appear in the video for the single. "That was really cool," Stephen admitted later. "It started out that it was gonna be a sample, but one thing led to another. I was really happy to be part of that kind of crossover," he told *The Denver Post*'s Mark Harden.

According to Stephen, Public Enemy phoned in their parts and it was Spike Lee who put the whole thing together. "They couldn't quite get the beat to fit together so they needed me to come in and basically redo the part and not make the changes. I started singing it like I'd been currently singing it and the guy went, 'Mmmm, can you sing it more like you did back then?' 'Oh, so you want me to sing like a scared 20-year-old?' So I did a perfect imitation of myself, which is hard to do."

"[Spike Lee] couldn't have been nicer, and neither could the guy that I actually did the session with," Stephen recalled. "They were complete gentlemen, but they all had these lurid stories about these guys walking in dropping the 45 on the console. I guess I'm getting the mix right!"

There was definitely an exciting edge to the filming of the video too. Stephen remembered playing his part, as directed, outside the Saint Joseph Church of God in Christ with some hilarity. "We were doing the video shoot and they had me down in the neighborhood with my cowboy boots and I'm standing there with a '57 Strat, which, even then, was worth quite a pile of money. And they want a shot from across the street of me just playing. So I'm sitting there, I'm all alone, and this tricked-out Honda pulls up and these guys with gold teeth come pouring out and they come and surround me, and I said, 'Should I be afraid?' and he said, 'I am.' This black guy, 'I am.' He said, 'Spike Lee? Spike Lee, okay cool,' and they got back in their car. That was right in the middle of all the drive-bys down here, so it's like, they want to film while I get assassinated. Is this a career move to get killed?

"I thought it was fun and they treated me like a king, and the other thing about those guys, when they sample, them guys pay! I mean you don't have to ask once and you get the cheque the next day and they will not tolerate any Hollywood accounting. I wish they could come and teach the rest of the business.

"I loved it ['He Got Game']. Everybody thinks about the song ['For What It's Worth'], it's some special thing–oh so meaningful and grand and special. Bollocks! It was just its time. It was a thought and I threw it out there and it's lasted all these years."

Around the time of the 'He Got Game' track and movie release in late spring, Crosby, Stills & Nash cut some songs for a new album that Stephen said "will likely come together in little bursts."

"I think it's more efficient. You go in and work on what you know you're going to do, but then get out of there and take stuff on the road and play it live a little bit.

"If you can sell a brand-new song from the stage, then you're somewhere already," he told *Mojo*'s Dave DiMartino.

Meanwhile, work on a comprehensive Buffalo Springfield box set had been reaching its conclusion, with Neil Young at the helm. When Stephen and Richie Furay got the call out to Neil's ranch to assess the selection, Stephen brought Neil up to speed with what CS&N had been up to in the studio. When he heard a new song Stephen was readying for an album and discovered the three were funding the project themselves, his curiosity piqued. Never a fan of even the slightest corporate record company pressure, Neil was impressed with the unhurried control Crosby, Stills, and Nash were using to create something new. The relaxed methods encouraged him to drop in on their studio recordings and he was soon sharing his own new songs with them. A gently evolving CSN&Y project was taking shape again, almost by accident.

CHAPTER 31
Looking Forward

"The songs we were doing were a little long on mellow. I thought we needed a bit more energy, so I asked Neil if he would come down to play on a few tracks" was how Stephen explained the trio transformed into a quartet once more.

"Mellow" remained a good description of what the four of them were recording at Neil's Redwood Digital (the Neil-penned songs were done here) and at Conway Studios, Ocean Studios, Stray Gator Sound, and Ga Ga's Room in L.A.

It was immediately evident that the songs Neil was bringing to the project were of a more intimate, down home quality than on the quartet's last album *American Dream*. And matching the songs, the atmosphere around them was very much better. On Neil's 'Slowpoke,' CSN&Y captured the perfect, but never too perfectly recorded, harmonies that had sanitized some previous recordings. Here there was a simple rustic rawness to this and other Neil Young songs that sparkled brightly, with the right amount of CS&N polish on top. Neil's favorite session musicians (Ben Keith on pedal steel and Spooner Oldham on keyboards, among others) brought sureness of touch to proceedings, but his biggest contribution to the record was his recording method. No overdubbing, no reworking or fixing glitches, and no multiple takes. The organic 'real' feel they had briefly captured on a song like 'Helpless' from *Déjà Vu* all those years ago had been rediscovered. "That was sort of like that last Springfield album," Stephen pointed out. "Neil came in with finished pieces, and then we complemented them, and then vice versa. And then we cut some new ones. And it almost happened. We were just a couple of songs short."

The lack of any truly stand-out songs from Stephen accounted for some of that shortfall. While Graham Nash delivered the stately 'Heartland' and the impressively catchy 'Someday Soon' and David Crosby delivered some of his best vocals yet on his very personal 'Dream For Him,' Stephen's tracks left little lasting impression. The exception was 'No Tears Left.' While musically less than riveting, it did at least have a biting lyrical intensity not expressed by Stephen in a while. The song was an indictment of how his golden Woodstock generation may have gradually turned out to be false Gods to the young generation of today. "Put yourself in their shoes," he told *Mojo*'s Dave DiMartino, "and listen to all this preaching and shit that they're having to endure from our generation. Then you add the political reality that they're basically pissed at us that from the '70s on we spent all of our money and then all of their money. I found myself on their side–I'm still enough of a rebel, enough of a miscreant, you know?"

On a largely acoustic album, Stephen may have wanted Neil's rock and roll side to come out to play and beef up the album a shade. But Neil was content to deliver his quieter side. His song quota constituted the gentle, almost fragile, 'Looking Forward,' 'Out Of Control,' 'Queen OfThem All,' and the aforementioned 'Slowpoke.' It was left to Stephen to counter with–in addition to the strident 'No Tears Left'–the uptempo 'Faith In Me' and the lyrically scathing 'Seen Enough,' inspired by the structure of Bob Dylan's 'Subterranean Homesick Blues.'

Stephen acknowledged that being around Neil Young once more had helped stretch his own thought processes when writing again. "Having Neil back is just so great for me," he admitted.

The album's 12 tracks were all new. There were some nearly great songs, but the overriding quality was in lead vocals and harmonies as good as any they had done as a quartet before. It would have been intriguing to hear those terrific vocals on two extra songs they experimented with rehearsing up for the album. At the press conference later they revealed that the old Byrds hit 'Turn Turn Turn' and Buffalo Springfield's 'Rock and Roll Woman'–with Joe Walsh guesting on guitar–might have graced the final selection.

Progress on the project was slow, but despite Graham Nash breaking both legs in a waterskiing accident and a last-minute change of title from *Heartland* to *Looking Forward*, the album got released on October 26, 1999. And, notwithstanding Graham's disability, the physical state of the quartet must have been vastly better than it had been during the making of *American Dream* as, astonishingly, this time a tour was rumored, discussed, and then booked.

A San Francisco press conference at the St. Francis Hotel saw the four announce a 41-date CSNY2K tour to kick off in the New Year.

Looking Forward, packaged with an album cover shot of Stephen's three-year-old son Henry in the recording studio, wouldn't make the impression hoped for and it stalled at Number 26 on the *Billboard* 200 (Number 54 UK). *The Los Angeles Times* thought that *Looking Forward* "demonstrates anew that old hippies don't burn or fade away, they just turn insufferably preachy," in a reference maybe more directed at Stephen's songs.

But there must have been a core to the new material that had encouraged optimism within the band, and the resulting tour would kick-start a healthy and happy period of cooperation between Crosby, Stills, Nash, and Young that would sustain them through many years on the road together.

CHAPTER 31
CSNY2K

Health, happiness, and togetherness were given as key reasons for the commitment to tour once again. Stephen had another explanation for why CSNY2K was happening 25 years after their last tour together as a foursome. "We also had to wait for another presidential impeachment and an unpopular war," he joked, referencing the Nixon era and newly elected President George W. Bush.

"Every once in a while we fly in formation, and that's what we're doing now," was the positive description of Crosby, Stills, Nash & Young at the beginning of the 21st century made by Neil Young. And as leader of the project, he also gave the press at New York's Pierre hotel an insight into what fans might expect to see when they turn out for the 35-city US tour. "I mean, this band can sing like The Byrds and jam like the Dead," he said.

Playing large arenas, the tour would last from January to April, harnessing all the new technology of better sound systems and big screens, attracting 551,000 fans, and grossing $42 million in ticket sales in the process.

With a good deal of faith in their latest material, the four would mix old and new on the CSNY2K tour, with Stephen's '49 Bye-Byes' from *Crosby, Stills & Nash* and 'Faith In Me' from *Looking Forward* played at every gig. The four were enjoying themselves. There were to be no petty arguments and no break-up, leaving the door open for more reunions in future.

On the face of it, there was nothing remarkable about the next Crosby, Stills & Nash tour that began in August 2001. Admittedly, they hadn't hit the road as a trio in four years, but they were in good shape and raring to go, invigorated by the receptions and feelings of warmth generated by the CSNY2K shows. One month into the tour and in Denver, Colorado, for another show on the 27-city tour, Crosby, Stills, and Nash, like the rest of the world, were shocked by the news coming in from New York on September 11th. Responding to phone calls in their Hotel Teatro rooms, they watched the terrorist attacks as the whole scenario played out live on TV.

The full horror of the attacks meant that America began to shut down, and the tour was simply the last thing on the trio's minds as they headed home to L.A. to be with their families. In the event, only three dates were canceled and Crosby, Stills & Nash were the go-to band of troubadors once more, reflecting the news and trying their best to soothe the nation on TV appearances post-9/11, such as *The Tonight Show With Jay Leno*. Before resuming the tour proper, they played a poignant concert at their 'local' Greek Theatre, where Stephen's usual show-closer, 'Find The Cost Of Freedom,' began proceedings this time.

When CSN&Y took to the road a year later, every ticket price donated a dollar to the various charities set up to help the victims of 9/11. This tour saw an even greater unity among the four of them, borne out of the tragic events they'd witnessed and reacted to.

Stephen's involvement with Neil carried through to the release of the *Buffalo Springfield* box set in 2002. "Listening to it all with Neil, it was really overwhelming," said Stephen. "I had sent all of my stuff to [Neil's] ranch years ago … so that nobody would buy the studio, find it, and say it was theirs. But I hadn't listened to it for a long, long time. I was absolutely overwhelmed. There was so much talent in that band. For an old guy like me, getting a little long in the tooth, it really kicked up my confidence," he revealed to *Post-Gazette* staff writer John Hayes.

Another boost to his confidence or knock to his ego, depending on how he took the news, came with the publication of *Rolling Stone* magazine's 2003 list of the 100 Greatest Guitarists Of All Time. Stephen was ranked Number 28, sandwiched between Mark Knopfler and The Stooges' Ron Asheton.

Ken Weiss saw at close quarters just how 'great' Stephen's dexterity on guitar could be. "Watching him play made it clear he was not just someone who practiced a lot. No, it was far more than that. The connection he had to the guitar in his hands was perfect, his hand and fingers seemed to know just what to do to make it sound as it did–and he appeared to do so without trying very hard. It was magic. I never saw anyone play as he did–not before or since–with the possible exception of Jimi Hendrix. The difference, however, was while Hendrix played with highly sexualized reckless abandon, although perfectly executed, Stephen played with fully structured and seemingly controlled phrasing–even as he apparently flew around the neck by the seat of his pants. That combination of structure and instant invention at once was quite a feat; and he did it brilliantly–every night."

The midway point in the decade saw Stephen admitting he was feeling his age. He was finding it increasingly hard to recognize his younger self and attributed his calmer, less angry, approach to life as the by-product of a happy family set-up. As many do in their sixties, he was increasingly drawn back to his childhood surroundings in the south and bought a home in Gainesville, Florida, in 2004. That same year, in line with the Stephen Stills Children's Music Project, he donated $100,000 toward the construction of a hall for the University of Florida's marching band.

Although he admitted to happily losing 10 of his 60 years when he walked out on stage, he still found the touring part of his life difficult. "If it wasn't for the audience, it wouldn't be worth doing at all," he said during a radio interview. "You can be in a $2-million bus, but after three days it's a bus."

The deaths of a few close friends and associates was also taking its toll. In spite of their past estrangement, Bruce Palmer's death in 2004 was still a sad moment to reflect on. "He had a style with the bass. He had a Bill Wyman kind of Motown feel put underneath everything, and it made it work for me," he'd said of his former bandmate.

Palmer had been the heart, soul, and glue that had stabilized Buffalo Springfield, despite his own erratic personal behavior.

A greater personal shock for Stephen was the news that Gerry Tolman had been killed in a road accident in Los Angeles in 2005. Manager of Crosby, Stills & Nash and Stephen individually, Tolman also played guitar with Stephen's band and wrote, performed, and produced with Crosby, Stills & Nash.

On a happy note, his children were now finding a measure of success themselves in their music careers. In 2004, daughter Jennifer Stills was a guest vocalist on Ray LaMontagne's critically acclaimed debut album *Trouble*, and her song 'Good Intentions' was included in the soundtrack to the movie *The Prince & Me*. Son Chris, who had already released his debut album *100 Year Thing* on Atlantic Records in 1998, now readied a follow-up, *Chris Stills*. Honest enough to admit that he had secured some gigs on account of his name, Chris also illustrated the problems associated with having a rock star father. "I had an interview with some lady in New York, and she just refused to talk about my record and just wanted to talk about my dad and his cooking," said an exasperated Stills Jr to the *Los Angeles Times*.

"When I told my dad what I wanted to do, he said, 'Just go to college, please, don't do what I did, look at me!' "He was totally against it," said Chris, who never did make it to college. "He tells me to keep eyes in the back of my head, don't trust anybody, and keep your publishing [rights]."

Always well advised in looking after his own publishing, Stephen's first solo album of the 21st century, *Man Alive!*, was released in the fall of 2005 on Titan Pyramid Records. It was the first, and will possibly be his last album cover to include artwork– a shaky self-portrait sketch–by the man himself. Where it differed most from its predecessor, *Stills Alone,* 15 years earlier, *Man Alive!* enlisted the help of just about every American musician that had sessioned for him before. Russ Kunkel, Joe Lala, George Terry, George 'Chocolate' Perry, Mike Finnigan, Joe Vitale, Herbie Hancock, Graham Nash, and Neil Young were all credited. There were even some backing vocals by daughter Jennifer.

The mixture of songs collected over quite a period of time

meant that some had been hijacked from the *Man Alive!* album for other projects. “Had [CS&N] not reconciled, ‘Southern Cross’ would have been on it and a couple of other ones,” Stephen was reported as saying in an interview with Alan Sculley.

“Some of the other things that are part of our show would have been on it, and it would have been finished a long time ago. But it wouldn’t be the same. It was what it was. It is what it is.”

Man Alive! featured Neil Young playing guitar on ‘Round The Bend’ and ‘Different Man.’ The latter featured Stephen and Neil howling to great effect on a duet of the traditional country-blues number.

‘Round The Bend’ was a tough track to get right and get the best of Stephen and Neil’s guitar work, as Stephen explained: “He said, ‘OK, let me hear this song that’s about us.’ So I played it for him. And he brought his electric guitar, so obviously he had it in mind that he had to have a piece of it.

“Joe Vitale [producer] was running the machines,” Stephen recalled. “He says [to Neil], ‘Try playing it from the top. You’re on and you can add little flourishes.’ Neil would not turn the volume up on his guitar until I was done singing, absolutely refused … That was so respectful and kind and thoughtful of him.”

‘Round The Bend’ ended up with a wonderful piece of interweaving Stills/Young electric guitar work. “If we start playing leads it gets really ferocious and it looks like we’re trying to outplay each other,” Stephen admitted. “But actually what we’re doing is we’re tapping into our own inner anger, the repressed [stuff]. This is cheaper than therapy and we just get going. And we try to lift each other. There’s nothing competitive about it.”

CHAPTER 32
CSN&Y: Relevant Again

Stephen and Neil would get plenty of opportunity to 'tap into their inner anger' on the next occasion CSN&Y hit the road. The controversial *Freedom Of Speech Tour* in 2006 was the band's most politically opinionated yet. So much so that the music, at times, became a sideshow to the massive media coverage the four were getting as a result of their political stance on the government's handling of issues surrounding the ongoing Iraq War.

The large-scale tour later spawned a film, *Déjà Vu,* that was part music but mainly a commentary on President Bush's ineptitude over the war. Bush was trashed, veterans were praised, and Crosby, Stills, Nash & Young were headline news again.

The concerts themselves were edgy, exciting affairs. Even some of the band's most ardent fans didn't go along with the sentiments coming from the stage. Much of the music from the tour was based around Neil's most recent solo album, *Living With*

War, which included a whole raft of Iraq War commentary songs, recorded hurriedly in two weeks earlier that year. When Crosby, Stills, Nash & Young began singing the new songs in cities across the US, there was booing and even walk-outs by ticket holders at some venues. Stephen was also unsure whether Neil's exaggerated approach was hitting home in the right way. As he admitted in his book *Waging Heavy Peace*, "Stephen was uncomfortable with the political nature, singing songs like 'Let's Impeach The President' and 'Living With War,' which were written as if they were from a raving political maniac."

Stephen felt that the band's role on tour should be more as chroniclers than preachers. "It went down well for the most part. There were a couple of cities that I warned them about, you know, they just don't like being lectured to, and why don't we tone it down just a little bit," he told Simon Harper.

It wasn't a fear of upsetting people he was alluding to. He wanted a more intimate platform for his political views. The *Déjà Vu* movie showed him doing just that at one point, encouraging people in someone's backyard to support a local political candidate.

Reports acknowledged that the four were sounding better than ever and came to the obvious conclusion that CSN&Y were, all of a sudden, relevant again. Then Vietnam, now Iraq–they had a cause to fight for, once more, and the old songs 'Ohio,' 'Teach Your Children,' and 'Long Time Gone' were all getting a terrific reception on the tour. Aggressive and strident, these concerts were charged with an electricity and sense of purpose that had been absent since the early Seventies.

The tour's worst moment for Stephen came with a nasty fall on stage during 'Rockin' In The Free World' at the Toronto show. Embarrassed but undaunted, he continued playing in a prone position down by the footlights before leaving the stage for a couple of stitches in a hand wound. Fortunately, the fall only ended his participation at that show and not the remaining dates.

When the movie was released in 2008, *Empire* magazine were full of praise for an "exceptional rockumentary."

There was the inevitable dig at the band being "hippy millionaire grandpas," but *Empire* went on to acclaim the electric atmosphere generated by the four. "Woodstock survivors will weep to see how old the Sixties' town criers are, but thrill with pride that they still kick ass and won't shut up."

After the hullabaloo surrounding the tour had died down, there was some sad news for Stephen, in particular, to digest. His career-long mentor Ahmet Ertegun had died after suffering a fall at a New York City Rolling Stones benefit concert six weeks earlier. The man who once described CS&N as "one of the great phenomenons in rock 'n' roll" and felt the only artists comparable were The Rolling Stones, Bob Dylan, and The Beatles, had been in a coma since suffering the fall. The legendary music industry boss had had a special influence over Stephen's music. The respect for one another survived some inevitably difficult periods. Stephen was devastated when Crosby, Stills & Nash left Atlantic Records, a move he described as "heart-wrenching." But the friendship between the musician and the record company man never waned.

"Every once in a while they would change teams at Atlantic," he would later reflect. "The new guys would go, 'Oh, we don't know you.' Ahmet would say, "But Stephen's my guy.' He always came to the shows, even when we weren't with him. That struck me as the classiest thing in the world."

On April 18, 2007, Stephen grasped the opportunity to commemorate their special relationship when appearing at the 22nd annual Rock and Roll Hall of Fame induction ceremony at the Waldorf Astoria Hotel in New York. As Neil Young announced from the stage at the tribute to the late Atlantic Records co-founder that night, after singing 'Helplessly Hoping' with David Crosby, Stephen Stills, and Graham Nash, "Ahmet was our man. I just hope that today's musicians have someone like Ahmet, because we were really lucky." Stephen and Neil then performed the Buffalo Springfield number 'Mr. Soul.'

That spring, Stephen's fans got to find out a little more about Stills the family man. Stephen's wife Kristen and son Henry appeared in a documentary movie *Autism: The Musical*. Henry had been diagnosed with Asperger's Syndrome from an early age and Kristen would become a prominent campaigner on behalf of autism science. As *Autism: The Musical*'s executive producer, she received an Outstanding Nonfiction Special Emmy Award.

There was an enforced slowdown in Stephen's CS&N activities in 2007. Joe Vitale, who was now an important part of team Stills, explained why to *ClassicRockRevisited.com*: "We just canceled our whole year. We may come back in the fall but we had to cancel for now due to David Crosby having to have shoulder surgery."

Of his work with Stephen's solo band, Joe was optimistic that the two would hit the road soon. "We are going to do several dates together. We dug into the old catalog. We are going to be doing a bunch of Manassas stuff. We are also going to be playing some Buffalo Springfield and some of Stephen's very early solo work."

In July, the result of the one-night solo recording session Stephen completed in 1968 was released as an album. The set of 12 pre-CS&N demos, titled *Just Roll Tape*, got an enthusiastic thumbs-up from fans and music critics. The tapes of the session might have been lost forever had musician Joe Colasurdo not stumbled upon them when rehearsing at A&R Recorders shortly before the studio closed for good in 1978. Having identified the 'Stephen Stills'-named boxes, he began the process of getting the tapes back to Stephen, which, through the help of a friend of Graham Nash, Dan Curland, and Nash himself, took many years.

"I feel like, oh my God, that guy sang high back then," joked Stephen on hearing the release of *Just Roll Tape*. "And I did that at two in the morning. I don't mind telling you, I don't have that energy right now."

On December 17, Stephen's health was the focus of widespread attention when he announced on CNN's *Larry King Live* TV show that he had been diagnosed with prostate cancer. Caught in the early stages, surgery followed on the day of his 63rd birthday (January 3, 2008). Wife Kristen was happy to announce that "Stephen's procedure went remarkably well and he couldn't be better. He will be home by noon tomorrow and the pain will be minimal."

And when Stephen spoke to Simon Harper a while after the operation, he had this to say: "I'm completely cancer free. The procedure actually sort of gave everything a chance, and I've lost 30 pounds quite easy, like it was nothing. I'm 180 [pounds] or thereabouts all the time now–it's easier on my knees, I'm fitter, I just feel great."

Typically, he was relaxed and in good humor when interviewed by Mary Colurso for *The Birmingham News and AL.com* about age-related issues: "Getting older is not for sissies," he confided.

"A wonderful thing happens when you turn 60. Some things just don't bother you. You don't care at all."

"I've been using a teleprompter so I can call up all of these obscure songs," he revealed. "It just makes life really easy for me."

Of the hours at a time exposed to loud music in his 20s and

30s that damaged his already impaired hearing, he had this to say: "As my hearing loss increased, I experimented with hearing aids but they were so cumbersome, I hated the feeling of having a big piece of plastic in my ear. I also thought they would block up my ears and cause me to miss the ambiance of the room and the crowds."

It was Neil Young who suggested Stephen try a modern design, behind-the-ear hearing solution called Dual. "I fell in love with them immediately. They were so light, they enhanced the frequencies I needed and let the ambient sound come in."

He was certainly in fine fettle for an important date at London's Shepherd's Bush Theatre in the fall. The concert, released on CD and DVD a year later, saw him tackle a testing set list. The *Record Collector* review was an honest reflection of a performance in which Stephen fed off a loyal audience willing him to succeed: "The voice is a little rougher, the range a little more restricted, but the music still pours out. After 'Suite: Judy Blue Eyes,' Stills slings on a Strat and, joined by an electric band, proceeds to rock the audience like they haven't been rocked in a while."

Stephen clearly enjoyed his return to London. He even chatted between songs, reminiscing about his house in Surrey. "Maybe it has something to do with being a grandfather, I don't know," he told Simon Harper. "I find myself more willing to have fun with it. I tell stories to the audience now."

Shortly after this there was a musical reunion with ex-wife Véronique Sanson and son Chris on the stage of the Paris Olympia. Then Stephen followed up a suggestion by former girlfriend Judy Collins to record something together in 2009.

"I saw Stephen in Cleveland at the Rock and Roll Hall of Fame last year, and I told him about the new album I was working on called *Paradise*. I thought it would be great if we did a duet together, because after all these years we had only collaborated a handful of times. He played in the backing band on *Who Knows Where The Time Goes* and performed at a few of my concerts during the time when *Life* magazine was doing a cover story on me, so there are a few photos of us from that era, but we had never actually recorded a song together.

"Stephen thought it was a great idea, so he came over to my home while he was in New York City for an event and we began working on the song. I had thought we were going to sing the beautiful song 'Four Strong Winds,' but when he arrived he told me he wanted to do 'Last Thing On My Mind.' I love the song, so we both sat down and played our Martin guitars and in about one hour it was done. It was absolutely wonderful–my husband was photographing us while we played, and it was a very magical, romantic experience."

Not quite so romantic was an anecdote from the 'Last Thing On My Mind' recording that Judy recounted in her autobiography *Sweet Judy Blue Eyes*.

Under the watchful gaze of Judy's husband Louis, who was snapping away with his camera, Stephen commented on the state of Judy's bare feet, reminding her how she used to admonish him for wearing tight cowboy boots that would surely give him bunions. Stephen revealed how she had been right to warn him and how he had had his bunions removed, before boldly announcing: "I see you haven't done a thing with yours!"

In the fall of 2009, fans of the *Manassas* album were at long last able to sample more of the atmosphere that made the 1972 release so special. A collection of outtakes and the fantastic early bluegrass demos that Chris Hillman, Al Perkins, and Byron Berline had first tempted Stephen with were put out on one disc, titled *Pieces*.

"It was great to go back and remix some old tunes from the vaults," Stephen told Max Bell, "to remove the unnecessary echo, tidy up the duff lyrics. Also to listen again to those players like Chris 'Curly' Hillman, Joe Lala, and Al Perkins. We were the first country-rock-bluegrass-steel-Latin band. And we were darned good."

Of the never previously released songs, 'Witching Hour' stood out the most. Stephen's snaking, sinewy guitar and perfectly pitched vocal would have graced the original album, but failed to make the cut. "It's about the reason I took off from CSN&Y in the first place," he observed. "Like, 'I'm being used here, and I'm not sure why.' And when it comes time to get down to it, I'm the go-to guy. That's the witching hour, when you make up songs."

Plans for a new CS&N record were made in 2010. Tentatively titled *Songs We Wish We'd Written* by Graham Nash and produced by Rick Rubin, the idea was to round up and cover the trio's favorite songs, such as Pete Townshend's 'Behind Blue Eyes' and the Jagger/Richards classic 'Ruby Tuesday.' The new album got off to a promising start with those two tracks cut at Shangri La in Malibu, but the legendary Rubin was reportedly overly autocratic with CS&N about song choices and the project eventually fizzled out.

The continuing tours with Crosby and Nash saw Stephen play London again in the summer of 2010. Ever the Anglophile, he had by this time become quite a fan of British sport and cricket in particular. On Saturday July 3, he was a guest in the BBC *Test Match Special* commentary box for England v Australia at Lord's, where he briefly met lyricist Tim Rice, who remembered an opportunity missed. "I was waiting to be interviewed by Aggers [Jonathan Agnew] regarding a cricket charity. I saw this bloke who I vaguely recognized standing at the back of the box, and if I remember correctly he and I shook hands and exchanged first names–nothing more. It was only some time later that I realized it was Stephen Stills–maybe I heard his interview or read that he had become a cricket nut when in a UK hospital. I missed a chance for a good chat there!" admitted Rice.

As Stephen revealed in an interview with Max Bell: "I loved it all, the fresh mown grass and the spring air. I played cricket; I even know the rules. In fact I still watch the big matches on Sky."

Another completely random digression involving Stephen occurred when the movie *Scott Pilgrim vs. The World* was released in 2010. In it, actor Mark Webber played a character called Stephen Stills, created by the author of the *Scott Pilgrim* graphic novels, Bryan Lee O'Malley. By way of explanation, the author described where his influences lay when creating what actually turned out to be a gay Stephen Stills in his books: "I feel like a lot of kids who maybe get the Nintendo references don't necessarily get all the music stuff. I guess I just wanted to put the rounded sides of my interest in there. When I was starting the book, I was listening to a lot of '70s music and country-rock–that Neil Young and Gram Parsons school of music … I'd been listening to all that, tracing it back. It all goes into *Scott Pilgrim*. It's kind of my whole synthesis of everything I care about."

Anyone tempted to delve further into the far-out world of *Scott Pilgrim* will be pleased to learn of another interesting character in O'Malley's books, called Young Neil.

In June 2011, Stephen was back in Buffalo Springfield, albeit briefly.

"Neil and I were sitting down at lunch one day and were talking about 'Let's do something fun,'" Stephen informed *Rolling Stone*.

"I said, 'Let's do Buffalo Springfield at the Bridge School.'"

That gig proved such a success that, amid much excitement and a rush of nostalgia, the band reunited for six concerts in Oakland, Los Angeles, Santa Barbara, and the Bonnaroo Music & Arts Festival in Manchester, Tennessee. The line-up consisted of Stephen, Neil, Richie Furay (now a Colorado church pastor), bass player Rick Rosas (replacing Bruce Palmer, who died in 2004), and Joe Vitale (who took over the drum stool from Dewey Martin, who'd passed away in 2009). Interestingly, the set list was almost all authentic, pure Springfield, with only Neil's 'Rockin' In The Free World' added. According to disappointed band spokesperson Richie Furay, the group had expected to do a full-length tour in 2012, but with Neil involved in other recording and memoir-writing commitments, the Springfield reunion, though well received initially, just faded away.

Another reunion of sorts took place at the Saban Theatre in Beverly Hills in February 2013. Here at a Writers Bloc event, Judy Collins, joined by Stephen, sat in two comfortable chairs reminiscing about their shared experiences together back in the day. When it came to the inevitable chat about 'Suite: Judy Blue Eyes,' there was a simple heartfelt end to the conversation. When Stephen turned to the subject of one of his finest pieces of writing, he said: "I don't know how to thank you for that song." To which she replied, "Nor I you."

Having played at plenty, up until now, Stephen hadn't strictly speaking ever hosted a benefit concert himself. In April 2013 that all changed when, with wife Kristen, he organized the Light Up The Blues concert for Autism Speaks.

"It's the first time I've hosted a large benefit," Stephen admitted. "Usually Graham [Nash] and his organization have done this for all kinds of causes. I've never fronted one. Something like this is supposed to take a year to put together, and we decided to do this over the holidays. It's an adventure, but certainly nothing I'm not familiar with."

The Stills' have some stellar support in their new venture. While movie star and musician Jack Black hosted the event, Chris Stills, Lucinda Williams, Ryan Adams, Rickie Lee Jones, and Stephen's old friend Don Felder performed at the concert with, naturally, Crosby, Stills & Nash headlining.

There was a nostalgia rush for Stephen's fans (and Stephen himself) with the release of his box set *Carry On* in early 2013. The 82-track collection covered his music dating back to a Costa Rica recording of his song 'Travelin'' in 1962.

Stephen seemed reluctant to take much credit for *Carry On*, which was produced by Joel Bernstein and Graham Nash. "They did the lion's share of the work on the project," he admitted to Brian Ives for Radio.com.

And when quizzed about the choice of *Carry On* for the title, he had this to say: "For lack of a better name, quite frankly. There was a British saying from the war, 'Stay calm and carry on.' That's where I got the title, 'Carry on then, don't make a big fuss about yourself.' That's sort of my attitude about this. I don't want to make too much a fuss about this. I'm not going to be parading around in a boa, that's not me."

CHAPTER 33
Back To The Blues

"The blues band of my dreams" is how Stephen described a new project he'd been working on in 2013. Creating the new group only came about when he began enlisting the help of some key musicians to make a blues album he had been itching to record for years. "So I got together with Barry Goldberg, and I wanted another really great blues guitar player who's better than me so I could learn from him because, you know, I'm always over-achieving," joked Stephen. Then when he discovered that John Mayer couldn't join the project owing to throat problems, Stephen searched for a guitarist/vocalist. "And I ended up with Kenny Wayne Shepherd, and it was like a bromance from the get-go."

Barry Goldberg was an old friend from the Sixties who Stephen had played with alongside Mike Bloomfield on the *Super Session* LP, and Kenny Wayne Shepherd was a 36-year-old guitarist and singer-songwriter with a big reputation. Hitching up with him came about through a mutual friend who owned the Indianapolis Colts football team. "When my manager [Elliot Roberts] first suggested him, I was like, 'Who?' He said, 'You know him, he's really great.' And I said, 'Sorry, I don't know who you're talking about.' I was at a casino, yelling into my phone, and I turned around and there was literally a marquee with an eight-story poster outside the window with his picture on it that said 'Friday and Saturday: Kenny Wayne Shepherd.' I went, 'Oh, the kid from the football.' It was one of those great human moments where grandad finally connected the fucking dots."

Added to the mix were Kenny's drummer, Chris Layton, and bass player Kevin McCormick from the CS&N band. "And we just started fiddling with this stuff," said Stephen, "and the songs started pouring out."

The recording project quickly became a band called The Rides. "The name comes from the fact that me and Kenny Wayne are both automobile nuts, of the Jeremy Clarkson persuasion," explained Stephen. "We're not Prius people, let's put it that way. I've got a 1990s Bentley, which I adore–it's just a very fast living room–and an X5. They're both pristine and get terrible gas mileage."

By the fall of 2013, The Rides had released their debut album *Can't Get Enough* and began touring. The album was an immediate success, peaking at Number 39 on the *Billboard* 200. And it wasn't just the guitar-playing that sounded great. Stephen now had a vehicle for the raw, whiskey-soaked bluesman's growl he'd been restraining in Crosby, Still & Nash and let rip on down and dirty tracks like the terrific 'Roadhouse.' The response to the music on the road from new wave blues fans and diehard aficionados to The Rides' live shows was unanimously good. "We had so much fun playing on stage ..." Stephen explained, "lots of freedom. Kenny and I found a wonderfully exciting knack for playing lead at the same time without a real 'arrangement,' just sort of instinctive guessing, from watching each other's hands. Neil Young and I used to do this with Buffalo Springfield. And the grooves are always right on the money, never rushed or jittery."

There was also a nice tip of the hat to the 'Surrey Boys' when Stephen assessed the popularity of The Rides. "But we need to come to Britain if we want to be known, because this country has honored the blues more than any other."

Earlier in the year, Stephen had tried to assure people that he wasn't going to make a fuss about his back catalog box set. He was now looking forward, not back, with his exciting new band The Rides gaining attention. But in September a fuss was exactly what was made of him at the Americana Music Honors & Awards show, where he received the First Amendment Center/ Americana Music Association "Spirit of Americana" Free Speech Award. It was an award previously given to Johnny Cash, Steve Earle, Judy Collins, and Joan Baez, among others. Looking back, it seemed, was something he just couldn't escape.

Back at the Royal Albert Hall with CS&N in London in October, Stephen was still in blues mode. "I'd like to thank the elderly person's council for allowing me to do that," he joked after playing some blues guitar that the rest of the band had only heard for the first time during the afternoon sound-check. In top form during their run of Royal Albert Hall shows, on the third and final night they treated the audience to a run-through of their entire 1969 debut album.

More memories, of Crosby, Stills, Nash & Young this time, were unleashed in 2014 when *CSNY 1974* was released. A live four-disc set and DVD of the historic stadium tour 40 years earlier, it reminded everyone who cared just how big a deal the quartet were back then. There were more good feelings of great days gone by when Stephen and Manassas were inducted into the Colorado Music Hall of Fame alongside Firefall, Poco, and the Nitty Gritty Dirt Band at a January 2015 ceremony at Denver's Paramount Theatre. Sadly, a week later, news came through of another rock and roll casualty when Stephen's favorite drummer, Dallas Taylor, died of complications from viral pneumonia and kidney disease, aged 66.

If fans of CS&N thought they'd seen it all in the trio's roller-coaster career, they had to think again in 2015. Stretching credibility perhaps further than their appearance at the Rock and Roll Hall of Fame induction in formal dinner suits, Crosby, Stills & Nash were signed up as the ship's entertainment on a transatlantic crossing of the ocean-going liner the *Queen Mary 2*. The seven-night crossing from New York to Southampton in September saw them perform their greatest hits, engage in question and answer sessions, and sign autographs for the passengers. It seemed like an incongruous direction to take for a band that even 10 years earlier had, with Neil Young, alienated some fans through their politics and controversially singing about impeaching a president.

But, as Stephen explained, the *Queen Mary* gig did have its advantages. It turned out to be an excellent way to travel to Europe for a tour. "You sing an acoustic concert for the passengers, and you get to bring all of your gear, all of the crew and everything, and you're in Europe. You can do a European tour in a very cost-effective manner. And, of course, they give us the really posh rooms. It's a pretty neat deal. James Taylor turned us on to it. I mean, we'll see ... We could run into the tail-end of a hurricane, which on a boat that size is actually kind of fun."

CS&N survived whatever the Atlantic Ocean had to throw at them, but a year later their professional and personal relationship hit the rocks. Another CS&N split story? This one was different. The March 4 statement from the *4WaySite* website, gleaned from Dutch newspaper *Het Parool*, seemed final. "Graham Nash says his two-year fight with David Crosby has brought Crosby, Stills & Nash to an end," the paper reported. "And he's accused Crosby of treating him like dirt, after he previously opened a rift with Neil Young. Young announced in October that he'd have no more to do with his CSN&Y colleagues, leading Crosby to comment: 'That's like saying there are mountains in Tibet. We know, Neil. We already knew.' He then admitted Young was 'very angry' with him, probably for calling his girlfriend Daryl Hannah a 'purely poisonous predator'–although he later apologized."

Stephen appeared to be the only member untouched by the falling out–aside from the lack of any future CS&N or CSN&Y activity.

The Rides had a new album to release, and in May *Pierced Arrow* further enhanced the blues trio's reputation. Back in the spring of 2015, fans had seen a preview of one of the album's stand-out tracks when Stephen's latest Light Up The Blues: Autism Speaks annual benefit was held at Pantages, Hollywood.

The excellent rock ballad 'Virtual World' was performed by Stephen and Neil Young and featured some of the duo's best guitar work, with Stephen's young son Oliver playing congas in an Argentina soccer jersey behind them. It was a wonderful performance by two old friends comfortable in each other's company. The Rides' album track version of 'Virtual World' had equally great dual guitar work by Stephen and his new sidekick, but was also a perfect example of how well Kenny Wayne Shepherd had taken on board Stephen's idea to attempt twin vocals with him. "There was something so magical to me about harmonizing with this man, who is so well known for this kind of thing," says Shepherd. "Crosby, Stills, Nash, and now me!"

AFTERWORD

Stephen Stills' enduring popularity is actually quite easy to explain. Fans will defend him to the hilt. Go on the review websites, social media, YouTube, anywhere and you'll see just how indignant they become if Stills gets so much as an unfavorable comparison to Neil Young or even an indifferent review. People identify with his tortured side. He's suffered many maulings at the hands of the press, which helped build those defensive shields down the years. Like any of us, he can't possibly justify some crazy things said and done when you're 20-something. His propulsion to rock stardom came at a time when musicians were grabbing control of their music, contracts, decision-making away from the record companies, and he, more than most, pushed his manipulation of the system to the max.

As one of a new breed he gained all the encouragement he needed from Ahmet Ertegun to create something that he probably thought (and certainly Atlantic Records could imagine) might turn into the American Beatles. Crosby Stills Nash & Young grabbed a nation's older teenagers' attention like no other band had done before, by creating a new sound, even new cultural values, and fusing Beatles and Bob Dylan. Hardly surprising, then, that Stills began trying to live up to the rock-star hype.

Always out to impress, but always looking to play and learn with anyone he thought would make him better, Stills built himself up but eventually lost control, and the CSN&Y mothership became a vehicle musically managed by either Nash or Young.

His story is one of an immensely talented but flawed individual trying to recapture that creative spark, energy, and control he saw slipping away. The arc of his career was in no way a straightforward steady decline. He has at least one solo album and the Manassas debut that rank alongside any of the great things he has done with CSN&Y.

His acceptance that he's never going to top 'For What It's Worth' or 'Suite Judy Blue Eyes' came a while back, and unlike his guitar-playing, which just got better over the decades, his song-writing did not, as he explained to Paul Rollo. "Those first passionate ones are really special. And later in life you might get deeper and more resonant and more crafted, but they're not as free as those first ones. You end up out-crafting yourself. You get too cute. Losing the point. Getting contrived. Which is why I admire Bob Dylan so much. He's managed not to do that."

Andrew Loog Oldham summed it up best when reflecting on the lack of lyric-writers writing about the world these days. "Everybody is so wrapped up in their teched-up, isolated world that they only know how to write about themselves. Where's the new Sam Cooke, Stephen Stills? Who will write the anthems that bind, and how, even if they are written, will those songs get through?"

It's a sentiment Stephen would no doubt agree with, having explored the subject in the best of his recent songs, 'Virtual World', for The Rides.

Stephen's commitments with The Rides, the occasional on-stage guitar duels with Neil Young, and his solo shows are probably enough for now. Are CSN and CSN&Y finished? This time it really appears so. He had been part of something more than just a great band – something that only a few musicians experience. There had been ideology, there had been protests – Crosby Stills Nash, and sometimes Young, had tapped corrupt authority on the shoulder and voiced a generation's hopes and fears.

A good proportion of the masses at Woodstock must have felt part of a dramatic shift in youth power. Perhaps Stephen Stills felt it too for a week or so in August 1969 or even in the summer of 1974.

"There was a time when I thought Crosby, Stills, and Nash could rule the world," he admitted. "But I never said we could save it. I just said, 'There's something happening here.' I suppose I just tried to keep things open-ended. I tried to do what I was doing in the best spirit of the troubadours."

Job done, Stephen.

ACKNOWLEDGEMENTS

Howard Albert, Max Bell, Byron Berline, Chris Charlesworth, Mary Colurso, Martin Downham, Michael Eaton, Andy Fairweather-Low, Pat Gibbon, John Haeny, Bill Halverson, Al Perkins, Andy Prevezer, Jeffrey Puckett, Sir Tim Rice, David Seinfeld, Brian Southall, Dolf van Stijgeren, David Tangye, George Terry, Nick Warburton, Neil Watson, Ken Weiss, Graham Wright, Mark Young

Broken Arrow – The Neil Young Appreciation Society magazine. Editors Alan Jenkins and Scott Sandie

So Far – The fanzine so lovingly put together by the ever-helpful Andy Langran

BIBLIOGRAHY

California Rock California Sound: Anthony Fawcett (Reed Books)

Crosby, Stills & Nash: Dave Zimmer (Omnibus Press)

Crosby Stills Nash & Young – The Visual Documentary: Johnny Rogan (Omnibus)

Delta Lady - A Memoir: Rita Coolidge with Michael Walker (Harper)

4 Way Street - The Crosby, Stills, Nash & Young Reader: Edited by Dave Zimmer (Da Capo Press)

The Great Rock Discography: Martin C. Strong (Canongate)

The Greatest Albums You'll Never Hear: Edited by Bruno MacDonald (Aurum Press)

Guinness Book Of British Hit Singles & Albums: Editor David Roberts (Guinness)

Jerry Garcia - Folk, Bluegrass And Beyond: Ken Hunt

BIBLIOGRAPHY

The Last Sultan - The Life And Times Of Ahmet Ertegun: Robert Greenfield (Simon & Schuster)

Life: Keith Richards (Weidenfeld & Nicolson)

Live Aid - The Concert (Sidgwick & Jackson)

Neil Young – Zero To Sixty: Johnny Rogan (Calidore)

Off The Record - An Oral History Of Popular Music: Joe Smith (Warner Bros. Books)

Prisoner Of Woodstock: Dallas Taylor (Thunder's Mouth Press)

The Road Is Long... The Hollies Story: Brian Southall (Red Planet)

Rock Atlas: David Roberts (Red Planet)

Rock Chronicles: Editor David Roberts (Firefly)

Rock On The Road: Mick Gold (Futura)

Ronnie: Ronnie Wood (Macmillan)

Sweet Judy Blue Eyes - My Life In Music: Judy Collins (Crown Archetype)

To The Limit – The Untold Story Of The Eagles: Marc Eliot (Little Brown)

Top 40 Albums: Joel Whitburn (Billboard)

Top Pop Singles: Joel Whitburn (Billboard)

Waging Heavy Peace: Neil Young (Penguin/Viking)

Who I Am: Pete Townshend (Harper)

Wild Tales: Graham Nash (Penguin/Viking)

Woodstock - The Oral History: Joel Makower (Sidgwick & Jackson)

INDEX

INDEX

INDEX

INDEX